Life and Love
in Nazi Prague

Photo 1 *Marie Bader at her desk.*

Life and Love in Nazi Prague

Letters from an Occupied City

Marie Bader

Translated by Kate Ottevanger
Edited by Kate Ottevanger
and Jan Láníček

BLOOMSBURY ACADEMIC
LONDON · NEW YORK · OXFORD · NEW DELHI · SYDNEY

BLOOMSBURY ACADEMIC
Bloomsbury Publishing Plc
50 Bedford Square, London, WC1B 3DP, UK
1385 Broadway, New York, NY 10018, USA
29 Earlsfort Terrace, Dublin 2, Ireland

BLOOMSBURY, BLOOMSBURY ACADEMIC and the Diana logo
are trademarks of Bloomsbury Publishing Plc

First published in Great Britain 2019
This paperback edition published in 2021

Cover design: Terry Woodley
Cover image Bridge of King Charles, Prague, Czechoslovakia, 1940
(Archive Photos/Getty Images), and private collection

ISBN: HB: 978-1-7883-1256-1
         PB: 978-1-3502-3775-9
       ePDF: 978-1-7867-3629-1
      eBook: 978-1-7867-2623-0

Typeset by Integra Software Services Pvt. Ltd.

To find out more about our authors and books visit www.bloomsbury.com
and sign up for our newsletters.

Dedicated to
Marie and Ernst
Edith and Grete

In a letter written by a relative who survived, appended to this collection, the author writes that 'Our children are grown up now and the hard school of Auschwitz taught them a lot. You can be sure that everybody who came out of Auschwitz did learn how to fight in life.' The protagonist of this moving and powerfully engaging book, Marie Bader, did not survive. But her letters constitute not only an important source on life in Nazi-occupied Prague but an exemplary case study of how Jews during the Holocaust struggled to maintain their sense of self in the face of increasing persecution.

Dan Stone, Royal Holloway
University of London

Marie Bader's letters offer a captivating, if poignantly tragic, glimpse into the life of Jews in Nazi-occupied Prague. Neither she, nor her beloved addressee in Greece, survived the war, but we are fortunate today to be able to read her remarkably vibrant and strikingly perceptive efforts to describe to him her hopes and fears as she negotiated with verve, and even humour, anti-semitic repression and the impending threat of deportation. Thanks to the especially skilful editing and scholarly annotation of her letters, general readers, students and experts alike will find much here that is thought-provoking and will have great difficulty putting the book aside.

Benjamin Frommer
Associate Professor of History, Northwestern University

Contents

List of photos

Foreword

'Oh my treasure, do you know how I long for the smell of a wood, for the smell of fresh air?'

So wrote Marie Bader from her tiny flat in the Karlín district of Prague on 25 September 1941. Her letter was one of 154 written between the autumn of 1940 and April 1942.

Their recipient was Ernst Löwy, Marie's second cousin, with whom an intense love affair was developing, albeit one separated by hundreds of miles. Ernst was living in similarly restricted circumstances, but in the very different environment of Thessaloniki in northern Greece.

Ernst and Marie had known each other from childhood, but it was only with the deaths of both their spouses that a mutual strong attraction – noticed previously and frowned upon by their respective families – was finally able to develop and thrive.

Both were severely restricted in their freedom of movement, and, though willing to risk the little stability each enjoyed, were unable to achieve the reunion and stable life together that both hoped for, so that the love affair developed in words on paper.

This volume of letters gives an insight not just into this story of late-flowering desire – Marie was fifty-four at the time the letters begin – but also into the anxiety and uncertainty felt by Jewish people at that time, when families were so often dispersed to different parts of the world and the future for those still in Europe was so unsure.

The correspondence has a special connection with the Imperial War Museum, since Jeremy Ottevanger, Marie Bader's great-grandson, who discovered the letters in his parents' attic, is a close colleague. It was my privilege to meet with Jeremy's parents, Kate and Tim, to discuss the book in its early stages, and it was a special pleasure to see the project grow from an idea to a full publication.

Kate Ottevanger undertook the considerable task of translating and editing the letters, and writing a highly informative introduction. It cannot have been easy to work out the details of a complex set of family relationships, and how the shifting events of the Second World War impacted on all of Marie's relatives and acquaintances, but this Kate Ottevanger has achieved with consummate skill. Her Afterword – in which she describes further groups of letters to and from her grandmother and probes the impact that the unravelling of her grandmother's last two years has had on her and her family – is exceptional for its depth and insight into our understanding of exile, loss and identity.

In Jan Láníček, moreover, Kate found a co-editor of considerable ability who, as well as adding a valuable historical perspective, has provided a well-researched post-script, explaining the likely fate of Marie Bader. To work on a project of this kind must have been a challenge and to have the perspective of a well-networked expert from the country of Marie Bader's birth was fortunate indeed.

I know from my past work with the Holocaust Exhibition here, how rare it is for letters to survive from that period – but in particular full sets of correspondence. This volume will be of value to historians, scholars of literature and the general reader, for the detail it provides on wartime Jewish life in Prague, in particular how different elements in the population responded to the Jews under threat, and for the particular optimism, thoughtfulness and insight of one woman who endured that terrible time.

Suzanne Bardgett
Head of Research and Academic Partnerships
Imperial War Museum, London

Acknowledgements

My thanks go first to Erika Kounio Amariglio who, after initial hesitation, generously agreed that our grandparents' love story should be made public. Without her blessing I would have struggled with my conscience. Her daughter, Theresa Sundt, has kindly provided me with family photos. Suzanne Bardgett of the Imperial War Museum, through her enthusiasm and her belief in the importance of the letters, encouraged me to cross that bridge of conscience and I am most grateful for this. Sir Martin and Esther Gilbert were also among the first to appreciate the significance of this collection. I must thank, too, Chris Szejnmann of Loughborough University for his support and in particular for putting me in touch with Jan Láníček, without whose wide knowledge of their historical context these letters would have been so much less meaningful.

Thanks, too, to family and friends – you know who you are! – who have backed this venture through all its stages. I am especially indebted to my husband Tim for his constant assistance and for his relentless detective work which helped broaden our knowledge of so many of the characters who appear in the letters. And last, but certainly not least, I would like to thank our son Jeremy for discovering the letters in the first place.

Kate Ottevanger
November 2018

Introduction

The discovery

In October 2008, we made a remarkable discovery. Rummaging about in the attic, our son Jeremy opened an old suitcase which had been there for over ten years, ever since I cleared my aunt Grete's house in Sheffield, following her move into a nursing home. In the suitcase were several items of photographic equipment including an old camera, glass photographic plates and negatives. Always interested in old objects, he pulled them out to examine them further and saw underneath a package, wrapped in brown paper, on which was written, in Grete's hand, 'Read some of these, 18/5/53'. Removing the brown paper we found a further wrapping, pale blue this time, on which was written in pencil: '*Briefe von Marie Bader, entweder vernichten oder durch Edmund Benisch, New York, Bay Shore, 81 Brook Aven. an Maries Kinder senden. Benisch ist Cousin von Marie.*' ('*Letters from Marie Bader, either to be destroyed or sent through Edmund Benisch in New York, Bay Shore, 81 Brook Avenue, to Marie's daughters. Benisch is Marie's cousin.*')[1] Inside the blue package was a collection of 154 letters, roughly two-thirds typed, the rest handwritten, all but two from Marie Bader to Ernst Löwy, the remaining two from Ernst to Marie.

---

[1] Edmund Benisch is referred to by the familiar name of Eman in Marie's letters.

Marie's background

Marie Bader was my maternal grandmother, mother of Grete, born in 1909, and of my mother Edith, who was born in 1911. Marie was born in 1886 in Zebau in Bohemia (Czech: Cebiv), then a part of the Austro-Hungarian Empire. Her parents were Moritz and Louise Rosenberger and she had a younger sister, Irene. In her twelfth year the family moved to Karlsbad (Czech: Karlovy Vary). On Christmas Day 1906 she married Emil Bader, a man eleven years her senior, who came from Znaim in Moravia (Czech: Znojmo). Marie and Emil set up home in Karlsbad, a Bohemian spa town which lay in the heart of a region populated mostly by ethnic Germans, known as Sudetenland, an area which was to take on great significance later.

Emil was a wholesaler of groceries, supplying shops in villages and small towns across northern Bohemia. He had been helped in establishing his business by his more practical and business-like friend Gustav Lípa, who later became Irene's husband and was to become far more successful in business than Emil. During the First World War Emil was enlisted in the Austrian army. While he was in a supply rather than a combat role, what he witnessed at the Italian front marked him deeply for the rest of his life. After the war, in independent Czechoslovakia, he had less interest in or energy for his business and it fell to Marie to manage the business through the postwar depression in order to ensure an income for the family.

An energetic and enterprising woman, Marie recognized that there was a market for convenience pudding mixes and baking powders, such as those already developed by the German company Dr Oetker. With Emil she set up their own business, EBE Karlsbader Nährmittelindustrie (Karlbad Foodstuff Industry), producing baking powder, pudding powders, bicarbonate of soda, vanilla sugar, packs of spices for pumpernickel and various flavourings. She also produced little recipe books suggesting ways of using her products.

1936

The business thrived, but in 1936 came a time of crisis for Marie. In January her elder daughter, Grete, had a breakdown, following the collapse of her marriage to Otto Reichl and subsequent divorce. Grete and Otto had been living in Berlin where Otto, also a Czech citizen, worked at the Pergamon Museum. When Hitler came to power in 1933 Otto, like other Jews in public service, was dismissed and he and Grete returned to Czechoslovakia where Otto vainly sought work. The lack of work was doubtless a contributory factor in the collapse of the marriage but whatever the reason, its ending had a serious effect on Grete who, following her breakdown, was admitted for some months to a psychiatric institution.

In May 1936, before Grete had fully recovered, her father Emil died of liver cancer. It was a devastating time for Marie. Her marriage to Emil had been a happy one, despite the strain of keeping their business going after his return from the war. Now Marie was suddenly on her own, with an ailing daughter to support.

At this point precious support appears to have been offered by her cousin, Ernst Löwy, a friend from childhood and six years older. Ernst and his wife Theresa, known as Thesa, also lived in Karlsbad. He and Thesa had a daughter, Hella, who was married to a Greek Jew, Salvator Cougno,[2] whom she had met when studying in Leipzig, and they were now living in Thessaloniki. The Bader and Löwy couples met regularly in Karlsbad, where Ernst practised as an architect.

When Emil died, Marie wanted to accompany his body, contrary to custom, to the place where it was to be ritually prepared for burial, but she was discouraged from doing so. It appears that Ernst intervened on her behalf giving rise to gossip in the community. Whatever the explanation, this intervention led to a rift between Marie and the Löwys and there followed a period of over three years during which she had no dealings with Ernst and Thesa. It is possible that Thesa was jealous, or even that she sensed an unconscious attraction between Marie and Ernst, referred to more than once in the letters. A shared train journey to Leipzig, which was such a happy memory for Marie, gains retrospectively a new significance.

---

[2]Erika and Heinz, Ernst's grandchildren, use the more recent transliteration of Kounio in their books.

Stormclouds over Karlsbad

The next three years, 1936–39, were hard. Marie had lost her husband, her daughter was ill, the business under severe strain, contact with the Löwys broken and, meanwhile, the clouds of National Socialism were gathering. Sudeten Germans were openly showing their sympathy for Nazism which had taken hold in neighbouring Germany and the anti-semitic Sudeten German Heimatfront (later Party), formed in 1933, was agitating aggressively for their claimed grievances to be put right. Karlsbad had a very large ethnic German population and Marie, like other Jews, must have been acutely aware of being caught between the Germans, whose language and culture they shared, and the Czech majority in the Czechoslovak state, led by President Tomáš G. Masaryk and his successor Edvard Beneš, who were known to be friends of the Jews.

With Hitler enjoying absolute power only a few miles away, the Sudeten Germans, under their leader, Konrad Henlein, were becoming increasingly menacing. Marie's assistant, Ernst Müller, was a Sudeten German. He knew how the EBE Karlsbader business was run, he knew the recipes and the client base. He would have seen that the writing on the wall was not favourable to the Jews in the Sudetenland and must have anticipated the rich pickings for Germans once they had achieved their dream of being part of Germany and once the Jews had been expelled. Impatiently anticipating that moment, he set up his own company, 'Müller's Karlsbader' in 1937, stealing, according to Marie, her recipes, her staff and her clients, and taking over the trade name 'Karlsbader', as Marie writes bitterly in March 1942.

Expulsion

In March 1938 Hitler marched into a receptive Austria and annexed it to the German Reich, increasing the insecurity felt by Jews in the Sudetenland, now surrounded on three sides by the Nazi regime. Following this success, Hitler turned his attention to Bohemia and Moravia. In October 1938, following the Munich Agreement which had given him the green light to do so, Hitler sent his troops into the Sudetenland, immediately incorporating it into the Reich.

Marie, together with her mother Louise Rosenberger (referred to as Mutti in these letters) and her older daughter Grete, had to leave Karlsbad and move to Prague, where Edith was already working. They were among more than 20,000 Jews who were forced to flee the Nazi annexation. Marie had three months to liquidate her business, the proceeds of which provided her with sufficient to live independently in Prague. They encountered a hostile Czech environment in Prague, opposing the influx of a large number of German-speaking refugees from the borderlands into the rump state. Politically and economically broken, the Czechs first of all looked after the ethnically Czech population and slowly excluded the Jews, especially those of German culture, from society. It took more than two years before Marie officially received a residence permit in Prague (see the letters of 9 January and 11 February 1941).

Marie and Grete rented a flat in the northern suburb of Bubeneč, while her mother Louise went to live with her other daughter Irene and son in law Gustav Lípa in their smart flat in Pařížská, in the quarter of central Prague where a large number of Jews lived. From 1 April 1939 Marie rented the flat at Terezínská 24 (Theresienstädtergasse), in the suburb of Karlín, from which these letters were written.

On 15 March 1939, German troops and tanks entered Prague, and those parts of Bohemia and Moravia not already absorbed into Germany by the annexation of the Sudetenland were declared a protectorate of the Reich.

Jews were now in even greater peril. Marie's younger daughter Edith married my father Franz Sternschuss[3] in October 1938, perhaps sooner than they might otherwise have done, realizing that if they had to leave Czechoslovakia, it would be better to do so as a married couple. In April 1939 they received permission to leave the country but not yet to enter Britain. They first went to Milan in Italy. Edith had secured a post in domestic service in England (this was one of only two categories of work for which women refugees could get entry and work permits, the other being nursing)

---

[3]Franz's parents Hede and Rudolf Sternschuss appear frequently in Marie's letters. Hede, Rudolf's second wife, was a non-Jewish German and thus not only a protection for her Jewish husband (whom she refused to divorce) but also able to offer some help to her stepson's in-law family during the war. This she, and later her mother and sister, did courageously.

and was able to go ahead, after a few weeks, to her live-in job in Sheffield. Franz, on the other hand, could only enter Britain if he had a sponsor. Such sponsorship was slow to come through and he was stuck in Milan, waiting for his visa. But theirs is another story. Grete secured a position as adult escort on a *Kindertransport*. With a British visa she left Prague by train on 11 May, arriving at Harwich on 13 May. Unusually, she was allowed to make the single journey out of occupied Czechoslovakia and did not have to return, which other *Kindertransport* escorts were required to do.

England was not the only country for which Marie's daughters sought visas. Honduras and Panama were among those which issued permits but the cost of visas and of travel was high and there were rumours that visas were not always honoured once the refugees had landed. For Marie's generation it was even harder to have to choose whether to leave. In earlier letters to Grete and Edith written in 1939–40 she still talks of possible ways to emigrate and even in her letters to Ernst she mentions learning Spanish and gives Ernst the address of the Spanish consul in Prague. Nothing came of this. There was also Mutti, soon to turn eighty, who had only a slim hope to be able to emigrate. Had Marie and Irene decided to emigrate, they would have left their old and frail mother to her fate in the hands of strangers. This was a decision that only a few desperate people were willing to take.

The Thessaloniki connection

Ernst and his wife Thesa had also fled Karlsbad for Prague after the Munich Agreement, but on 14 March 1939, following weeks of rumour and speculation about Germany's intentions and the day before Hitler's troops marched into Prague, they set off for Greece to join Hella and Salvator and their children Erika and Heinz in Thessaloniki, where Salvator ran a photographic studio.

Thessaloniki had a very large Jewish population, numbering more than 50,000 in 1939. The Jews of Thessaloniki were Sephardi and many were descended from the community which had been expelled from Spain at the end of the fifteenth century. Their language was Ladino, a Romance language derived from old Spanish and heavily influenced by Hebrew, Aramaic and other languages of the Levant. Their food traditions, whilst conforming to Jewish laws, differed from central European Jewish cooking. (Hella later told Bea Lewkowicz, who was researching into the Jewish community of Thessaloniki, that Salvator's family did not approve of the marriage as she was an Ashkenazi Jew.) For Ernst and Thesa this move was an upheaval and required considerable cultural as well as linguistic adaptation. It is clear from the letters, written after Thesa's death, that Ernst missed the familiar dishes from Bohemia, as Hella was now cooking in the style of the community she had married into. Ernst's nostalgia for central European cuisine is a recurrent, if minor, theme in the letters.

Renewed contact and the awakening of love

Thesa Löwy died just before Christmas 1939. For over three years Marie and Ernst had not been in touch, but Ernst wanted Marie to know. He asked his brother Emil, who was still in Prague, to tell her the news. Marie wrote a letter of condolence and it seems to have been that letter which initiated this intense correspondence and which unleashed the suppressed and hitherto unacknowledged love between the two of them. Marie also wrote to her daughters in Britain to tell them the news of Thesa's passing, hinting tantalizingly at the causes of the rupture in their relations and suggesting that they too write to Ernst: '*Now, I want you to write a nice little letter to Uncle Ernst .... You do know that Th[esa] died. He is very sad. He wrote to me that she always spoke about us and [he] explained all sorts of things. Apparently she suffered a lot at the time from the break she initiated. Since knowing how ill the poor creature has been for a long time, I now understand and have completely forgiven her the injustice she did me. I am so sorry for her, and for him too, because it was a very good marriage. I beg you to send him your condolences.*'

For whatever reason, whether it was climate, food, the paucity of German speakers or sharing their daughter and son-in-law's home, Ernst and Thesa regretted moving to Thessaloniki and would have liked to return to Czechoslovakia (or rather, to the Protectorate of Bohemia and Moravia). After Thesa's death there was tension between Ernst and his daughter and on various occasions Marie found herself advising him on how to deal with the situation. It is not clear how much Hella knew about her father's love for Marie. With so many letters coming from Prague, sometimes twice a week, she may have suspected something but Ernst had not put her fully in the picture.

Marie and Ernst were both reluctant to let their families too much into their love and for Marie this caused her to reflect on her relationship with both her mother and her sister with whom she had been very close up until this point. Now she felt keenly how precious her independence was just at a time when Jews were being restricted to an ever narrower area of the city and when eviction was, for Marie, a constant worry. The tensions in the family are tangible.

Life in Prague under the Nazis

Although Marie was careful in writing about conditions in Prague, reading between the lines one nevertheless detects the slow strangulation of the Jewish community. For example, on 13 September 1941 she wrote '*I am afraid I will soon not have a typewriter.*' What she did not say is that she had received a form from the *Kultusgemeinde* (the Jewish Community in Prague, which played a central role in executing Nazi decrees) on which she had to declare whether she owned a typewriter and that she had handed in this form that very day, stating she had a Continental 340, in average condition, and that it was currently in her possession. This followed an order by the *Reichsprotektor* (head of German administration) that Jews had to hand in their typewriters and bicycles. In silent confirmation of this, the letter she wrote on 1 November is handwritten, as are all subsequent letters.

Typewriters and bicycles were not the only possessions which Jews had to give up. Ski equipment, musical instruments, fur coats, warm clothing and radios were all confiscated. Access to certain public places and entertainments was banned – not just swimming pools (August 1939), theatres and cinemas (February 1940), and parks, (May 1940), but even stretches of the banks of the river Vltava (September 1941) – and access to public transport severely restricted (by stages, from September 1940 onwards, see letter of

22–23 January 1942). More and more items in the shops could no longer be sold to Jews: trivial or inexplicable items such as apples, onions, garlic, fruit and nuts, whether fresh or preserved (hence Ernst's offer to send her nuts and raisins), shaving soap (and even pork!), and from February 1941 shopping hours for Jews were restricted to between 3 and 5 p.m.

For Marie the complaints of the Prague Jews at the deprivations they faced paled in comparison with what the refugees from the Sudetenland had already suffered and she was distressed by the selfishness revealed in many people. On the other hand, she commented on the kindness of many ethnic Czechs with whom, coming as she did from the Sudetenland, she had hitherto had relatively little contact. Marie's ability to communicate in Czech, even if she was not fluent, was crucial (letter of 25 July 1941). The situation was more difficult for the Jews who spoke only German, a language already resented by the Czech population before the war. These sentiments further increased when German became the language of the occupier.

Determination to go to Greece

A major theme in the letters is Marie's longing to join Ernst in Greece, in fact an unrealizable dream. Livia Rothkirchen writes '*The outbreak of the war put an end to free emigration from the Protectorate and made it difficult, if not virtually impossible, for individuals to leave.*'[i] It is unclear whether Jews in one occupied territory would have been allowed to travel to another occupied territory. She would have needed an entry permit for Greece before she could apply for an exit permit from the Protectorate, and then a transit visa for Yugoslavia. The changing military situation after the outbreak of the Greek–Italian war and later the German invasion of Yugoslavia and Greece further complicated the plans. Marie spent much time and energy trying to assemble the necessary documentation. Official information was obscure, contradictory and endlessly frustrating. Against all the odds, Marie engaged in a hopeless battle with bureaucracy, constantly struggling to believe in a future with Ernst.

On several occasions she wrote about a possible proxy marriage, which would then have given her the necessary marriage certificate to strengthen her application to join Ernst. Again, documents are required, sometimes needing to be translated into German (such as Thesa's Greek death certificate) and then notarized by a lawyer.

Stoutly independent, Marie's one worry, if she could get to Greece, was that she would have no resources to contribute to her upkeep. From her replies to Ernst it is possible to infer that he too found his dependence on his daughter and son-in-law irksome and there is even a suggestion that he felt his son-in-law, Salvator, resented the cost of his upkeep, although Ernst had money and occasionally found work.

The Cougnos owned a vineyard a few kilometres outside Thessaloniki where Ernst spent some time working. Perhaps to avoid a life of dependency, Marie fantasized about the two of them living a simple life there with a goat, chickens, even a little pig, and growing vegetables and fruit.

Her dreams reveal how much Marie missed being able to walk in the countryside and enjoy nature. Cooped up in Prague and banned from parks by the edict of 17 May 1940, one of the few places where she could walk was the Jewish cemetery. Recalling the walks her family and Ernst's used to make together, she yearned to be able to do this again with him.

Managing the censor

Each letter bears, in pencil, a number applied by the German censor and, up until the occupation of Greece, a few of the earlier ones carry the stamp of the Greek censor as well. Marie was conscious of the fact that her letters were being read by a stranger and she skirted around issues about which she might not be able to write. Prohibitions on Jews attending theatres, concerts, walking in parks, travelling or shopping at certain times are not explicitly mentioned. Again, one must read between the lines, as for example when, unconvincingly, she told Ernst she was no longer interested in going to the theatre or when, in March 1942, she wrote that they did not miss fruit. Grete and Edith become the nameless 'friends' who live in 'Chicago', rather than Sheffield.

On several occasions she urged caution because of the censor and when topical events, such as a disturbance referred to in August 1941, cannot be explained, she suggested Ernst obtain copies of the Prague German language newspaper *Der Neue Tag* to read about developments.

Sometimes Marie wrote so cryptically that the censor, having just obliterated three lines of her letter, told her '*Write unambiguously!*' or, on another occasion, wrote '*Please be brief!*' As Marie was the sender of the letters, the censor's comments could only reach her if Ernst passed them on to her. With a playfulness bordering on cheek she commiserated with the censor who would have had to cope with six sides of her handwriting if she were without her typewriter. This humouring not only shows Marie's non-confrontational character but that she instinctively understood the value of appealing to the censor's human feelings, when the whole thrust of the Nazi regime was to dehumanize its operatives as well as its subjects. Marie reminded the censor that he, too, was allowed to be human.

Being aware that some letters might be withheld by the censor – as some in fact were – Marie advised Ernst to keep copies of his letters to her as she did of hers to him. Some letters only got through with a page or two missing, a sentence obliterated, or, in one case, a section cut out with a sharp blade. Another letter was returned to her because it was too long.

Strict censorship allowed only soothing messages to get through and Marie was cautious when she wrote of deportations to occupied Poland, which began in the second half of October 1941, shortly after the arrival of SS General Reinhard Heydrich as Acting *Reichsprotektor*. However, the fact that she believed, and wished Ernst to believe, that people were being sent away to work, shows how well German propaganda was working as this was the illusion the Nazis were deliberately fostering. Maybe she already subconsciously realized the gravity of the situation, but did not want to admit it or trouble Ernst with her concerns. This possibly helped most of her letters to get through, the majority intact. It is only towards the end, when deportations were in full swing, that an increasing number of letters have pages missing.

The severely controlled correspondence with people who had been sent to Łódź (renamed Litzmannstadt by the Germans) in October 1941 and the sending of food parcels helped maintain the idea that people would be able to earn a living. Marie believed she would be able to offer useful skills. Only once, in the letter written on the eve of reporting for deportation to the Theresienstadt ghetto (Terezín in Czech), did she momentarily wonder whether she might be wrong in her belief, but then hastily ruled that out.

This brings us to another theme in the letters which may have met with the censor's approval: Marie's firm intention not to break the law. Repeatedly she stated her intention to stick by the rules imposed by the Nazi occupiers, whatever they might be, and when the order to wear the Star of David was issued, she professed unresisting compliance. The letters must therefore be read with a clear awareness of the presence of the censor and perhaps a certain admiration for the propitiating comments addressed directly to him and for Marie's determination to express her love despite the unwelcome eavesdropper.

How developments affect Marie's writing

One thing which strikes one forcibly in reading the letters is the change in tone, mood and subject matter, often quite abrupt, within one and the same letter. The more one becomes aware of this the more one realizes how significant the shifts are. I think there are three main explanations.

The first is a wish not to let personal anxieties become a worry which Marie will not be able to dispel until a subsequent letter (and with the fear of letters getting lost or being confiscated by the censor, the content of each needed to be as complete as possible, to avoid misunderstandings and to cover every aspect of their epistolary conversation). There may possibly also be an element of diverting or disarming the censor. The second explanation is her reaction to the grim events occurring in the Protectorate, to which she can often only allude with caution. A third contributory factor to the tone of the letters is the tension evident when letters and cards are not getting through, particularly in the spring of 1941, after the German invasion of northern Greece on 6 April and entry into Thessaloniki on 9 April, of which there is no mention.

On the emotional level, then, the tone can shift from a discussion of the problem of obtaining documents to a joke, a bit of playfulness, or a puzzle. Anxious advice on how Ernst should care for himself turns to tender dreams of their future, uncaring of the censor's intrusive eye.

As regards the background events and developments, the most extreme moment comes in the autumn of 1941, following Heydrich's arrival in Prague on 27 September. Two days later he ordered the immediate closure of all synagogues, putting an end to Marie's hope (letter of 15 September 1941) of celebrating New Year there. She told Ernst that she would have to begin wearing the 'emblem', (compulsory from 19 September). Typically, after a momentary lapse, when she confessed to feeling alone and miserable, she composed herself and imagined the two of them together, with her teasing and 'pestering' him.

On 10 October Heydrich convened a meeting with top Nazis, including Adolf Eichmann, in Prague Castle, to discuss 'the solution to the Jewish problem'. The decisions taken by this conference were immediately announced at a meeting with Protectorate journalists. Marie, having evidently heard the news, postponed saying anything about the 1,050 people (in fact 1,000) to be deported from Prague until well into the letter she wrote that evening. It was a letter of warning, both about her likely future and about his. Admitting that she had been fearing such an event for some time she did what she could to reassure him. On 15 October she wrote two letters. The first is missing from the collection and one must presume it never arrived. In the second letter she said at the beginning '*I am all right so far and am now much calmer and more composed.*' Perhaps she meant that in her first letter she may have sounded agitated and said too much in it for the censor's liking and that is possibly why it never arrived at its destination. In the second letter she hinted at things she could not tell Ernst explicitly but again tried to reassure him, while on the 18th she wrote that two transports had left, one to Łódź, the other to Minsk (in reality again to Łódź), with a third leaving that day.

Marie likened the fear of the summons to the fear of the *plumpsack* man in a traditional children's game where none of the participants, arranged in a circle, can know who will be his next victim. This recurring reference to a children's game becomes a cover for a much deeper anxiety, to avoid the censor's attentions and perhaps also as a subconscious device to diminish her fear.

It is surprising how much she was actually able to tell Ernst, but the true terror and fear in the community and indeed within the whole population (there had been many executions after Heydrich's arrival) can only be guessed at. When one thinks how desperate life must have been one can only admire

Marie's efforts to divert Ernst with talk of other things. On 27 October she mentioned the possibility of suicide (but only after talking it over with him) but by the next day she was re-reading his letters and imagining herself in another world once more.

This period was clearly a terrifying one for everyone and the fact that there was no escape was becoming increasingly self-evident. It was now clearly not a matter of 'if' but 'when', but again she began to adapt to the inevitable and responded to Ernst's obvious distress by telling him (18 December 1941) to cheer up and suggesting that those who look to the future rather than the past find it easier to adapt to changing circumstances. The shift of the deportation destination from occupied Poland to Theresienstadt led to the hope that from now on the deportees would be able to stay in the Protectorate. Yet Marie soon realized that trains were leaving the Bohemian ghetto for further east (letter of 12 March 1942).

In January 1942, the postponed Wannsee Conference took place, in which plans for the destruction of European Jewry were finalized, while in Marie's own life the departure of her sister and brother-in-law demanded further adjustments. It requires little imagination to guess what the atmosphere in Prague was like, but both Marie's words of comfort to Ernst and her description of her activities with those organizing help for the destitute, give an idea of how she was able to confront practically the prospects ahead. Knowing, with the benefit of hindsight, the nature of the trap closing around her and her fellow Jews, we are given an insight into ways of coping with increasing powerlessness and dehumanization.

She continued to write to Ernst with considerable frankness, despite the prying, even potentially prurient, eye of the censor, expressing her love in all openness and describing a dream she had shortly before her own departure which is incredibly moving. In her dream she and Ernst receive a call from her daughters and agree to go and join them, transforming the preparations for Theresienstadt into a perfect reunion with her dearest ones. This dream, too, had to pass the censor: mercifully these last two letters were allowed to reach Ernst in their entirety.

Marie reported for deportation on 21 April. The night before, she wrote two letters, one to Ernst – the last in this collection – and one to her daughters, which reached them after the war.

The letters

Ernst did not start to save Marie's letters until October 1940, more than nine months after she had written her letter of condolence which broke the silence that had existed between them since 1936. It must have been around this time that their mutual love was recognized and declared because, on 7 October 1941, she wrote '*It will soon be a year, my sweet, since we declared ourselves.*' Thereafter he seems to have saved every letter he received – some never reached him. At some time after receiving Marie's last letter on 26 April 1942 – perhaps anticipating his own deportation – he bundled them up and indicated that they should either be sent to Marie's daughters or else be destroyed.

When they reached Sheffield is not known, but neither Grete nor my mother ever spoke of their existence. Indeed, I consider it doubtful that Edith ever read any of them: she would, I believe, have found it too painful and perhaps also an unwarranted intrusion. Is reading what are unashamedly love letters an intrusion? It may be, but they reveal so much about my grandmother's character, her liveliness, her strength, determination and independence that they deserve to be treasured by those of us who come after. The fact that Ernst wanted them to be sent to her daughters suggests that he wanted the story of their love to be known by her children so that something would live on after them, and possibly that he also wanted Grete and Edith to know how their mother had lived the last two years of her life, bravely enduring hardship while sustained by the hope of a happier future.

Kate Ottevanger

2019

Marie Bader's letters and the Holocaust in the Protectorate of Bohemia and Moravia

Marie Bader's letters, compiled in this volume, provide Holocaust scholars and the general public with a unique collection of documents on the life of the Jewish community in Prague during the German occupation. A leading scholar on the history of Bohemian Jewry recently noted that we still lack an up-to-date synthesis of the Holocaust in the Protectorate of Bohemia and Moravia in a single volume. The historiography in English is even less developed. The last major work in English on the subject was published in 2005 and it was predominantly based on research conducted before the opening of east European archives after the Changes of late 1989. Since then scholars have published a number of studies on the development of Czech and German anti-Jewish policies in the Protectorate, on Czech anti-semitic movements and their press, as well as on the emigration of the Jews from the Protectorate before 1941 and the history of the Theresienstadt ghetto. One of the key topics that still awaits an author is the social history of the Jews in the Protectorate. This edition of private letters presents a key source that future historians will have to consult.

I joined the publication team relatively late, long after Kate Ottevanger had translated Marie's letters from German into English. Kate did so with love for her grandmother, whose fate she had to follow until the bitter end. I helped with the explanatory notes, shared my opinion on the parts of the letters we should publish, and contributed to the introduction and epilogue. We have been able to explain most of the indirect references Marie makes in her letters. Nevertheless, we sometimes had to admit that nobody apart from Marie and Ernst would ever understand the meaning of her words. The fact that we could read only one side of the conversation – Ernst's letters to Marie did not survive – complicated our endeavour. Furthermore, Ernst began to save Marie's letters only after October 1940 and it is evident that not every letter Marie sent after that date was delivered. Marie kept Ernst's letters when she stayed in Prague, but burnt them shortly before her deportation, thus silencing one side of the conversation forever. Only two letters sent by Ernst survived and we include them in this book.

The edition consists of selected and abbreviated letters. In our editing, we were guided by two aims: first, we wanted to give space to the personal story of Marie and Ernst, to this love affair that, under the hardship of the war, blossomed between two old friends, distant cousins, separated by frontlines and about a thousand miles. Second, we intended to allow readers insights into the daily life of the Jews in Prague under the German occupation from the time of the gradual segregation until the large-scale deportations to the Łódź Ghetto and Theresienstadt.

The story is both deeply personal and more general. Marie felt alone in Prague. Her daughters escaped in time to Britain, and her relationship with Irene and Gustav, her sister and brother-in-law, became tense. Direct contact with Edith and Grete stopped soon after Britain declared war on Germany in September 1939.

Marie's circle of old friends from Karlsbad could not replace the close bonds of family. Conversation with Ernst by means of letters became part of her daily routine, and she spent evenings alone in her room composing long letters to her old friend and now lover. For fear that the correspondence would be withheld, many of the letters discuss mundane matters but, interwoven with the chit-chat, questions of far deeper significance, offering insight into the current situation, are touched on or only hinted at. The letters reveal a whole network of people who communicated within Nazi Germany, as well as from the Nazi-held territories to countries overseas. To send letters to Ernst, Marie used the help of her cousin Eman (Edmund Benisch) in the United States and her friends in Vienna. She also communicated with people in other towns and cities, and remained in touch even with those deported from Vienna to eastern Poland in early 1941. These extensive communication networks and the role they played during the Holocaust are another topic that still awaits its historian. Pieces of information soon spread in the community, especially at the time when the Nazi anti-Jewish policies became more intensive. Marie's letters show that the community was relatively well informed about the destinations of the deportation trains, though unconfirmed rumours were common. Marie seemed to have good contacts at the Jewish Community in Prague (*Kultusgemeinde*), especially with Abraham Fixler, who worked as a permanent liaison officer at the Nazi *Zentralstelle für jüdische Auswanderung* (the Central Office for Jewish Emigration) in the Prague district of Střešovice. That is why she knew about the prepared deportations from Prague and the provinces, as well as about pauses between transports.

Marie's letters display the coping mechanism of the Jews in the gradually shrinking public space and limited social life of German-occupied Prague. Together with memoirs, a genre still being published to a considerable extent today, the letters complement other published primary sources, including letters sent by Paula Czerner to the United States between 1939 and 1941, the letters of Henriette Pollatschek from the same period, and the private diaries of Peter Ginz, Eva Mändl (Mándlová) and Jiří Münzer. At the same time, Marie's correspondence offers a particular perspective, which is largely absent in the other publicly available sources. It surprised me how Marie, while keeping in mind the censor's ever-watchful eye, expressed her opinions quite openly. The letters are full of detail about Marie's life and daily routine, including her social life, reactions to the introduction of anti-Jewish laws and later a description of the Jews' concerns about their fate after the arrival of the acting *Reichsprotektor* Reinhard Heydrich, and the preparation for deportation to the east. The fact that Thessaloniki, where Ernst lived, was under the German occupation from April 1941 and Marie did not therefore have to send the letters to an enemy country could be one factor contributing to the openness. This became crucial after December 1941, when Germany declared war on the United States and Czerner and Pollatschek could no longer send long letters across the Atlantic. Marie remained in contact with Ernst until April 1942, when she was deported from Prague. The detailed description of the events between September 1941 and April 1942 makes the edition a crucial source for our current understanding of Jewish life in the Protectorate at the time of the deportations.

It is clear that Marie's fate by no means represents the typical Jewish experience in the Protectorate, if anything like that even existed. She was an outsider from several perspectives. She was a widow in a patriarchal society, who until the deportation kept her private room in an apartment building where Jews as well as non-Jews lived. This was at a time when several Jewish families had to share one flat and parts of Prague became off-limits to the Jews. She was a refugee, who had come to Prague shortly before the Munich Agreement of late September 1938, after which her hometown of Karlsbad became part of the Reich, and she only narrowly escaped the violence unleashed by the Nazi sympathizers during Kristallnacht in November 1938. As a refugee, Marie experienced being uprooted long before the Czech Jews in Prague faced a similar fate. Last, she was a Jewish woman who had identified with German culture even after the German state completely excluded the Jews and when the Czechs rejected any manifestation of the occupiers' culture, including public communication in German. In her letters, Marie is not critical of the Czech population, but she was clearly unable to establish any social contact with local Czechs or even Czech Jews. Her social circle consisted of her acquaintances from Karlsbad, who found refuge in Prague, and her sister's family and friends. Marie lived in a community apart from Czech society, though she quickly became aware of the changed situation and tried to perfect her spoken Czech. She was a strong woman, and managed to cope with all the challenges of life in the Protectorate facing a Jewish woman of German culture who was accustomed to a comfortable life, and only rarely doubted her strength and abilities. Her will to overcome all obstacles and even help fellow Jews in Prague contrasts with the mental collapse of those who were unable to cope with the challenges, including Gustav, Irene and Mutti. Marie's letters attest to the Jews' ability and ingenuity when facing the genocidal regime of Nazi Germany.

Jan Láníček

2019

Editors' note

The edition contains only selected letters Marie Bader sent to Ernst Löwy between October 1940 and April 1942. The editors shortened the letters to avoid repetitions and left out details not essential for the main story and for the history of the Holocaust. For fluidity of reading there is no indication of omissions.

The Letters

1

October 1940–April 1941

After the death of Ernst's wife Thesa, in exile in Thessaloniki at the end of 1939, Marie wrote to him, following a painful three and a half year break in their friendship, to offer her condolences. That letter was written in the spring of 1940, but it was only in the following autumn, when they had finally admitted their love for each other – become 'engaged', as Marie later puts it – that Ernst began to save her letters. At the point when we enter the conversation, Marie had already experienced more than two years of displacement, after her family escaped from the Sudetenland, including eighteen months of the German occupation. Soon after the invasion, the Germans and the Czech Protectorate authorities began to introduce anti-Jewish laws that restricted the social space of those considered Jewish. On 21 June 1939, the Reichsprotektor *Konstantin von Neurath issued a law concerning Jewish property, which introduced the racial Nuremberg Laws in the Protectorate. Other laws limited Jews' employment opportunities. They were barred from public schools, could shop only at certain times of the day, and were not allowed to visit public parks, restaurants, museums, public baths, theatres and cinemas. There was a curfew that forbade the Jews from leaving their homes after 8 pm. Marie often alludes to the restrictions, though she needs to be very careful because of the censor who checks every line she sends to Ernst. With the shrinking 'Jewish map'*[i] *and progressing 'social death',*[ii] *the renewed contact and relationship with Ernst offered Marie the possibility of escapism from the real world of persecution. Ernst at this point was enjoying the last days of peace before, in less than a fortnight, fascist Italy invaded Greece. Thessaloniki was not directly impacted by the fighting, but Ernst's granddaughter Erika remembered the changing life conditions and atmosphere in the city with the approaching winter: 'The newspapers kept printing big headlines about our army's victories. ... The first weeks went by and then the first casualties arrived. Feet with gangrene, amputated legs. The first dead, and then more and more ... All the terrors of war. The cold was getting more severe.'[xii]*

Karlín, 17/10/1940

My dear Ernst

Your letter of 8 October came yesterday and I want to answer it straightaway. I myself can't understand why I am in such a hurry to reply, but my thoughts are constantly with you and I want to chat with you. My God, how has this become possible? How has it all come about? Who would have believed that this could happen at our age? I'm not ashamed, I think it is beautiful that despite one's age one can feel so young, both you and me. I'm so happy and *soooo* delighted with the contents of your letter. Many thanks for your sincerity and your trust in me. You restore so much to me, you lift me up as no other person is able to do. I can easily bear all sorts of unpleasantness and, as you gather, I really do throw my head back and say to myself: 'And now let's look ahead, life is worth living, it's beautiful to be alive.' I can rejoice like a child over your love and kindness and oh, how beautiful it would be if you were here with me. I too am now seized by a great longing and how do I deal with it? By writing to you and by imagining that you're sitting here next to me now, we're telling each other all sorts of things; there's laughter, joking and discussion. And then I shake my head at what I'm doing. Is it really me? How can this be happening? Am I doing something wrong? No, I tell myself, when I think of my reasons, and you know them! And so I thank fate for giving me your friendship. I'll keep and look after this precious thing as my most valued possession, to treasure it in days to come in my own manner. And so that I may succeed I will ask God that we may remain healthy and cheerful, so that we really do meet again!

After you cleared up all the doubts that arose from your letter, three letters ago, I am not sulking any more, as you can see. I can give you my hand and we are absolutely friends again, but I really must tell you why I was very unhappy. When I wrote to you that no-one is allowed to trouble our friendship you answered that perhaps the main cause would be the great distance, because one is subject to external influences.

I accept your assurance that nobody reads my letters to you. That is as it should be. They are our affair alone, which can't interest any third person, and so I can write to you much more openly if I know that.

Don't let yourself be undermined by the times. It is absolutely not possible in the situation we live in to grumble when one is living with and dependent on one's nearest relatives. The times are so exceptional and the difference between what is one's own and what is another person's has been so heavily blurred, compared to what it was before, and he who has been less affected by fate must quite obviously share with the other. I find it is much harder for the one who takes than for the one who gives; it can all change again. Your dear [daughter] Hella is a wonderful woman, to judge from your descriptions. She's making your life smooth and pleasant. She always impresses me in the way she does things. I think it's just wonderful that you are able to live among such lovely young people and that you can spend this temporary period in such a beautiful country. As you describe so interestingly, there is everything in profusion there and much is so cheap, and your vineyard![1] – it must be so nice to spend a day there. The mosquitoes are less pleasant. We too have sufficient provisions, the rationing works impeccably, there is perfect order and fairness in it and I am quite content.

From America[2] we have news from the 'friends'[3] that Edith and her husband, brother-in-law and sister-in-law are renting a house near their town. The men are working at their jobs. They didn't write where Grete is and I'm actually

---

[1] The vineyard was a small piece of land, twelve kilometres outside Thessaloniki, which Ernst's son-in-law bought before the war. With the help of Ernst, they built a small dwelling there. The family visited it every weekend.

[2] Marie's cousin in New York, Eman Benisch, is acting as a postman for letters between Britain and Czechoslovakia.

[3] Throughout her letters, Marie refers to her daughters Edith and Grete as the 'friends' and writes as if they are in the USA, not Britain. She never mentions Sheffield (where Edith is working) by name but occasionally calls it Chicago. Edith, being the younger of the two, is often referred to as 'the little one'.

most worried about her. Today I am sending you Ulli's[4] address because I'm afraid that some day you may not be able to write to me any more. I simply couldn't imagine your letters stopping and I do believe that you would want to avoid that. So please make a note: Dr F. U., Geneva, Switzerland, 44 rue des Pâquis. He'll be able to give you news of the conditions in the country from which you have no direct news.

I have to stop soon, as there's not much more room. If you have time and want to, write a diary for me and send me a page from it sometimes, because I want to know a lot about you and I'll do the same and tell you things from the last 4½ years of my life which seem worth while to me. Please give my greetings to all the family. Write to me as soon as you feel you want to. For me it can never be too soon. I send you very much love and I think of you all the time.

Your Mitzi

Thessaloniki, Odos Koromila 3,
26/10/1940

My dear Mitzi

Many thanks for your loving letter of the 17th October, which I received today. I read it three times so as to be sure I wasn't dreaming that it was all true. My thoughts were with you the whole time and I must admit that it was that letter and no other that I was looking forward to. Any other would have been a great disappointment for me. I'm not as surprised as you are at the fact that we love each other. It was present even in our youth and was only repressed by our understandable reserve. When people love each other their love will out, and in that I played my part in full. Nevertheless, I am not as confident as you but I hope I will become so. Yes, you're quite right when you say that life is still a precious thing, but will it be granted to us to make this thing a reality?

---

[4]Fritz Ullmann (1902–72) was a cousin of Marie's mother. The address given is that of the headquarters of the World Jewish Congress and of RELICO (the Relief Committee for the Warstricken Jewish Population) in Geneva, where Ullmann was based during the war as representative of the Jewish Agency. He was a committed Zionist, who maintained contact with Jewish communities under the Nazi occupation. He was widely praised for his efforts to help the Jews of Czechoslovakia.

I hope and wish for it perhaps even more passionately than you because I was certainly aware of it before you were. I thank you again and again that as soon as you became conscious of it you expressed your feelings. You yourself have already answered the question of whether it was wrong, but it is more than just *not* wrong, it is a *duty*. I am only afraid, my darling, that you think too highly of me, but for me, the more highly you think of me the better.

As far as my health goes, I feel well and will try to remain so. But although I don't often show my feelings, I am nevertheless, like most people, very receptive to love, because it is pure. So now you will understand why I was always writing in my letters that I want to come back. Perhaps the war will end soon so that there will still be time for us to be happy. You mustn't talk so much about the burden of age. I don't believe there is any reason to be ashamed but to be joyful, at any rate for ourselves. You know full well my thoughts on family but all that is unimportant. Only absolute selfishness is healthy.

I take as understood your promise never to interpret my words as intending to hurt you since it is obvious that I don't want to do that. Both sides must understand these words we may say to each other in the light of the situation which exists between us. Stick to that principle, no-one may interfere, whoever it may be. If I expressed some thoughts about this it was really only from worry and anxiety because you've several times been subject to these pressures. It is in my nature always to speak as I think and if no loving word passes my lips, it's not with the intention of hurting. I know that you were surrounded by much tenderness and love, which were also expressed in words. You can't expect that from me but actions will replace words. If you remember that, dearest Mitzi, you won't feel disappointed in me. It's particularly right at the beginning to give of oneself naturally and not let any false expectations arise. Really, I don't need to write that because we've known each other long enough and I've never pretended otherwise. I know that you need a lot of love and tenderness but I can only be sincere .... .

I couldn't finish this letter yesterday and today, as I continue it, war has broken out between Greece and Italy.[5]

---

[5]Italy invaded Greece on 28 October 1940. The invasion was a failure and the Italian army was forced to withdraw. Thessaloniki was not directly affected.

The text ends at this point. The rest is missing.

Karlín, 22/10/1940

Sent before Ernst's letter of 26 October was received.

My dear Ernst

Well, that was a pleasure this morning to have your letter in my hands, because I had calculated from the date of your last one that the next letter

Photo 2 *Ernst Löwy.*

wouldn't arrive for another three days. First of all, my deepest thanks for your good wishes. I too could wish myself a bit of happiness. One must just hope and trust to the future.

There's only one bitter pill in your letter and that is your terrible loss of weight. It really won't do, my Ernstili. If you were here I would soon feed you up. If I knew that Hella wouldn't mind, I would send her a few good recipes for dumplings. What do you think, my darling? Can I risk it?

I've seen Dr Gallus and his daughter[6] quite frequently. Things are probably going as well for them as for other people. I'll find out and let you know.

Would you like to have the Jewish newspaper from here?[7] I don't in fact know whether I'll be allowed to send it but it would be useful for you to be able to read it because I see it's not years but decades that you've been away from here.[8] Forgive me if I am so frank. I can't always express myself as I would like to but that's how it is.

The 'friends' have just sent us greetings for our family Saturday, which gave great pleasure to everyone. The couple are living in a country house near Chicago. The house has been put at their disposal by a friend of the family. The little one is a good little housewife, the big one has a job. They seem to be living very happily. I am so glad about it.

Now I must give you a picture of some of the types of people here to help you imagine them. There is one kind who simply can't come to terms with conditions today. As long as they themselves were not affected, they thought that fate would not touch them as it did others, that everything would remain as it had been for them and that the war had nothing to do with them. But when the time comes for them to be tested, then they are desperately unhappy, they destroy the happiness of home and family and the husband and the whole family around him become ill or unable to work, etc. I've no time at all for

---

[6]Judr. Ervín Gallus (*1882), his wife Valerie (*1891) and daughter Eliesa (*1917) were later deported to Łódź (on 21 October 1941), where they perished.

[7]*Jüdisches Nachrichtenblatt – Židovské listy*, was a weekly published by the Jewish Community office (*Kultusgemeinde*) between 1939 and 1945. It published new anti-Jewish laws, issued by the German and Czech authorities, and promoted the idea of Jewish emigration, as well as retraining courses.

[8]Because of censorship, Marie only hints at the changes in Czechoslovakia since Ernst and Thesa left in March 1939.

this sort. The next type face the times sensibly and calmly, prepare themselves quietly for an alternative career, both husband and wife lower their standard of living, accepting everything as it must be accepted and simplifying life for themselves and others. But neither type can imagine themselves in the position of a refugee. They thought that we[9] were the only ones to be tested; they, the so-called Czech Jews, were privileged and saw us as intruders and I always disliked that very much because views like that don't fit with my way of seeing things. But now everybody is in the same boat, which is right and just. On the other hand I'm impressed by those older people who bravely take up various training courses to learn everything possible about manual skills. It is truly moving and admirable what those people do. Ernstili, you would be astonished if you saw professors, doctors, lawyers working, mostly with great diligence and thoroughness, for example at poultry farming, studying the theory and preparing themselves for exams, among them sometimes men well over sixty years old.[10]

Now it's time for our personal chat. First of all, please don't forget your photograph. I am looking forward to it. I won't talk about being in the dumps again because I won't do anything any more that you don't want – that's the first thing I want to say. Again, it's you I have to thank for my confidence because I know that you need it and I know that by helping each other to stand up tall, our friendship will blossom in the way I want it to.

How would it be if we wrote to each other twice a week, whether there is an answer or not? Then we would always have something to look forward to every third day. I think I could then contain my yearning a little. Only I don't know if my longing for you isn't too great. If it is, then just say so. There would be an awful lot I could tell you about what I lived through in the last four and a half years when we weren't speaking to each other and you could also tell me all sorts of things about any period of your life.

---

[9]Marie referred to Jewish refugees from German-occupied Sudetenland and Jews of German nationality and language as opposed to Czech Jews in Prague. In this letter Marie refers to tensions between Czech Jews and Jewish refugees from the Sudetenland.
[10]The Jewish Community office in Prague organized various classes so that people who hoped to be able to emigrate could learn foreign languages and acquire marketable skills.

Please give my best wishes to the young ones and the youngest. I can only urge Hella to use the greatest energy in fattening you up!

Warmest greetings from your Mitzi.

Thessaloniki, 13/11/1940

My dearest Marie

I received your letter of the 22nd today and I'm hurrying to answer straightaway. I hope that in the meantime you have received mine of 26/10 and I'm very curious to have your answer, although from what you write I haven't the slightest doubt that you agree entirely with my feelings. In the meantime Greece and Italy are at war and because of that I can't write to you in as much detail as I would like. I'm all the more sorry because you write to me, my darling, that my letters are your greatest pleasure. You can stop worrying about my weight. Since I've been following your advice I'm eating more and have already gained some. I've consulted a doctor several times recently and he's quite happy with my lifestyle. Your well-intentioned suggestions to Hella can't unfortunately be carried out because the others wouldn't eat the dishes, quite apart from the impossibility of preparing them. I think that it would be very good if I could have my clothes and underwear, as well as my bed and table linen, sent to you. If you can arrange anything (they are at Sebert's[11]), then do. If you need authorization, then let me know, so that I can write about it to my lawyer there. Could you use the furniture and the other things? You know what there is, so I don't need to describe it to you.

I thank you very much for the news about Gallus. I understand you very well when you write that I seem to have been away from you for decades but what if it were different? I'm always glad when you've got good news of our friends. I always got on well with them and always will. Your observations about people are right and were already true when I lived in Karlsbad but take comfort, people are the same the world over and selfishness is highly developed everywhere.

---

[11]Sebert was a property management company in Karlsbad.

I don't want you to obey me blindly, and the you that I know and love won't want to either. I know that I have found in you the best and dearest comrade, which makes me proud and happy.

The civilian population ask me for a lot of advice about the wartime restrictions and I find the day too short. Please don't be angry if I act according to current restrictions and end this letter and often only send you a card. They're now demanding that one reduces letters to cards if possible so as not to overburden the inspectors.[12]

And now, my dearest, have no worries and stay well.

With warmest greetings, Ernst.

Karlín, 15/11/1940

My dear Ernst

After an anxious wait, your letter of 26/10 arrived at last. I see that you had only just received my letter of the 17th. Which merciful censor should I thank for the wonderful chance that the letter arrived? My God, how happy your letter makes me!

Darling, I thank you for your cheering words and if God grants us life and health we will see each other again as soon as it is possible. My memory of life with Emmerl[13] is so beautiful that my dearest wish was for a continuation of such happiness, so when then, quite unexpectedly, I recognized that I loved you dearly, how could I hide it from you? The thought that there, far away, a warm heart was beating for me was just too beautiful.

I hope confidently for an early reunion. One of the two of us will risk the big journey just as soon as we may. Nobody will be able to stop me, I know that now, let alone will anyone dare to try to influence me. Those times are over and I'm determined to build our future happiness with a sure hand.

Three days ago your brother Emil was here for lunch. A while ago I invited him to come and eat with me. Recently he just invited himself. I thought that

---

[12] After the outbreak of the war with Italy Greek authorities evidently increased the control of civilian postal communications.
[13] Marie's late husband Emil Bader.

was delightful, so natural and sweet, and I was so happy to see him. And just guess what we talked about most of all? Weren't your ears burning? I read him bits from your letters and he just shook his head over your good style. Then he showed me pictures of you and I let him give me one, and now it's my companion. Emil looks well, has very sensible views and accepts his fate.[14] Apparently his people are well, both here and over there, and he just has to be content with that.

A month ago I was given notice for my flat because I am a German [-speaking] Jew and the owner would prefer someone Czech. That is a very hard blow for me because I'm no longer allowed to take a flat on my own. According to the present regulations I have to take a room with someone else.[15] That is hard and painful for me, as if the ground had been cut from under my feet. So from 15 January 1941 I will have a room, with my furniture, at the Lípas',[16] but I think of it with dread. Granted it's better to be a lodger with my own people than with strangers, because they would also have to take other strangers. I was so upset about this that I became ill, but I'm quite better now, and as I lost some weight I feel much healthier and livelier than before. But now that I have the certainty that one day we will belong to each other entirely, this question of accommodation worries me less. What do I care when I think of you!

Ernstili, the times are serious and hard, and that is why I am writing especially openly, though rather embarrassed, in front of my friend Eman.[17] However, I'm doing it because I think that, particularly now, one shouldn't be too secretive with one's feelings, so that in this way one can find enough endurance and morale to get through these anxious times and it is satisfying

---

[14]Emil Löwy (*1875) is living apart from his non-Jewish wife. It seems that they were still formally married at the beginning of the war, which protected Emil against deportation. In November 1941 (part of the letter sent on 19 November 1941 is not included in this edition) he was living in an old people's home in Prague. Whether his wife divorced him or she died, he appears to have lost his protection and was deported on 24 October 1942 to Theresienstadt and from there immediately to Auschwitz (on 26 October), where he was most likely murdered immediately upon his arrival.

[15]There were increasing restrictions imposed on the Jews in Prague. They could live only in certain districts (in Prague 2, Prague 5 and parts of Vinohrady, see the letter of 25 September 1941) and several families had to share an apartment.

[16]Gustav and Irene Lípa. Irene was Marie's sister.

[17]This letter was sent via her cousin, Eman Benisch, in New York.

to know that at least in this way I can say how much I love you. I could say a lot to you but I don't want to annoy the censor too much, so I'll stop.

Greet your loved ones. I send you a dozen sweet kisses. I hug you warmly in my heart.

Your Mitzi.

Karlín, Sunday, 17/11/1940

Dearest Ernst

I have had a very busy day, with numerous guests, a lot of work, but also much pleasure. It was a family get-together, at my place this time, and other good friends invited themselves round for a little chat. Now I am alone again, but no, not alone, now comes the most beautiful moment of the day. In front of me is your picture, which otherwise I carry about with me, and now it is time to chat with you. There you are, sitting near to me. I look at your hands, then I answer some of the things in your letter of 26/10 which I didn't deal with yesterday. So you want to protect me from disappointment? And you remind me of your reserved nature. I know you, Ernstili, and am quite aware of it. I also know that I am a little excitable and that I should be a little calmer – well perhaps that may yet happen. I got to know you thoroughly on several occasions and have never forgotten the lovely time we had when we travelled together to Leipzig. Nor the sad moment when they carried Emmerl away and you didn't let them stop me from going with him. You were the only one who understood my mind and knew that to be there was the right thing and what I wanted. Oh Ernstili, I felt no other person in the world knows and understands me as well as Ernst Löwy does.

Even as a child I was only drawn by kindness. That's why I was so attracted to Emmerl and gave myself to him totally, because I loved his honourable and kind nature so much. I would never have been capable of going behind his back, his boundless trust deserved my total commitment, it moved me, and I did everything to deserve it. Yes, if it had been different, if he had behaved in a nasty, unkind way, I would have become stubborn and rebellious. One can get anywhere with me through kindness.

And now I would like to deal with something else: you have good reason to mention you fear that I might let myself be influenced. Ernstili, you don't think that I still live in the same conditions as when I lived in Karlsbad? My love, much has changed since then, both the people and the times. Today, everyone is preoccupied above all with his own affairs, people are far less interested in each other than they used to be, everybody's head is too full. And what about me? I have paid a heavy price for what I have learnt in my widowhood, but in my thinking and in the way I deal with life I have become very emancipated and independent, almost recklessly so. I don't let anyone tell me what to do, above all not now when on occasion my sister and brother-in-law show kindnesses towards me. That is exactly why not now, because the price to be paid for having life made easier for me is that my freedom to think and act for myself is taken from me. That is a price that no attentions can be worth.

And as for our relationship, Irene knows that we are in correspondence, and so does Mutti.[18] They also know, because I told them, that we love each other, that our greatest aim is to be united. Mutti is delighted but Irene is hurt that I do not ask for help and don't tell her anything more, that I keep everything secret and don't show her any letters, in a word, that I am not taking her into my confidence enough. But I think that she is pleased too because she and her husband have always liked you.

So have no fears about me. But I need the same reassurance about you. I have such a foreboding that somebody, either there or perhaps here, might some time whisper suspicions. That is why you must also make a promise: that you will only think and believe of me what my person itself presents to you. The unpleasant vexations of that time[19] would not have got so out of hand if my mother and sister hadn't, quite against my wishes, got themselves involved. That was still possible at that time. I was so crushed by sorrow that I hardly knew what people were doing. I certainly didn't want this nasty behaviour, this gossip in the town. Unfortunately, that is how my mother behaved in other cases too and then there were always the most horrible consequences. But

---

[18]Louise Rosenberger (*1861), Marie's mother, lived with Marie's sister and brother-in-law. She was murdered in Treblinka in October 1942.
[19]The time of Emil's death and its aftermath.

because I was her child and loved her I was always weak and never managed to criticize her way of doing things.

Now my mother is an old lady, nearly 80 years old. She loves you as she always has, has never been angry with you, and rightly so, and neither has Irene. On the contrary, it is thanks to my mother that we found each other. It was your wish that Emil should inform me of poor Thesa's passing. Mutti spoke once with Emil and heard that I was to be told. She brought me your address and said 'So there you are, now you can write to Ernst. I think he deserves it from you and your husband.' My good one, I hope you are not angry that I am telling you this today in such detail, but it has to be done in order to be fair. I don't really know what reason you have or had to be so mistrustful. I think you must mean Mutti and Irene – there must have been an awful lot of gossip at the time about which I am probably the one who knows least. I will still always strive to bring peace and harmony between those who are dear and precious to me but I will never require you, if it is not your wish, to enter into any closer relationship: we two, however, must always be in agreement in front of others.

More times in my life than I can recall, my mother and sister have shown me loyalty and self-sacrifice; I must acknowledge that, whatever their failings. I would really have no right to judge too harshly, that would be wrong of me. Therefore I will try very hard never to disappoint them in my love for them, and I hope that in the end, for my sake, you too will not find it too great a sacrifice to make it up with them. I leave the decision to you. Once again I say, first and foremost, we are for each other, only then for others, and only when we are agreed in our views do we take those of others into account. You are going to say that the unnatural mother says nothing about her children. Well, I know you always loved each other a lot, there was harmony from the beginning. I am almost certain that they will not come back to their homeland but find one in a far off land. They will put down roots somewhere, it seems. And I will absolutely not influence them because I have no right to do so. You know that I was always a good mother and will be so again, but they don't need me any more. I will never be able to mean much to them any more, but God has not forsaken me; he has given me your love!

Now I want to answer a point you make. You write that you hope you will be able to pay [your children] back everything, that is, the expense you are causing now. Well of course, Ernstili, you will. You are still young and as a man you will be able to work hard and achieve things. Just wait! You will sweat. Just think how much there will be to rebuild after the war. There will be an enormous amount of work everywhere, just for you and your profession. Then it will be easy for you to pay back that little bit, so don't worry. Just take it easy and wait calmly until your time comes.

Finally, I just want to say that I am using the opportunity to write in such detail while it is still allowed. I wrote the first three sheets fourteen days ago and then we heard that communications were interrupted. I have just enquired at the main post office and learnt that communications are still functioning so I am posting this letter to you today, 29 November, and send it trusting to luck. I would like it very much if you could send me a card twice a week – you will understand that one worries.

And now keep well, my good one. Loving hugs and kisses from

Your Mitzi.

Karlín, 26/11/1940

My dear Ernst

That was a glad and happy moment when I held your letter of the 13th in my hands. Thank God for the good news.

Today I can give you some good news about me too. First, after the success of my publicity, I now have some students, male and female, who are working with great enthusiasm and I am delighted with their success and mine.[20] People are paying me all sorts of compliments about the excellence and quality of my teaching and I am very happy and so are the rest of my family. I also had the satisfaction that what was left of our previous [EBE][21] production is highly sought after and its outstanding quality is most highly

---

[20]Marie's students were learning how to make *Oblaten* (*oplatky*, wafers).
[21]EBE Karlsbader Nährmittelindustrie (see the Introduction).

praised in those circles where once I struggled without success. Were it permitted, I would now have a wide market here. That isn't possible but the public recognition makes me feel it would be possible, if it were necessary, to succeed somewhere else.[22]

The second and actually more important point is that I can't actually move out of the flat on 15 January because the landlady has no right to give me notice, as I am obliged to remain in the flat since no other is being offered to me. I told her that and hope that now I will be allowed to keep my beloved nest, where I am so happy, a while longer.

Write to me regularly as long as you are able, and if my dear Eman has discovered his kind heart, which will be full of sympathy, I am quite certain he will surely do all that is possible. I can be much warmer in my letters to you in front of him, because as I remember him from my youth, he will understand how it is. We were the same age and grew up together. He was always very cheerful and full of fun and although he has been gone for 38 years he is still a faithful, dependable cousin and friend.

Many greetings to all the Cougnos[23] from me, keep well, cheerful and content. I hug you in my imagination and send you a dozen kisses and am

Your Mitzi.

Karlín, 7/12/1940

My beloved Ernst

I am settling down this Saturday evening, the one evening when I have enough time and inspiration to chat with you, which is my best relaxation. Today I am particularly longing for you and I really don't know how I will put up with that for any length of time. I am at a loss for an answer.

This afternoon I was invited to some friends. It was very lively and cosy. Times have changed so much and people too. It amuses me very much to see men I know doing the housework so well, things like clearing the table; it is terribly funny, but

---

[22]Does Marie consider joining Ernst in Greece?
[23]The family of Ernst's daughter Hella.

suits the times if they help their wives with the housework and shopping in their ample free time.[24] I went home at seven o'clock. When I see the many couples, everyone together, and me struggling along on my own, when I can so well picture you by my side, indeed when I cannot imagine any future other than with you, then something nasty takes hold of me that I never knew before. And you know, my darling, what that is: huge jealousy of all those who are in couples, laughing and joking, and then I have my work cut out to suppress those tormenting thoughts. I have never felt jealousy in my life, but now I'm actually experiencing its reality.

From now on I will write to you twice a week. If you can, do the same; one definitely has to expect things to go astray here and there. It is wartime and one has to be grateful that some things get through. Please send me the address for a possible intermediary again, one never knows when one might need it.

Today I had a real meal, the sort you like, crackling and liver, etc. Oh how I thought of you and the times we ate things like that together and all sorts of teasing went on. Actually I sometimes got really cross with you because I often didn't know whether it was serious or a joke. I can see before me the look of irony on your face, your mouth would take a particular shape, something would come out that made me prick up my ears, that was meant for me in some way. Yes, what happened to those times?

Today I bought two primulas in flower because now, in the winter, none of my houseplants are in bloom. I imagine that they come from you and they make me very happy. It is an extravagance, I know, but these are the cheapest and people must have some pleasure. I will be told off, but that doesn't matter much to me. In my sitting room I have a large modern window with lovely foliage plants and now my flowering plants among them. They make me very happy and when I come home they are what I see first. In front of this window stands my desk with various photos of my loved ones and now you are ranged among them. But that is still too little, I want to have you with me completely.

---

[24]In several letters Marie describes the changing gender roles in Jewish families caused by the gradual segregation and the fact that men, previously much more prominent in public life, lost their jobs. For example, on 6 August 1941 (not published here) she wrote: 'Here it is commonly the men who go shopping because they usually have a lot of time. If the women have to queue they can't get everything done on their own in the short time available. Don't think I am suggesting something to you which is degrading.' See also the letters of 10 March 1941 or 18 July 1941.

Continued on Sunday 8/12

After being with my people almost the whole day long,[25] I am alone again. And that is good because that is when I'm happiest. I can converse with you in my mind; the atmosphere at their place is, unfortunately, mostly tense and uncomfortable. They get very worked up about things that don't worry me. I have left all that behind long ago, but they still have to experience it and deal with it.

I have re-read my chat with you from yesterday and think today that it isn't quite right but I'm not going to change anything. Please don't take anything amiss, it was just a passing mood I was in. I think I once wrote to you that Uncle Paul,[26] with his wife, brother-in-law and mother-in-law emigrated to São Paulo, Brazil, from Paris via Portugal. In the summer he lost a lovely, promising child, a girl of thirteen. They left in deepest sadness. Now I have had a letter saying that it is so beautiful there and, although he has no work as yet, he has some very good friends, a brother-in-law in New York, and Oskar in Milwaukee, where Paul's son is too. Obviously it takes a time in a foreign country before one gets used to it but it makes one glad to get news which is even half-way good. Paul is pursuing the hobby which was his favourite as a boy – catching butterflies. That reminds me, too, of my childhood and youth because I was only half a year younger than Paul and in the holidays we would from time to time go hunting for butterflies in the Udritscher forest[27] – that is, we would look for caterpillars, which I did not like. He collected them in matchboxes and I had to carry them. I always wanted to know if they were still alive and looked inside. Mostly they lost their heads then, and then there was trouble!

Max[28] is in correspondence with Mutti and I usually add a few lines. He is separated, his two lovely children visit him from time to time, but only briefly. He seems to feel very alone. A while ago he asked me for my opinion on whether it would be a good idea to come here. Until now I couldn't decide how

---

[25]Marie regularly joined bridge parties with her friends, many of them also refugees from Karlsbad.
[26]Paul Buxbaum, one of her mother's brothers, left Czechoslovakia before the war. Oskar and Max, both in the USA, and referred to further on, were his brothers.
[27]Udrčský les (in Czech) near Karlsbad.
[28]Max Buxbaum, Mutti's brother.

to reply to such an important question, but now I have written that it would certainly be better to stay in his warm nest as his sisters are hardly in a position to offer him the peace and comfort he is looking for, because today everyone has enough worries of their own. It is surely better that he stays where he is.

Dear Ernst, give all your loved ones my greetings. Keep well, be healthy, cheerful and happy.

Love, Mitzi

Karlín, 9/12/1940

My dear Ernst

At the word 'my' there comes a warm feeling in my heart and I think: really mine, yes, really mine. What a wonderful thought! Today began so beautifully. Very early I got ready to take a letter to you to the post, but instinctively I knew that there would be news from you. And there was. And now in the evening, after the day's work,[29] I am sitting here again and writing to you.

Ernstili, you ask whether we will see each other again. Yes, of course! How could I bear life if I didn't have that hope? And it won't be so very long. I want to be together with you by spring, at the latest. That is my greatest wish, dearest. Some day mankind will make friends again, every war has an end, so this one too will end one day, and then, and then? Then there will be a *wieder-wiedersehen*! It doesn't matter where it is, I don't care at all. I won't be afraid anywhere in the world if you are with me.

I am glad that so far you are happy in your country; that pleases and comforts me. May God continue to protect you all. I pray fervently every day for you and for my 'friends'. When I open my eyes in the morning the first thing I see is your photos, my first words are to ask God to protect you and them.

You mustn't write anything to me which could lead to the letter being confiscated. I don't want to know anything except things about you, about what you are doing, about yourself, that is enough for me. And then about

---

[29]Marie refers to her daily routine of washing, cleaning, cooking, shopping and visits to officials or lawyers.

your loved ones, Hella and the family. Otherwise, nothing else interests me at the moment. I am also writing only personal things, as you see, because I dearly hope that in this way I will not annoy the censor.

And now, my darling, I am going to sleep, to dream about you as I usually do, so good night! Greetings to Hella and everyone.

I hold you close in my mind, send a dozen sweetest kisses and remain

Your Mitzi.

PS What does dear Hella think when there are so many letters from me?

Karlín, Saturday, 14/12/1940

My beloved Ernst

There is no doubt that fate has destined us, after so many hard trials, to enjoy the most wonderful happiness which is normally only reserved for the young. How could we refuse to recognise this? Thank God there is still time left for us. You believe, Ernstili, that our mutual attraction had existed for a long time. Well, my darling, I would have to go back a long way. I can't do that in a letter but you know a lot of things better than I do. In many things I am simple or stupid. I will only say today that it was a severe trial for me when I had to forgo your friendship. It was hard and bitter to bear and I suffered unspeakably, but I deliberately avoided any situation which might have caused trouble. I still think about our Leipzig journey – how beautiful it was!

It has not yet been decided about the flat but I will probably have to move out. That is a whole chapter and it makes me sad. I am going to do my best to please my lords and masters and I hope I will succeed.

Continued on Sunday 15th

Just think, we have 13 degrees of frost here. That's pretty cold! Can you still imagine it? I was out from 9 in the morning because the little daughter of an acquaintance is leaving in the next few days with the Youth Emigration Group to Palestine.[30] She came to the Lípas to say goodbye. Partings like that are like

---

[30]The Youth Aliyah (Jugendalijah) organized the emigration of children and the youth to Palestine, which was under the British rule. The efforts continued clandestinely even after the outbreak of the war (as part of Aliyah Bet).

funerals and I felt very upset too. Of course there were other parents present, two couples whose children are there already. In the afternoon we were with friends to play bridge and I laughed a lot because one lady was so funny and original. You know how heartily I can laugh – I haven't forgotten how, thank goodness! It was really enjoyable. But they are all complaining that, according to them, I am so absent-minded. What can be to blame for that? Have you any idea what the cause is? Yes or no? But don't get big-headed (as you say!)

If you should write to the 'friends' in Chicago, I have no objections either, if you think it is right (and only then) to prepare them about us. They will be very glad, I think.

Ernstili, I am not at all worried about our future prosperity. It is as you said: we will manage. I have total confidence in you and besides, I will be there when you need me and, in any case, in your work too I will always be your comrade. Perhaps as your typist if you pay me well and behave yourself. What do you think? In the long run I would like to live a simple, quiet life because everything will be very different, since people have learnt that a lot is superfluous and that a simple life is actually in many ways much more attractive and comfortable.

And now, in my imagination, I am standing on tiptoe, I pull your head down towards mine, kiss your forehead, your eyes, your cheeks and then your mouth, and then all of them again. That is exactly one dozen kisses. Good night then. I will have beautiful dreams about you. Greetings, please, to all your loved ones.

With tender love, your Mitzi
Comment from the censor: 'Please keep it brief!'

Karlín, 19/12/1940

My beloved Ernst

So that you shouldn't worry, I am answering your letter of 7/12 immediately. I am relieved that you are to become a member of my family.[31] I think the way

---

[31]Ernst apparently wants to announce their intention to marry but does not hide his feelings about Irene and Mutti following their part in the rupture in 1936.

you intend to do it is the right one. I can accept your attitude towards Mutti and understand you. That is why I will do what you wish and never refer to this subject again or attempt to bring about a deeper relationship between the two of you. Besides, Mutti told me 'I will be content if you are happy; I don't demand any personal relationship.'

I don't really want to discuss the matter further now, but I must tell you one thing: my mother and sister have indeed always been very good to me, and here in Prague too, but for a long time I have been living in a different world from them. The relationship we used to have disappeared a long time ago. The fact is that very few people have adjusted to this troubled time. Since the children left I have been quite alone mentally. I sometimes feel hurt by my family's behaviour and no longer feel that they have a real understanding of people and things. On the whole the times have proved me right, so that I continue to have confidence in myself. Now I have found in you a friend and loved one who, despite hard times, expresses kindness and love and respect for humankind, such as I would expect from those to whom I can show my heart and who understand and sympathize with me.

I am very glad to hear that Thesa thought well of me and I can say that I always meant well, honestly and sincerely by her. I believed I understood her and never had any intention of hurting her. I have long ago made my peace with her in my mind. I do know that you were the best and most decent husband. How could I ever have judged you as anything else?

Recently I had a beautiful dream which I want to tell you about. It was dusk, we were sitting in a cosy corner when there was a sudden rustling; a little apparition flew up to us, sat down at our side, it was little Cupid himself! He spoke to us and we said to him with one voice, 'We wanted to thank you, good one.' He answered 'Yes, dear children, but that's not enough for me, that is why I have come, because I want proof of your gratitude.' 'And what should that be?' we replied. 'Well listen,' he went on, 'each of you has left behind here and there, in different places, objects and knick-knacks which you loved dearly but which you won't be able to use for years and I gave these things away to others among my charges so as to complete their happiness. In payment for your gratitude I wish you to assure me that you won't complain to anyone of this, won't make any criticism either spoken or written, nor will you blame anyone;

in short, that you will accept the situation without grumbling and not tell your families and friends a word about it! You must know that I granted you a special blessing and have found you worthy of enjoying exceptional happiness, so now you must decide for yourselves.' For a while we looked at each other and then you said 'Good, it will be as you wish' and I said 'If that's what you want, I am willing.' Then Cupid lifted his little wings high and was gone. I woke up and thought to myself that it was a beautiful dream; it could even happen in reality. How do you like it?

Dear one, I know the time is coming which reminds you of very sad days.[32] My feelings and thoughts are with you, but please, and this time for love of me, take care of your health, keep yourself well for me, I beg you. In a few days it will be Christmas.[33] I always had very lovely memories of it. This time I will be thinking a lot about you, will write to you and look forward more eagerly than ever to the time when we will be living together.

A happy new year, full of good cheer! Let's drink to our health together. And now the most heartfelt hug and love without end.

Mitzi.

Karlín, 24/12/1940

My dear Ernst

There was no news from you this week and that doesn't please me at all, but that's how it is. It may also be that my news to you does not arrive, not through my fault but because of your specific wish that it should be sent by ordinary post.

How will you spend the festive season? If you can, tell me what you did. I'll spend one day at the Lípas' but this evening I am staying at home, against their wishes, but I prefer it so. I have also been invited to a tea party on the second day of Christmas. At the moment there is a hard frost, real Christmas weather. There is snow as well and we need better heating in the apartments.

---

[32]Marie is referring to the first anniversary of Thesa's death.
[33]Marie several times refers to the celebration of Christmas, but at the same time to the effort to stick to Jewish traditions. This was a common feature of Jewish identity in Bohemia.

I hope you received my letter of the 19th and will have understood from it that your possessions which were at Sebert's were sold a year ago. I hope this news doesn't surprise you because it has happened everywhere as all the flats and warehouses had to be cleared. A large part of my possessions was also cleared in this way. I am not thinking about it any more because what I have here is enough for me and I wouldn't have had room for any more. In the final analysis, we have both lost far more important things including our dearest ones, so don't be upset and don't think about it.

The 'friends' sent us greetings again and told us that the men got a pay increase and that things are going well for them in Chicago, so one has to be happy about that, at least it's a little ray of hope for the festive days.

This time I am being brief so that the letter is passed to you by the censor more easily. May you and all your loved ones stay healthy and cheerful, happy and content. Keep well, dear Ernst, think a little about me, then our thoughts will cross. I hug you warmly and send you a dozen sweet kisses. Greetings to the Cougnos.

Your Mitzi.

Karlín, 28/12/1940

My dear Ernst

Your letter of 7/12 was the last news from you up till now. Please, Ernst, if, God forbid, you are ill, ask Hella to write me a few lines. It is too much of a torment to be completely without news of you, when up to now you wrote to me so regularly. Or are you annoyed or angry with me about something? You would tell me, I hope.

The Christmas holiday is over. I know you had the anniversary of poor Thesa's death and it was surely terribly sad in the house. My thoughts were with you a lot, but also with her. I recalled more vividly than before many little incidents when we were all together. I see her before me as if it were yesterday, how she loved eating breaded lamb cutlets and how you always warned about moderation and a suitable diet. She told me various things about Jurgo the dog, how he loved to hop into bed with her but that Ernst mustn't see it because he didn't like it, and how she laughed when Jurgo drank all the milk in our sitting room.[34] She could laugh till she cried about this heroic deed, and when you angrily prepared to punish him and we had difficulty calming you down. What a drama that was! And it was all so harmless.

How different it is today. I also had our dog Harry here, the one I bought for Greterl at her request when she came home from the sanatorium. I was just glad that she wanted something again. Harry was a lovely animal but very wild and impetuous. When we were here in Prague and he was still in Karlsbad, she begged until I gave in and let the dog come. Greterl had a great deal of pleasure from him here and so did I, but for me he was also a great trial, particularly after Greterl left. He had very little freedom here and it was awkward for me to walk about all the time with that big animal, while my family were always complaining about him. On the other hand, I was very attached to him as I was quite alone, but it was no use, I had to give Harry away; which was very hard for me. But it is marvellous for him, as he is wonderfully cared for.

What happened to Jurgo? When I met Thesa here in Prague, shortly before you left, I innocently asked her about him and the poor thing burst into tears and we both got upset. We said goodbye, it was the last time and for ever.

The 'friends' are now remembering me more often. Yesterday the friend[35] of the older one sent a telegram at her request with greetings and new year wishes from her and news of their welfare. Isn't that nice of her? It's as if she had guessed that just at this moment I have a lot of worries and need a little joy to help me bear this period more easily.

Today we had a family get-together at Edith's parents-in-law.[36] The father is pining for the children and also has all sorts of unnecessary worries. He has a very sensitive nature and is also constantly unwell, which makes me very sorry. The children are not to know that. The only thing which could make him better would be to see them again. Be glad, dear Ernstili, that you were at least spared this anxiety which gnaws at a person's vitals.

---

[34]Jurgo was the Löwys' dog.
[35]A reference to Käthe Brock-Strauss, a good friend of Grete Reichl (Marie's daughter), who managed to get to the USA with her husband and children.
[36]Hede and Rudi Sternschuss.

Monday a.m., 30/12. I left the letter until this morning and was hoping for news, but unfortunately in vain. Keep well, my love. As long as you're in good health. Warmest hugs and kisses. Greet all your loved ones.

Your Mitzi

Photo 3 *Marie's daughter Grete with her dog Harry, 1939.*

Karlín, 31/12/1940

My beloved Ernstili

The arrival of your longed-for letter of 14/12 today, the very last day of the year, put me in a very happy, confident mood for the coming year. Can you understand that, my dear? It is New Year's Eve, our town is thickly blanketed in fresh snow. Although I was invited to spend the evening and stay the night at the Lípas', I preferred to stay at home so as to be able to be with you in my thoughts.

I was very worried about you because of the long break but the contents of your letter made me very happy. I agree with you completely that we should only speak of personal matters in our letters, that is fine with me. But then, now and again, when I re-read my letters, I am a little embarrassed because they talk of almost nothing of substance and I wonder what this serious man will think of me, the whole letter being such a lot of nonsense. Then I shake my head and laugh at myself. This is how it is with me: I write exactly as if I were talking to you, without thinking about what I want to write, a letter like that is meant to replace a conversation or a cosy little chat. That's why there's all that nonsense, you see?

I am sure, dear Ernst, that in our future life together we will often argue and discuss. It won't always go smoothly. I know how you are, but I am not afraid of you any more, as I once was. I didn't always understand you and was sometimes embarrassed and confused (which may happen again) when I saw you on the point of pulling that ironic mouth. Then I knew I should watch out, something was coming again. I never really trusted myself to answer because I didn't want to arouse any suspicion and so I usually stayed in the background. But you can look forward to later on, my little friend. I have got my own weapons and then you won't be able to laugh. We won't fight in anger, won't want to, but in battles of the intellect I will give way, because you are the cleverer one. In the battle of love I am almost afraid when I hear of your lust for battle, but he who dares wins. Let's wait and see what happens. You may well be right that I am not always the easiest partner because I fight back, but it is usually you who starts it.

You mustn't have any inhibitions. Why should you? You see, I have already got to contradict you. Because I do not on principle regret what I once did – that's out of the question. It may well be, as you believe, that there was nothing we should have done differently in the actual situation. Our mutual attraction had existed for a long time, each of us knew our duty, each had enough self-control to contain his feelings. When they told me that you were missing my condolences, every feeling of bitterness vanished. I wrote to you immediately with an overflowing heart and without reserve, without realizing myself how glad I was to write to you. So it was indeed you who made the opening move, but then it was I who straightaway grasped the outstretched hand. Your letters then gave me pleasure. I wrote that to you, but I still didn't suspect, didn't admit to myself, just how dear those letters were to me. It was again you who at certain moments showed me the way back to life. There were two or three letters where again and again I came across something which made me sit up and listen. I had to think it over and then say to myself 'He is right, in fact. I will take it to heart.' Do you remember, Ernstili, when you wrote to me that life belongs to the living, memory to the dead? From that day on I found my way back to life – that is to say, you led me back. Then came a letter which admitted great anxiety because my letters were not getting to you. That's when I knew for the first time that everything was clear between us.

I was wondering whether the frequent letters weren't making things awkward for you with Hella. A pity that you can't talk about it with her but that's how it is. You are both made of the same stuff and similar characters find it hard to agree. That can't be changed. But, darling, when we are together again there will be so much talking, just wait! Then you will be able to tell me everything to your heart's content. And if you don't, I will do so anyway and then your heart will open up, I know for certain. And I can be silent too; if you all think I can't manage it, that isn't true.

You ask me if I wasn't sometimes unhappy in our marriage. How should I answer you? If my situation had been different, I could no doubt have developed quite differently. Much was hard for me in our early marriage, it wasn't an easy life that I led, but Emmerl's great kindness of heart, his boundless love and his good character helped me over many difficult periods. My attraction to you dates from my earliest youth. Emmerl sensed this once and warned me straightaway. That is why sometimes I deliberately moved away from you when you made a joke – did you ever notice that?

Dearest, I could still write for hours to you but I am at the end of the sheet of paper so I am off to bed. Keep well, now I hold you close, hug you in my heart and send you a dozen kisses. Many greetings to all the Cougnos.

Lovingly, your Mitzi.

On the same date as the last letter, Ernst wrote the following to Marie's daughters in Sheffield:

Thessaloniki, 31/12/1940

Dear Gretl and Edith

Your mother wrote to me that she thinks this postcard will reach you at this address. She is always glad to hear from you. Perhaps it will be quicker to write to her *via* me, and if that isn't possible, let her hear from you now and again. I hope you are both well. I am in regular correspondence with Mitzi. It's giving both of us a great deal of happiness. She's just worried about you and also about her flat. She would then have to move in with the Lípas. I hope that we will all meet again one day. The English are doing well at the moment and better every day. Well done them! Very best wishes from the Cougnos and especially from me. Yours, Ernst Löwy

Karlín, 4/1/1941

My beloved Ernstili

Today I was hoping to have some news from you but there was nothing. The present snowy weather may be hindering traffic and the post. We have mountains of snow by the sides of the roads here and anyone who doesn't have to go out, doesn't. Since yesterday I know for certain that I can keep my flat, indeed must keep it, and that the owner cannot demand that I move out because she has absolutely no right to dispose of it and that I may only move out with the permission of the *Kultusgemeinde*,[37] but they do not allow it. The owner did not reply at all to my letters, she served me

---

[37]The Jewish Community office (*Kultusgemeinde*) became the main intermediary between both the German and Czech authorities, and the Jews in Prague. Although before the war the *Kultusgemeinde* predominantly organized the religious life of the community, their role increased during the war, when they became the main administration unit that managed all aspects of life of the Jewish community, provided social services, organized labour and administered the accommodation of the Jews in Prague. Ultimately they were responsible for the registration of the Jews and later for the organization of

legal notice to quit and kept me on tenterhooks. I was already resigned to my fate and was getting used to the idea that, if I had to, it would be better to share a room with my mother at Irene's rather than be a lodger with a strange person among strangers, but it would certainly have affected my nerves badly. Finally I remembered a young friend to whom I hadn't spoken for over a year. I knew that he would be able to give me exact information before I paid the rent for the next quarter. I wrote him a few lines and hey presto! in a few hours he was at my place, a real knight, thoughtful and kind. He explained everything in detail and, as he is also an authority on these matters, I am at peace at last, and the four families in the house too. Now I can breathe again.

How marvellous it is when one is in trouble and realizes that there are still really good friends, true, unselfish, decent people. Already here in Prague people who owed me nothing at all have shown me true friendship. I feel uplifted and honoured. I want to learn from it and if I should ever again be in a position to help others or advise them I will do it willingly.

Monday 6/1,

Ernstili, you didn't take me quite seriously when I said we would meet in the spring. The time when we meet again will be our spring, even if it happens in June, and in any case, my energy, which is a bit low at present, won't be able to manage anything before then, so we must just grit our teeth and wait. If only it depended on me!

When I think back to the World War with all the problems and burdens which that time brought me, it too came to an end. I was just 28 when the war began and it immediately laid on me great burdens, anxieties and physical hardships. My one comfort and the constant refrain of my hopes and plans was the phrase 'when the war is over'. And finally it happened and then came times which, at least in part, fulfilled my hopes and expectations. We two are not yet so old that we have to give up hoping – I certainly don't feel like that.

---

deportations to the ghettos. They also had to secure the Jewish property confiscated by the Germans. The Jewish Community office was fully subordinated to the *Zentralstelle für jüdische Auswanderung*, the main German office in charge of the so-called 'Jewish question' in the Protectorate. See Chapter 2, footnote 61.

And your letters are also so sweetly full of anticipation and cheerfulness. That makes me as happy as a child.

What do you think of this long letter? And the Herr Censor! May he forgive me this once. Next time I will be more modest.

Keep well, dear Ernst. I hug you closely,

Your Mitzi

Karlín, 9/1/1941

My dear Ernst

Here I sit again today and imagine that you are here now. The idea becomes so real to me and then the writing starts. I have then a secret, cosy, peaceful and calming feeling enveloping us both. I see you sitting here, smoking and reading, all worrying thoughts having vanished from your face; we have forgotten all the hideous ugly things we have experienced, forgotten everything around; there is always something to tell, to discuss; everything is as if it has always been so. It is a wonderful method for me, Ernstili. But soon I will try sending a card. Sometimes I worry that my numerous long letters may in the end give you problems and I don't want to make things awkward for you in any way.

I am very glad that it is no longer so cold for you. Here it is deepest winter with a great deal of snow. On 24 December I had very vivid thoughts, as I told you. I think too that Thesa would have no objections if she knew that we had found each other. As for me, a year ago I suspected nothing, was interested in no-one, wanted to remain alone for ever and curtly rejected every overture. So it must be fate, it had to happen. Don't reproach yourself with anything, you have not chained me to you – I feel equally responsible.

From yesterday I am officially a resident of Prague.[38] I have been struggling for it for a long time and am very glad to have something sorted again. The 'friends' sent us greetings, they are very good and I am very happy about them. With time one becomes very undemanding. You can imagine how I feel about

---

[38]It took more than two years after her escape from the Sudetenland before the Czech authorities confirmed her residency status in Prague.

them sometimes, how frightened I am for them and how I have to fight to keep my longing under control. Who would ever have thought it? Oh God! I could sometimes scream for pain, but then I think 'Can I be ungrateful?' When I have you, then I will accept things quietly.

I think that on the whole people [here] have changed little. Those who were kind and good still are and those who before were angry and useless have remained so. As for me, I have become indifferent to much. I have changed a lot in many ways, particularly my idea of possessions and money, etc. has changed enormously. I think that one lives more peacefully with few possessions, and with less worry. Nevertheless, I have plenty of understanding and sympathy for others. So many sad experiences have cleansed me or educated me, but not, heaven forbid, embittered me. I remain cheerful and confident, because I know for sure that the dear good God will not forsake me. What happened to us raises me above the everyday and so I hope we will soon have a joyful *wieder-wiedersehen!*

And now good night, sweet one. A dozen kisses, a very loving hug.

Your Mitzi.

Karlín, 14/1/1941

My dear Ernst

Your letter of the 2nd came today. As always the contents gave me great joy. The instruction 'Keep it brief' was meant for me, not you, and I must finally control myself and start to write less.

The difference in our ages shouldn't really pose a difficulty for us, the years are taking care of that and can't be denied. For me you will be right just as you are. I only wish that you could recover some of your happy, contented nature. I simply cannot believe that there is never an occasion to laugh in your circle. There are nothing but young people around you and in any case your existence, as I imagine it, is not too difficult. For me it is a different matter, brought about by my situation. Probably the many trials have drained me or made me indifferent. I became quite fatalistic and am often envied for remaining on the whole so calm when other people get so upset. My life at present isn't particularly rosy but I don't admit it. It is only a waiting period and I want to spend it as well as possible, preserving myself for the coming, more lovely time with you. And in making this effort I help myself get over a lot. If I find myself in merry company I can be very jolly with them. It does one so much good and one forgets for a time one's various worries. So, Ernstili, don't just smile, try laughing heartily sometimes, grow young again with your grandchildren and have as much fun as you want with them.

I will tell you about my flat in my next letter. I've had to fight hard again to keep it, whether with permanent success I can't tell you today.

The main thing for me is that my new pupils are capable, that I make progress and have success. That spurs me on and most important of all is that I keep on getting news from you.

And now, my dear one, I hug you most lovingly and am

Your Mitzi

Karlín, 17/l/1941

My dear Ernst

Your letter of the 5/6 made me endlessly happy. In it, my dear, you are particularly sweet and lovely and if you were here now and as loving as you are in your letter, you would be amazed at what I would do to thank you, with a woman's nicest kind of gentleness and kindness. Just think of an older Edithel. She is, after all, my child and once I was just as gentle and soft, so I want to caress you and embrace you as lovingly as Edith to show you how I thank you. I think your ideas and plans are enchanting and I know, too, how serious you are about them. In the meantime I would just be glad if we could see each other, wherever it was. But we must be patient. So listen, dear one, I'll make a suggestion: we will roam through the world as wanderers the whole year long, for almost no trouble or deprivation is too great a price. But we would have to choose countries where one can always make short walks because I am no long distance hiker and I wouldn't be able to keep up with you.

You guessed right about my dream. I just wanted to give the unpleasant news about Sebert gently. It annoyed me a lot that I had to tell you it. Thank you very much for not seeing it as a tragedy, just like me. I'm so glad.

I will stop now, but I will just tell you that the matter of the flat has been settled in our favour, so we are staying here, thank God!

My sweet one, I hug you closely,

Your Mitzi.

Karlín, 20/1/1941

My dear Ernst

Another Sunday evening where I am using my free time to have a chat with you. When I look at your letters and mine I can see your intellectual superiority because you say everything in a few words, while I write a lot and there is nothing in it. If I wanted to, I could do it a bit differently but I'm not going to because I enjoy just chatting with you. I want to come back to the second paragraph in your letter of the 5/6. I need to think a lot about how it came about that we have hardly spoken to each other for five years. I can only understand it as you explain it that our mutual inclination was dormant in us from early youth, that's why the feeling of belonging to each other revealed itself so completely.

In my thoughts I have grown so accustomed to living with you that, whatever I do, I weigh up what you would say about it, asking for your advice, as it were. When I work I imagine that you might come in through the door and I go to greet you. When I walk in the street it is always with you. Even when I'm in company my thoughts keep slipping back to you and sometimes it is difficult to hide the smile which slips over my face. If people noticed it they would think I wasn't normal. When I wake up in the morning I imagine quite distinctly that you are near me and the knowledge that you are certainly thinking of me as well brings me calm and a joyful start to the day's work.

Continued on 21/1

The first two days of the week brought no news from you, perhaps tomorrow? I tore up a card that I wrote to you. I don't know, I just can't do cards. I have nothing to put in them.

Today I had a really good laugh with my small circle of friends. We were exchanging memories of earlier times and various stories were told. At last I saw my brother-in-law [Gustav Lípa] looking lively again – otherwise he has become very silent, very withdrawn – and I could hardly stop laughing.

Gretl's friend cabled to say that the 'friends' are well. That makes you happy, doesn't it? By the way, I just want to tell you this once how much they always liked you, how they admired, respected and valued you. Did you know that? And if kind fate brought us all together again, which I fear may be unlikely, there would be a lot of love and tenderness around you and I would face strong competition, hard to beat!

Our vast quantity of snow has finally given way to milder weather. The streets and roads of Prague are swimming in water but many hundreds of people are busy clearing things up.[39] I am glad the great cold has ended. I hope that for you it is already nice and warm. Is spring coming?

And now I'll finish, my good one. Good night! I hug you lovingly.

Your Mitzi

Karlín, 25/1/1941

My dear Ernst

Unfortunately I can't send you the prayer book you want. Don't be cross, but I am not at all keen on any more praying. That's why I can't bring myself to get hold of one. I hope you don't think I am being unhelpful but there is nothing to be done. In fact, Ernstili, you have been away from us for a long time and sometimes I become conscious of it.

People often ask me now how it is that I look so well, so different from how I looked before, probably much more lively, so you see, people notice that I am happy, my soul is reflected in my face.

Always yours, Mitzi

---

[39] Around this time hundreds of Jewish men were forced to clear snow off the runway at Prague airport, as well as from other sites in Prague. The authorities often used Jews who were out of work as forced labourers to clear snow and for other public works.

Karlín, 29/1/1941

My dearest,

This week I am again without news from you. I know that you have written but this knowledge can't still my yearning. Well, perhaps tomorrow. Recently we have had a very hard frost. Almost a month of this year is over and that means we are one month nearer to seeing each other again. I am well and have a lot to do.

The day before yesterday I had a happy surprise. The doorbell rang and there at the door stood my nephew from Brno, Fredy, the son of Emmerl's sister. I hadn't seen him for five years, nor his mother, and there was plenty to tell. He has to hand in his emigration application [*Emigrationsmappe*] here.[40] The past came back to me very vividly. Life is at once quite different when there is another person in the house and it is only now that I realize what I am missing all the time. But I thought, what if you had come instead of him?

By the way, before I forget, I am to greet you from the 'friends' in Buenos Aires. Today I actually only wanted to write just a card, so I will finish now. I am completely

Your Mitzi

Karlín, Sunday 2/2/1941

My dearest Ernst

Again it is the lovely moment when I can give attention exclusively to you. I have been away from home since three o'clock on Saturday afternoon until this evening. On Saturday afternoon I was at architect Eisler's for afternoon tea and a game of bridge.[41] You probably know the couple; they live in my

---

[40]*Emigrationsmappe* – this was a collection of the documents that people who planned to emigrate had to complete and submit to the *Zentralstelle*. It included their personal details, as well as a declaration of the assets, and confirmation that they did not have any outstanding debts, among other documents. Fredy (Alfred Kessler) did not manage to emigrate in time and perished in the Holocaust (deported to the Rejowiec ghetto in eastern Poland).

[41]Rudolf Eisler (*1874) lived in the same block of flats as the Lípas. He was deported to Theresienstadt in September 1942. He died in the ghetto on 25 December 1943. His wife Eliška (*1898) and daughter Doris (*1922) perished in Auschwitz.

sister's building. It was very enjoyable and they're good company. In the evening my family had a guest, my young friend that I wrote about recently, and I had to be there, at the wish of the others. There too it was cosy and then I couldn't go back home,[42] so I stayed the night as their guest and was spoilt like a child. In the morning I was brought breakfast in bed, the newspaper, everything as it used to be at home on Sundays. Then I felt like having a little cuddle, wanted to slip into Mother's or Irene's bed, but a feeling of shyness prevented me. Why? Because I was thinking constantly of you, as I always do in my free time. I said to myself, no, if I can't snuggle up with you then I won't do it at all. And postponed is not cancelled. … And then we went out for a lovely walk. There was a wonderful snowy atmosphere, so bitingly fresh and good for one, and in the afternoon we had our reunion with the Karlsbad ladies at Frau Fischer's. That was very nice too. I didn't go home till evening but the whole time I was looking forward to this moment alone with you.

Today (Monday) I went to see Karel Struzi[43] and talked over everything necessary with him. I also got him to write about Sebert. I have seen everything and am now completely in the picture. You need have no more worries, I will deal with everything. You like order, as I can see, and you haven't left much work for others to do as you put it in the hands of others in good time.

There was a letter from my cousin Eman in New York. Apparently his daughters and son-in-law[44] are doing very well, he is pleased about that and I am also glad when I get good news about relatives and friends.

I hope that tomorrow I will get news from you. It's high time! I hug you warmly,

Your Mitzi

---

[42]Jews were subject to a curfew and had to be indoors by 8 pm.
[43]Dr Karel Struzi was a lawyer who handled Ernst's property affairs.
[44]This is a hidden reference to her own daughters and son-in-law. Eman only had one son.

Photo 4 *Wedding photo of Marie's daughter Edith and Franz Sternschuss, 1938.*

Karlín, 11/2/1941

My beloved Ernstili

Today was a lovely day for me. It's true, I'm in the middle of spring cleaning and last week I had the decorator in for two days and just at this moment, of course, I had some quite unexpected visits so that it was evening before the longed for moment came when I could be quite alone with you. And now it has come.

About my business, well, what should I tell you? It isn't so easy to give you a proper understanding because a long time has passed since our last talk. I have no substantial fortune so no worries about looking after it. My daily needs are provided for and up to now I have not gone without, and I know that the others would care for me if it were necessary, which is always good to know. Of course, I like self-sufficiency and independence more than anything and up to now, thank goodness, I have been able to maintain them.

Of my actual possessions, the real estate, which represents half of it, brings nothing in, but even without this I live carefree and cheerfully. At the time of my move I brought with me the equipment and everything that goes with it in

order to start up my business again here.[45] As I didn't get a licence, I asked for
a three-month permit to liquidate the business, which was granted. From the
proceeds I have managed to support myself since 1938. Of course, my dear,
good sister has helped a lot by giving me all sorts of pleasures, large and small,
in my everyday life; her generosity is boundless. And so this is how everything
has actually gone very well.

For the relatively high rent for my accommodation I have managed to get
a contribution by subletting and in fact, since I have been alone, my needs are
not so great. The house and business in Karlsbad are being looked after by a
manager whom you will surely know, Herr Walter Pleier.[46] The business is,
of course, being liquidated after my departure, which means the outstanding
debts are being collected and my obligations are being discharged, which I
hope has already been done. So I am now relieved of all worries and that suits
me fine. I have had my head full enough of business worries my whole life
long and I'm delighted that it can have a rest. I now consider myself 'Mrs Have
Nothing' and feel very well with it.

I am very proud of my certificate of citizenship. It was issued to me with
effect from 4 February and now I am no longer a refugee.[47]

I read your news about the children with great pleasure. It must be so
delightful for you to be able to enjoy them. There is hardly anything more
lovely than to see sunny, happy young people around you. I love these young
people with all my heart.

My sweet, the page is full. Oh dear God, may Herr Censor forgive me!! I
send you a warm hug and then a dozen sweet kisses and am completely

Your Mitzi.

---

[45]Her EBE company.

[46]Treuhänder (trustees) took over and administered confiscated Jewish property.

[47]See footnote 38. Marie's Protectorate citizenship application was rejected in October 1939 (http://
www.holocaust.cz/databaze-dokumentu/dokument/102890-baderova-marie-ztrata-statniho-
obcanstvi/)

Karlín, 15/2/1941

Answered on 18 May after the resumption of mail

My beloved Ernstili

I already wrote to you about my work situation. I wouldn't want to vegetate like this for ever but I hope I will get by like this until the end of the war. Don't worry, dearest, up till now I have had no problems. I had physical ones when I came here and had a lot of responsibilities and worries, but now that I have to take care only of myself, what problems can I have? And if I am honest – you will hardly be able to believe it – it is only now that I have partly been able to recover because the life I led after Emmerl's death was one I could hardly have borne for long; it was in every way too stressful and however awful it may sound, it is true that for this reason it was better for me that I was forcibly removed from the many stresses and worries.[48] My body has recovered enormously health-wise, my nerves too. I got rid of the rheumatic problems, took care of myself and 'last not last' (*sic*, in English), I completely changed my attitude to life, learnt to have different ideas about society, can laugh and be happy and full of hope, feel neither my years nor all that I have experienced which others find so hard to bear. For me that is over, you know already how I feel about that. And in the immediate future I will certainly not in any way be lacking anything, as far as human requirements go, so you have no reason to worry about me in the way you do. I hope I can feel the same about you, and when we are together, then we will be really rich, even if our pockets are empty, as long as we are healthy and good humoured, have a bit of luck and also some cheerful thoughts.

(*unsigned*)

Karlín, 16/2/1941

My dearest Ernst

My bridge ladies left two hours ago, everything is back in order and finally the longed for moment has arrived when I can be alone with you. Today I

---

[48]Marie is referring to having been forced to give up her business after the Munich Agreement.

had such awful cards that I was almost annoyed with you. I blamed you and yet I couldn't help smiling a bit at the same time. In short, it was you again who steered my thoughts in another direction to the extent that now I get no good cards at bridge or am too distracted when I play. So you can see, you bad one, what you are responsible for! Now I can see you laughing, or at least smiling.

I want to go back to your letter of the 25th: I will certainly do everything to look after myself and my health, as far as that is possible these days. First and foremost for this I need inner peace, which I have finally regained, apart from the great longing for you, and of course I am very much afraid for the children but I no longer count on always being near them. Despite these seriously difficult times, for the first time in five years I will greet the coming spring with enthusiasm, just as I used to in happier times. In recent years there was no way in which I could rejoice at nature in her glory, just because the horrible memories of the sad events of spring 1936[49] soured every joy for me. But now I can rejoice again in this most beautiful season which here in Prague too is a feast for the eyes.

Your feelings about possessions and money are completely in tune with mine. The only ones who should be pitied are those who through their own inabilities have not adapted to the present times, who are not capable of learning or contributing in any field and who are constantly hankering for the past, thus making themselves ridiculous. I would never dream of saying that at home it used to be like this or that. I don't think like that but accept the facts and concentrate on dealing as best I can with my present situation.

If, up to now, I haven't asked you about your current financial situation, it is, of course, only so as not to be too intrusive, although I believe I understand it from various remarks of yours. You too should not have any worries, it will get better for you again. I know your feeling of dependence on your child is gnawing at you but that is unfair and one could easily

---

[49]1936 was the year her daughter Grete had a nervous breakdown following her divorce from Otto Reichl, and when Marie's husband Emil died.

accuse you of being oversensitive. Later, when we are both able to work, we will give back everything to those who are helping us out now, shall we, my love?

Soon spring will be showing signs of arriving here too, and with it, according to my prediction, the time of our reunion should be getting nearer. It's unlikely to happen then, but one day our spring will come and then what a spring that will be. A real spring, I promise you!

Now I am going to sleep. In my thoughts I fall asleep in your arms. Good night, dear one.

A dozen kisses, tenderly yours,

Mitzi

Karlín, 4/3/1941

My beloved Ernstili

I had been feeling very worried and grown most impatient, when your letter of 12/2 arrived today after a nine-day interruption in the postal service and I thank God you are well and in good humour even if three weeks have passed since you wrote. I only hope the post continues to function, otherwise life would become almost unbearable.

My 'friends' haven't forgotten you at all and when they send me greetings it is clear that their greetings are just as much for you, darling. If I imagine the moment when the two will be able to put their arms around your neck and hug you like a real uncle and father substitute, then my heart already overflows with joy in anticipation of the happiness to come.

I was very amused by your answer about the problem of space;[50] it made me laugh heartily. You are a crafty, clever chap! It's just a pity that I can't answer as I would like to, since you like sincerity so much: I wanted that answer and am very pleased with it. I will definitely reject the negative solution to the space problem.

---

[50]Ernst suggested that he and Marie would have to share a room.

Tell me, my sweet, where is your brother Alois? Still where he used to live? A lot of people have gone from there.[51]

I am well, except when I have no news from you, then I am desperately sad and like a flag at half mast for those around me.

I embrace you most tenderly and send you a dozen of the sweetest kisses.

Your Mitzi.

Karlín, 6/3/1941

My beloved Ernst

So today I was at Dr Struzi's and can report that the message from Sebert about the sale of your property a year ago was in accordance with the legislation. S. didn't report anything else. After adjusting the valuation, a payment order will be made, and only then can one establish whether the party has made full settlement in law or not. ... ...

By chance I met your brother Emil there, who complained that he had no news of you and said that he had written to you. From there he went to Ilse[52] who seems to be getting on all right, as is her son. He also told me that your brother Alois wrote: he is in good health and cheerful. The worry I had for him in my last letter is no longer necessary.

Ernstili, do you also realize that we have been writing to each other for over a year? If you had been here the first anniversary would have cost you money, for at least one little flower stem! ... ...

And now, good night. I will dream beautiful dreams of you. Keep well, be healthy. I embrace you tenderly and kiss you.

Your Mitzi.

Handwritten footnote: 'Another warning from the censor. Keep it short!'

---

[51] Alois Löwy lived in Vienna, where the first deportations of the Jewish population took place in October 1939. Here Marie refers to the second wave in February and March 1941, when 5,000 Viennese Jews were sent to Occupied Poland (to the Lublin district and other smaller places). Marie's letter shows that information about the deportation spread very quickly.
[52] Emil Löwy's daughter.

Karlín, 10/3/1941

My beloved Ernstili

I received your letter of the 18th today and every letter which still arrives is
a gift for me, because I am in a constant state of anxiety.[53] … … … … … … …
… … … … … … … … … … … … … … …

If I tell you that there was no other way out for me you will find that
incomprehensible. Well, Ernstili, it would need a fuller explanation which I will
keep for when we are together. You will be amazed at what I experienced while
I pretended to be so energetic, far too much for an ordinary person, believe me,
Ernstili. But it is all past; I have learnt to think quite differently and can see now
that one can lead one's life in other ways and so far I am happy with that.

With you, spring really has arrived; here there is just a hint of it. In
humans this reawakening is so wonderful and so cheering, just beautiful.
It's only then that one sees the world in its true light, I think. The world
would be so wonderful, enough room for everyone and truly beautiful. Let
the storm rage, some day will come a time of blessed peace, please God! I
accept your proposal to consider me your little wife, your beloved. I do it
anyway because in my mind I am living totally with you. I am very proud, my
treasure, of your correctness and popularity, and the respect people pay you.
It is the only thing we own. Not long ago, at the dentist, a man was rude to me
because he thought I wanted to push in and be treated before him. It wasn't
true and he was wrong but he called me a liar in front of four strangers. I
was able to prove that he was wrong but I was deeply hurt, as if someone had
boxed my ears, and I was so upset that I had a nosebleed when I got home.
It is sad that there still are boorish people around so lacking in self control.

[Architect] Eisler, of course, has no work. There isn't any and everybody is
reduced to the same low level. Either they [men] take care of the shopping for the
household or they work at home dusting, tidying, etc. Many go on courses but
these don't fill the whole day. Usually the women do all the work alone and that's
when the men lend a hand. Good, isn't it? It often amuses me but one gets used to it.

---

[53]There follows a large gap where the censor has removed a section (apparently from the other side)
with scissors.

Ernstili, please keep copies of your letters so that we can keep a better record of our correspondence ... ...
... ...[54]

... ... What will I dream today? Goodnight now. I hug you tenderly, send you a thousand kisses.

Your Mitzi

Karlín, Friday 14/3/1941

My beloved Ernstili

Up until today this week hasn't brought me any news from you and my thoughts are therefore constantly with you. At the moment my mother is unwell, unfortunately quite seriously, and unfortunately a lot of it is her own fault. Frequent coffee drinking has given her high blood pressure which has led to her having a blood clot in her eye. The consultant prescribed a strict diet and treatment. If there is no pain and if no complications set in then she may save the eye, in which she has almost no vision because of glaucoma; otherwise she would need a serious operation which would upset me very much indeed. The thought that she may have to undergo such torture in her 80th year makes me tremble and fills me with worry and horror.

The 'friends' send greetings again, very cheering.

I had another wonderful dream about you but, as I am not sure that this letter will reach you, I won't recount it but will stop for today, embracing you tenderly in my mind and kissing you in the usual way and praying to God to take you into his protection. Tenderly yours for always,

Mitzi.

---

[54]The next section, about twenty lines long, has been removed.

Karlín, Sunday evening, 17/3/1941

My beloved Ernstili

It is Sunday evening again and I am alone at home after being away almost the whole day. Yesterday I was at a birthday celebration which was a very modest affair, but nice. There were twelve of us and we made pleasant conversation. My friends have got the use of only one room in their large flat and yet it was very prettily done, so one sees that people can adapt.[55] The gentlemen played bridge in one corner, the ladies talked. And today I was at the Lípas for lunch, then at my bridge party. …[56] My mood has sunk below zero, but only when I am alone, because I haven't had any news from you.

Here I sit now, with your picture in front of me. This little picture looks very seriously at the world and I am trying to imagine what you are doing at this moment. Everything possible runs through my head and I am stalked by disquiet and apprehension. I regret bitterly that, because this young girl[57] had to put off her visit, you couldn't have the picture from the Willinskis. I sometimes think that it is almost impossible that you can picture me as I am. I think that photos are the most beautiful thing that we have from our absent loved ones.

Dear one, do you still remember our expeditions in the car when you yourself were driving? Our main worry was your driving ability and we teased and made fun of you. Do you remember how you used to get angry? Once we were in Glatzen near Marienbad[58] and stopped at the edge of a lake. Photographs were taken – I think I've got the picture somewhere here. Have you perhaps got the photo with you, if you took such souvenirs when you went?

And in my effort to occupy myself with you I am delving more deeply into memories of when we were together in former times and shall I admit what I regret? Why did I never try to talk to you in more depth? Today I still can't understand why, when I occasionally met you later, in the years 1936–8, at the time when you both were cross with me, you just – what should I say? – just

---

[55]Several families had to share one apartment.
[56]The next sentence has been obliterated.
[57]This is probably the girl referred to in the letter continued on 15 December 1940, who was going to go to Palestine, where the Willinskis, mutual friends of Marie and Ernst, had emigrated.
[58]In Czech Kladská near Mariánské Lázně (Marienbad).

looked past me so angrily. What could I do about the whole affair which was based on fantasy?

I was particularly glad to hear from Emil that Alois sounded very well, unlike all the others in his circle who are very unhappy at the pain of separation because they don't like the Lichtmanns, Ashkenazis, Guens, Goligers, etc. at all.[59] I must say that I entirely sympathize with them and would almost prefer my V.[60] to undertaking this journey, but so far the question doesn't arise so let's hope for good things in the future.

Dear one, it is sweet of you to think of my love of flowers. From childhood that was my great weakness, flowers and birds. They are the most lovable of nature's creations and the sight of them delights me.

And now, enough, my treasure. Keep well and healthy. God be with you all. My thoughts are always with you.

I hug and kiss you tenderly. Mitzi

Karlín, Sunday evening, 23/3/1941

My beloved Ernstili

Imagine, my love, it was no dream but reality when on Saturday morning your little letter fluttered into the house. And as I was convinced that there would only be cards now I was particularly glad. And then the beautiful contents! I was so happy all through Sunday. I imagine what it would be like if you were at my side. Then everything becomes so lifelike that, when my outstretched arms fall back into nothingness, it is only then that I realize that I have been fantasizing.

On the 3rd you wrote that you regretted that earlier we had repressed our feelings and what did I write to you on the 17th? Something similar! Good, isn't it?

---

[59]Deportation to Poland. Marie uses code names for places in Eastern Europe (or for Eastern European Jews). The specific meaning of the terms is not exactly clear.

[60]Deportations from Vienna had already started. Marie was probably referring to Vironal tablets, which had been used by people wishing to commit suicide.

It is so sweet of you to worry about whether I have enough for my daily life – thank you very much, my love. Don't worry, I will have enough for a good while yet, till the end of the war, I hope. There is in any case no going out for pleasure, at most only a few male and female friends come, and then not until after coffee time, 'après', as we call it. Yesterday there were nine people at my place and it was really nice and cosy. Today, at Irene's, there were even more and different acquaintances. There was the merry Frau Neumann[61] with her coarse humour which only she can get away with – I laughed till the tears came. Oh Ernstili, it is good sometimes to be able to laugh so heartily. It really does you good. I always imagine how it would be if you were there too and I have a little pang in my heart that it cannot be, but one day it will! If I ever need anything, my sweet one, I will very gratefully take up your offer and I thank you again warmly with a sweet kiss. You can hardly imagine how good my sister was – and is – and how rude and ungrateful I often am to her for it, because it goes against the grain for me to keep accepting gifts. We see each other every day and if by midday she has heard nothing from me she rings up or comes over herself. They care for me like a hen for her chicks.

Ernstili, visiting the Willinskis[62] has become impossible and that is also why they couldn't send you the picture.

Are you very busy? How is the vineyard? And the young ones? And how will you be protected when the great heat starts? Are you already sleeping under a mosquito net? Are you careful enough about that? I'm afraid of malaria etc. because you weren't born there.

… … … … … … *(section obliterated by the censor)*

And now I am going to fall asleep in your arms. Goodnight, my beloved. I hug and kiss you tenderly.

Your Mitzi

Comment from censor: 'Write unambiguously!'

---

[61]Louise Neumann (1879–1942) was a member of Marie's bridge circle. She was deported on 10 June 1942 to Ujazdów in eastern Poland, where she perished.
[62]Palestine.

Karlín, 31/3/1941

My dear Ernst

I thank God and the most esteemed Herr Censor that your letter of 15/3 arrived this morning. As always, I was delighted and now I will feel much easier the whole week long. This is how I will make my thanks: to God, by offering half my midday meal (it isn't sumptuous but quite good) to the first needy person who comes here today, and I thank Herr Censor by respecting his order as an official, writing briefly as he instructed on your last letter. My God, that isn't easy for me, the well-known chatterbox.

Therefore, my sweet one, I am not going to go into all the points in your letter in detail, but tell you that I am happy to hear that you are growing round and are healthy, that you can laugh – that is wonderful, that's how I picture you – and that I am also healthy and share your thoughts. Soon it will be spring here too. Yesterday I was with our friend Dezsö Reiszman[63] who recently lost his wife so tragically. Didn't you know them both? It may be useful that his brother Geza lives in Vác, Hungary and knows you. He asks you to write to him some time, instead of Ulli.

Ernstili, I am not going to be afraid of your irony any more. I won't dream of it and will gladly let myself be spoilt. I wish we were already at the point where we could spoil each other.

But now I'm stopping, because I must! In my mind I hug you tenderly, send you 1,000 kisses and am yours alone.

Mitzi

PS. Darling, your last letter had the following order from Herr Censor 'Write briefly. Otherwise the letters will not be delivered.' Eman is a good lad. A pity he isn't a rich man or he would help to get us over.[64]

---

[63]Desider Reiszmann (*1883) was deported to Lublin, via Theresienstadt, in mid-May 1942. His brother Geza was reportedly killed in Auschwitz in 1944.

[64]To provide them with an affidavit, one of the conditions prospective emigrants to the United States had to fulfil.

2

June 1941–September 1941: Germany invades Greece

*T*he long gap between the last letter and the postcard dated 14 June can be assumed to be the result of the invasion of Greece by Germany in April 1941. The Italian invasion the previous autumn had led to a six-month war between the two countries in which Greece was largely successful, forcing Germany to come to the aid of its fascist ally and postpone plans to invade the Soviet Union. German troops entered Greece via Yugoslavia and Bulgaria and captured Thessaloniki by 9 April when Greek forces surrendered.

Greece suffered greatly during the occupation. The country's economy was already weak even before the Italian invasion of October 1940. There followed a ruthless economic exploitation by Germany. Raw materials and foodstuffs were requisitioned, shops cleared out, and the Greek collaborationist government was forced to pay the cost of the occupation, giving rise to inflation, further exacerbated by a 'war loan' Greece was forced to grant to the German Reich which severely devalued the Greek drachma. Requisitions, together with the Allied blockade of Greece and the ruined state of the country's infrastructure, led to the emergence of a powerful and well-connected black market. The food situation became critical in the summer of 1941 and resulted in the Great Famine which reached its peak during the winter of 1941–42.

Historian Mark Mazower writes: 'By November shop-shelves were bare and black market prices had soared' and that death tolls rose alarmingly and continued at a high rate until the spring of 1942. It has been estimated that approximately 300,000 people died during the Axis occupation of Greece as a result of famine and malnutrition. Mazower suggests that the famine may have delayed further persecution of the Jews 'because the military authorities understood the economic importance of the Jews for the city [Thessaloniki] and felt the famine was not a good time to disrupt trade further'.[1]

In the letters that follow there are many references to food shortages in Greece, which Marie considers to be worse than the situation faced by the Jewish population in Prague (as indeed it was).

Undated, received 4/7/1941

This letter is difficult to place as it is undated, but it is likely that it was written during the period when mail was not getting through, possibly in mid-April. Letters were being held up and this one wasn't delivered until after Marie's card and letters of June had arrived. Any letters Marie wrote between mid April and mid-June apparently never reached Ernst.

My beloved

It is already 18 days since I had any news from you. I know it can't be helped and yet it is terribly difficult to bear life like that. I keep re-reading your last but one letter where you say that we must keep telling ourselves that the other one is well and in that way banish all worries. Well yes, I am trying to, but it is very hard. I confidently hope that you and all your loved ones are well. My thoughts are constantly with you all. So far I am quite well, except that the anxiety about you completely ruins my existence. It is also very depressing that the 'friends' are so lazy about writing.

I met Emil briefly at Aunt Lidi's.[1] He is well, but also anxious about his brother. Next Sunday he is coming here with the aunts for a cup of tea and if

---

[1]Lydia Vogel (*1875), sister of Marie's mother. She was murdered in Treblinka in October 1942.

thoughts can reach over the great sea your ears will be burning that afternoon. And now farewell! I end my letter in the way you know, send many greetings to all our loved ones and am

Your Mitzi.

Postcard (by airmail) Karlín, 14/6/1941

Dear Ernst

Your card of 8/6 gave me enormous joy and at the same time I understood that, if it is possible, something will come from you in the next few days. I was all the more happily surprised that my hope and wish to have news of how you and your loved ones are was fulfilled. Now we will resume our exchange of thoughts. I hope that my mail will be delivered. Your brothers are well. Emil was here two days ago. I am in good health and live as usual. Apparently Alois has a lot to do. I am not very happy about the 'friends' because I haven't seen their handwriting for a year. That's really strange. I am always glad to have their greetings but I am no longer quite convinced [about their wellbeing] though I don't know why.

Warmest greetings to you and all your loved ones.

Your (*unsigned*)

Karlín, 14/6/1941

My beloved Ernst

Can you imagine how indescribable my joy was when today I got your card of the 8th? That's a weight off my mind and I can think and live again a little more easily. But thank you, my good one, with all my heart, for being so kind and sending me news so quickly, I shall never forget it. It tells me so much in every way. If only I could, how I would reward you for your kind and loving attentiveness. I was imagining all sorts of things, even though I told myself a hundred times that you, a former front line soldier,[2] would take all that happens calmly and collectedly. It's just very bad for the nerves to be without news for months when your letters are in fact everything that makes life worth living.

When eight days ago your belated letters of 1 and 3 April arrived, I knew that I would know at the latest by the 15th where you are. Our newspapers wrote that the post, including airmail, only went to Athens. So there was nothing left for me to do but to hope and wait. Yes, my treasure, that was a precious birthday gift,[3] believe me, and I thank you again for it and for your good wishes. I knew you wouldn't forget. Now I am going to beg you to write lots and lots about how you are, whether you still take your regular walk in the garden, whether you are already swimming in the sea, in short, everything you do.

My life goes on fairly monotonously. In the morning I am at home, in the afternoon between 3 and 5 o'clock the shopping gets done,[4] then I am with my family. Either we go for a walk or we are at Irene's, or at my place, sometimes at friends. From 7.30 I am back at home and then I do all sorts of work. I am so longing for a direct sign of life from the 'friends' but to no avail. I haven't seen their handwriting for a year and that hurts me very much. I am really very anxious and doubt the truth of what I am told. Or is it just my longing for them?

My mother is somewhat better, to the extent that the inflammation has died down and there is no immediate threat to life. That is a big step forward and one must thank God for it.

And because I am so full of longing for you at the moment I am going to end this letter because of the pain I have at knowing that [being together] simply cannot be. I send you my love, a dozen sweet kisses, hug you tenderly in my heart and am

Your Mitzi

---

[2] Ernst fought in the First World War.
[3] Marie's birthday was on 12 June.
[4] By this time Jews were allowed to shop only between 3.00 and 5.00 p.m.

Karlín, 17/6/1941

My beloved Ernst

Today I was at Tante [aunt] Lidi's and my mother, my sister and [aunt] Hulda[5] were there too. I am very sorry for aunt, she is not at all well. She is in a very bad way mentally, misses being active and the income from her little shop which she gave up. Fortunately she still has her flat, she lets part of it, stopped having a maid and does everything on her own. Of course she has lost a lot of weight which in her case was actually no misfortune, but being completely alone is terribly hard for her and in addition she has almost no money. That's really hard. I think she has always had a prejudice against me and I could hardly consider her as a close friend, but her situation as an old lady makes me very sorry for her and I am trying to comfort her and cheer her up, at least with words, and sometimes I succeed.

It is very interesting to observe how most people – I mean above all, people of our age, and a little younger and older – simply cannot get rid of their ideas of possessions and wealth, how hard they find their losses, how anxious they are about the future. They are still unable to grasp that we are living in completely different times, that worrying is pointless, that one has to leave God to take care of things. I often wonder whether I am perhaps irresponsible in that I am not getting all worked up about what might happen in the future. No-one knows what it will bring, so why should one spoil the present? Who knows whether one will live to see that time and in any case one is not obliged to carry on living. I can no longer spend my time worrying about the future ever since I realized that precautions, plans and preparations are pointless, that everything always happens very differently from how one expects. That is what our times have taught us.

Oh how I would love to see you and speak to you now. I feel as if I should be with you at this moment. To know that I can't be yours depresses me terribly and I am very upset by it.

---

[5]Hulda Wurm (*1884) was Mutti's sister. She was sent to Treblinka on the same train as her husband Artur (*1874) and sister Lydia.

Now I am going to stop. I embrace you with dearest love, kiss you ten times and am

Your Mitzi

Karlín, 22/6/1941

My beloved Ernst

And yesterday, Saturday, your letter arrived and I am once again so very happy!

I imagine the little house in the vineyard is delightful. If you can send photos, take one of it and of yourself working there, please, please do! I wonder whether you will be allowed to send the picture of yourself that you meant to send. Here no enclosures are allowed, the letters are handed in at the counter unsealed and are only sealed when they have been checked by the official. I can well believe that you used to think that I was 'not so joyful'. Firstly, most people only knew me in my professional capacity and there I certainly did not make the best impression, and secondly Emmerl didn't like me to behave in a free and uninhibited way in company, so that my true nature was never really seen except by a very small circle. I have to say it again: just picture for yourself an older Edithel – she is my child after all. Just as she behaves with those around her, exactly so will I behave with you.

You have almost too good an opinion of me, if you think that I am exercising my brain a lot. This is particularly not the case now as, since I have been busy working more with my hands, I have given up my Spanish and Czech lessons because they cost me too much and I couldn't afford the expense and even less the time for studying. But I have learnt a lot more Czech through contact with people, understand a lot and can even speak it if need be.[6]

Beloved, you write: 'I have a feeling it might be possible to come.' My heart stopped for a moment when I read that. And then *I* am supposed to decide whether you can leave again! That I should let you go again? Unthinkable! You have given me a hard puzzle to solve. I can't give you a definite answer today, but I feel already that I will have to say you should wait a little longer. You need

---

[6]Marie, as most of the older Jews who used to live in the Sudetenland, was not fully proficient in Czech.

have no worries about your upkeep during your stay here because obviously we would share everything.

You want to know what I have been doing the whole time. Well, I do a lot of work at home. On fine days we go to our favourite place where there are benches to rest on. That is the plateau behind the cathedral, the Hirschgraben, in a little hollow with a view of the Loretto Church, my favourite church.[7] We sit there and darn stockings, etc. And another place we go to be in the open is the old cemetery.[8] Here, too, the blossom is over, only the acacia is still wonderful – that will be the last of the blossom.

I send you an extra kiss for the birthday greetings you sent me. How lovingly you wrote to me. My treasure, for your birthday I hope I will be able to give you my wishes in person. Keep well and happy and write soon to your unspeakably-longing-for-you

Mitzi.

Karlín, 25/6/1941

My dearest Ernst

In your letter today, of 15/6, you say you are unhappy that you have still got no news from me. I hope that in the meantime you have been inundated by my letters. You ask whether I am healthy and happy. Yes, my treasure, I really am. Since I have been getting news from you again I feel quite changed. Please don't think I'm being conceited, but all the people I know ask me how it is that I look so marvellous – people notice it from far off. Apparently I look so much younger.

I am delighted with what you write about yourself and thank God that I hear such good news, touch wood, about you. If I were there I wouldn't allow you to go for such a hike in the heat of the midday sun, particularly at this time

---

[7] Jelení příkop (in Czech) behind the St Vitus Cathedral, and the Prague Loreta.
[8] Jewish cemeteries (especially the New Jewish Cemetery in Olšany, Prague-Žižkov) were some of the few public places accessible to the Jews after the introduction of anti-Jewish restrictions, when they were no longer able to visit public parks. Marie describes the limited public space available to the Jews.

– that is too much! But you must be feeling healthy and strong and your body has adapted itself brilliantly to the climate.

Do you know, treasure, what is now giving me pleasure? Now and again I send a 2 kg parcel to Poland, to some Viennese people who have emigrated[9] there. You should read their thank you letters!

In everything I do I see you around me. I see before me Haus Lanner[10] and our flat inside it. It is a Sunday evening, you are coming to visit. Then there is the sound of the doors on the ground floor, I hear your dear, booming voice, which always delighted me so, then the happy greeting, the strong handshake. Everything comes alive to me. And how will it be when we do see each other again? Can you imagine it? I can: it will be wonderful, as beautiful as paradise.

At the moment I am reading a book that you probably know but in case you don't, I recommend it to you. It is 'The Good Earth' by Pearl S. Buck.

How are things with Salvator's business?[11] Has he still got stock to sell, and how is it going?

What are the children, Mädi and Bubi,[12] doing? Mädi must already be a young lady. Irene, who loves teasing me and who knows too that I am very vain, keeps saying 'Just wait, you will soon be a great grandmother!'

Treasure, even if there was no news for a while you should not be anxious.[13] And now I am going to lie down and dream of you, the most beautiful dream a person can have.

I hug you lovingly, kiss you many times, and am

Your Mitzi

---

[9]Emigration is the accepted and official euphemism for deportation. Marie's references to the parcels she (and others) sent to the deportees in Poland evidence the solidarity in the Jewish community even at the time when Prague Jews had limited access to food.
[10]The Bader family home in Karlsbad.
[11]Ernst's son-in-law had a small shop with photographic equipment.
[12]Erika Cougno (Mädi) and Heinz Cougno (Bubi) were Ernst's grandchildren.
[13]The German-Soviet war broke out on 22 June 1941.

Karlín, 1/7/1941

My beloved

Today I received your letter of 22/6. Can you imagine how good for me your gentle solicitude is? Of course it hurts me to see my mother growing old and it's often very much on my mind. She longs so much to see the children and I hope for it for her sake above all. May God grant it. I don't actually know how it is for other people but my love for Mutti was boundless, and she was an exceptional mother, she was often able to help me over many hurdles. In times of trouble I often thirsted for a word from her which would resolve everything and when it came I could breathe again. That is how important her opinions were to me. But that has changed utterly, particularly since we have been living in Prague. Mutti has become hard, too hard to my mind, and too sharp in her judgments, so I can't feel close to her any more. It isn't like it used to be. Is it because of old age or circumstance, or both together? I always imagined an old lady as thoughtful and kind. When I sometimes come home disappointed I think to myself that perhaps it has to be so, so that I don't depend completely on my little old mother.

The 'friends' send their greetings again, but that is so very little. Each time one hears that they are supposed to be getting on well, I would just like to hear something more definite but there's nothing one can do. Whether your letters can take their place, well, that is a question! Just wait till I have you here, or I am with you, then you will discover the answer. Your letters are everything to me, you know that very well. Today I could express myself to neither of the children as I can to you. This bond is unique. But despite that I would just really like to know how they really are.

Something in your letter shows a certain discontent; try if you can not to get involved, especially if you can't change anything, I beg you. Please don't be offended, keep your good humour, don't let your good, decent soul be saddened. I will make it all up to you when we belong to each other, as far as I am able. It is delightful about Mädi, that she looks after you so well. She is a treasure of a child. And when we have our home, we will invite her and repay her many times over, treating her like our little child.

I have never baked potatoes in the open air, although I lived in the country until I was 12 years old. My childhood was very quiet, I was a great dreamer, played mostly with dolls and flowers. But I have another memory involving you from when we lived in Buchau,[14] when you and one of our uncles carried us around the Ringplatz as angels; can you still remember?

Your fruit is pretty expensive, but it *is* available. In other places it is both expensive *and* a rarity. You don't seem to have ration cards and can buy what you want.[15] Enjoying vegetables has now become common here too and I think it is a healthy way of life. One doesn't need to find a sanatorium for dieting, so every situation has advantages which one shouldn't underestimate.

Eman wrote to me that he has written to you. He is a fine scallywag, he makes jokes! He writes about my kisses to you, that he took some of them, but he is sending you some of his own instead. I laughed a lot! If he would only tell

Photo 5   *Mutti (Marie's mother, Louise Rosenberger).*

---

[14]Bochov.
[15]Marie is as yet unaware that there are severe food shortages in Thessaloniki.

me more about the 'friends'. They write to him every week. He always writes the same thing to me, just a few words.

Now I am going to go to sleep and will dream of you all the time. My sweet one, farewell. I hug you tenderly, send you a dozen sweet kisses and am yours alone.

Mitzi.

Karlín, 9/7/1941

My beloved

When I handed in my last letter to you I wanted to enclose the local Jewish newspaper, but unfortunately it isn't possible. I can't understand why one can't do it from here when you can receive the paper from Vienna.[16]

A few times I have meant to write to you a bit of news from home. Petter Louise walks dogs because he is too old for any other work. Laura Heller cuts out skirts. My little friend pleased me very much. I am very happy because I gather that she is working again in her former profession.[17] That would be a great step forward, also the knowledge that she is leading a proper, regular life. I was often chided for encouraging her too much in her studies and in languages and that I didn't teach her to be practical, etc. That was, of course, wrong but nobody could know what the future would bring. Above all, I knew that she took great pleasure in learning, in knowledge, in her evident results and successes. I could see fulfilled in her what was denied to me in my youth and I knew too that we often had the same taste in that regard. It is true that I didn't consider above all what the practical outcomes of her studies would be but I thought that if she had her doctorate and had mastered several languages she would always be able to earn her living. Now she already has two years' experience in a bank and recently the wide experience as a cook and maid in America.[18] So my treasure, you can imagine how I swell with pride when I imagine that I did advise my friend well, that she now apparently has a wonderful job, suiting her abilities.

---

[16] *Jüdisches Nachrichtenblatt, Ausgabe Wien.*
[17] Her daughter Edith. Edith had a law degree from the Charles University in Prague. She worked as a secretary in a bank.
[18] Edith emigrated as part of the domestics' programme, one of the few ways for young women to reach Britain before the war.

This week I am all alone in the flat because the couple [the Vaceks[19]] have gone away for a week's rest. It is very peaceful.
Continued 10/7

Today your letter of 2/7 arrived and I am very happy with what you write. I am very glad that you are not going on so many long walks in the great heat, so that you don't lose all your little bit of fat! The life you describe yourself as living is like ours in many ways now. I myself have yoghurt every evening – it isn't rationed yet – tomatoes often, cucumbers, and cheese if I can get it. For simplicity's sake I prepare meat once a week and make it last two or three meals. Apart from that I have vegetables, and from time to time, when I am not too lazy to prepare it, cake or dumplings, or Bohemian desserts, but it really isn't worth it for one person. One can make coffee from grain, with things added, and it tastes very good. I buy curd cheese as often as I can get it. It's a food which is much in demand and particularly useful for various kinds of dumplings. But I am very sorry that you have so little variety. Do shops close for everyone at the same time or only for some?[20] I obey all the orders exactly and have only one great wish, that I shall always be able to keep them strictly.

Ernst, if you could see your friend Motz from the coffee-house, and how thin and altogether unwell he looks, you would shake your head.

Mutti is suffering. She is uneasy all the time, mostly irritable and on edge, always offended if things don't happen the way she wants, and my sister doesn't have an easy time at all with her.

All yours, Mitzi.

Karlín, 14/7/1941

My much beloved
Today brought me your letter of the 5th which will make me full of joy again. I go about my work cheerfully, absolutely refusing to let my feeling of happiness be soured. And there are certainly enough unpleasant things, believe me.

---

[19]The Vaceks lived with Marie in one apartment. It seems they were not Jewish.
[20]Marie is wondering whether the German occupiers in Thessaloniki have imposed the same shopping restrictions on Jews as they have in Prague.

And now to your epistle: there's no need to fear that nature will impose her limitations, my treasure, as I know very well that we two are no teenagers. We are wonderfully suited in our ages. And as I see in the weekly wedding announcements in the Jewish newspaper, where plenty of people seek and find each other, we are perhaps no exceptions.[21]

How do I imagine our first meeting? Ha, my sweet, that *is* a question! The immediate effect of seeing each other again would be the same, wherever it might happen. To see you, to fall into your arms in the most natural way, the surroundings would disappear for me, wouldn't matter at all. To look for our home – mine, yours, another – would for the time being be unimportant. I would first look deep into your eyes, wait to hear what you wanted to say, or not, and leave it to you to decide what to do next. I would certainly be wondering over and over whether it is true, is it really him, is it not a dream? Next I would wish to spend a few days of complete peace with you, to hear all about you, to be able to look at you without interruption. I would need a long time to digest the reality, even when you were sleeping I would have to watch you and keep assuring myself that the dream had become reality.

And now, how did *you* imagine it? And where? That is a question only God can answer, because I don't think any human being can do that today. I would like most of all to stay here, but that doesn't depend on me, as you know, but on the end of the war and on you.

Erika enthuses about medicine. A fine thing to study, even if it is quite strenuous for women's nerves. I thought that she would soon be grown up, that was to be expected. I have learnt from my experiences of the education of the young and if I had grandchildren whom I had to counsel, there is just one thing I would advise. Whatever their future, both girls and boys absolutely must, from their earliest childhood, along with training for a job using the brain, become thoroughly competent in some kind of work using their hands. Then the parents will truly have equipped their children in the best way possible.

I don't deserve the praise for the money I spent on the Viennese: once one knows what unspeakable misery reigns among these people then it is indeed

---

[21]Other sources confirm an increasing number of weddings in the Jewish community with the intensifying persecution. This could be a social response to new hardships.

only one's duty as human beings to do one's little bit.[22] It's sad that you regret your decision to go to Greece. I can really understand it now and I am upset for you. But please don't forget that it was surely Thesa's heartfelt wish to see her children and it must be a comfort for you to have fulfilled that wish.

The landlady has given me notice again, but it actually isn't valid so I'm ignoring it.

And now, a sweet, gentle kiss, then a saucy one, then a few very passionate ones. I am not upset, so just stay healthy and cheerful and hopeful.

A tender embrace from your Mitzi.

Karlín, 18/7/1941

My dearly beloved

Your letter of the 9th gave me great joy, as always. It came just after an accident, which luckily had no serious consequences. The maid was clumsy and caused the bookcase to fall on me. Nothing much happened – just a bleeding knee, which put paid to my going out today, and then I became completely reconciled with the momentary shock and pain because a letter from you can do a lot.

Regarding your wounded feelings as a father, you really should not take offence, my treasure, because it helps no one and damages you, and me with you. Please don't forget that you and Hella have a similar nature, both of you mean well by each other and yet you can't treat each other as you would like. Neither of you is to blame; it is your nature which is the cause, as happens with people with such distinctive characters. There is no question of her not loving you, it just seems like that to you. Perhaps it is even jealousy? Just be patient a bit longer, then I will make up for as much as possible.

If I were in your position I would look for various distractions so that you have the diversions you need. Don't laugh at me, Ernstili, if I advise you to prepare some meals for yourself from time to time. Here many men deal with the cooking when circumstances demand it, so it would not be a dishonourable

---

[22]Marie is referring to having sent parcels to some Viennese friends who have been deported to Poland.

Photo 6 *Hella and Salvator Cougno.*

activity for you but simply good for your daily well-being and your health but also a distraction.

It will be another weekend without you. I am invited out tomorrow and Sunday but I don't enjoy it without you. When I look at a group of gentlemen I know I could so easily imagine you among them.

I embrace you very tenderly, kiss you many times and am

Your Mitzi.

Dearest, do you realize it will soon be a year since we admitted our love to each other?

Karlín, 22/7/1941

My beloved Ernst

Who can describe my disappointed face when this morning, cheerful and expecting your letter – due yesterday and therefore awaited with certainty and longing – I opened it and saw that there had been a mix-up. I received a letter from Athens from a daughter to her mama. Unfortunately the letter contains neither the address of the sender nor of the recipient. Perhaps the letter you sent to me will be returned to you and will then arrive as intended.

I have to smile a little at all this when I picture the face of the unknown mama getting your letter. What do you think, Ernstili? Will she see the funny side?

I am fairly well, I still have to use a stick as my knee isn't quite right yet. I was at the doctor's yesterday because I was worried I might have a torn ligament, but luckily I don't. I really had a very lucky escape because I might have been killed outright.

I long so desperately for you, so that I would prefer to stay at home all the time like a hermit because nothing makes me happy at the moment and now I will be lucky if I get something from you this week. How long will this situation last?

I will stop for today and hope and pray that you, beloved, are healthy and optimistic. I hug you most dearly, kiss you in my usual way and then long indescribably for you.

Your Mitzi

Karlín, 25/7/1941

My dearest Ernst

I really ought to leave out my second letter this week because I still haven't had one from you. Even if the mix-up was not your fault, you were a little bit to blame because your handwriting is very similar to the German lady's. But as you see, I'm not like that, so I will stick to my schedule. But I am just very sad and out of sorts this week and I have even cried twice, which is very unusual for me, just because nothing came from you.

Above all, I am annoyed at Irene, who regularly asks me 'Have you got any news?' I just say yes or no. When she heard that I took from your envelope a letter from a mama to her daughter [*sic*], she laughed heartily. She thought it was so funny; it felt to me like *schadenfreude*. I thought I was going to scratch her eyes out, I was so angry, but I didn't show it and every day when we speak to each other she mentions it and laughs all over again. What a silly goose, don't you think?

My injured knee is unfortunately still giving me trouble; I have been to the doctor who found nothing but I can only walk with a lot of pain, and walking, which I keep forcing myself to do, tires me quite a bit. And just at this very time I have to be running around incessantly because I have to find another warehouse. It is terribly difficult to find one, almost impossible. But I absolutely have to find one because I have a lot which must be stored, and also, if I had to move, I would really rather store my furniture etc., and only in the worst case give it away. I would rather not be parted from my things. Every day I go out looking, enquiring, putting up adverts. I am also worried about moving things into store, as on my own I can hardly do anything. Irene is helping me a lot in my search but up to now we have little in prospect. If you were here I know you would help me.

Dearest, this week I baked yeast cakes with quark, cherries and crumble. I tell you, they were so good that I even received rare praise from my mother and I was so pleased with this success. What would I have given to be able to put that in front of you!

There's no longer any free time in the afternoon because shopping hours are limited to between three and five o'clock. Then one really has to pull oneself together and go and buy something. You will rightly think that one person on her own surely doesn't need to shop every day, but one has to take care not to let one's suppliers forget that one is still alive, otherwise one is trampled on everywhere, because every day is fish day but not catch day, as the old saying goes, which means that one doesn't get every day what one actually wants.

My treasure, you can surely well imagine how funny all of that seemed to me at first, I who was used to sending for something from the cellar or the shop when I needed it, but even more so the strange behaviour of certain suppliers who show favour to one and not to another. As far as possible I have chosen nice people and I manage well with them. It is nevertheless a skill in a city like Prague, with its particular peculiarities, such as that a Jewish woman must absolutely speak Czech and they make it very difficult for her if she speaks German.[23] Yet today Prague is a city where both languages are equally heard. All notices are in both languages. I can make myself quite well understood but I make mistakes when I speak, which I find rather disagreeable as I was always very proud about speaking faultlessly in my mother tongue. But I must say that I often come across very good and nice-natured people, the working class people in particular have a kindness which is moving and exemplary. I have not yet, thank goodness, been insulted by anyone, either with a word or a look, and hope it may remain so. Naturally, I behave very discreetly everywhere and stand back as much as possible. It also gives me pleasure to be able to get this or that for Irene that she often can't get and then they are surprised that, while I have been here such a relatively short time, they have been let down by their old suppliers and are glad to accept my help.

Worries come back again and again ever since I have been here, and I still haven't found peace. The matter of the flat, in particular, plagues me – in the end, if I do have to move out, I will after all land up at Irene's. Of course, that hasn't been decided yet – I would only have to move out if someone applies to the magistrate for my flat and I must be prepared. The whole thing horrifies me and it depresses me very much. I tell myself that I can't ask anything for myself other than the fate that has long befallen so many others. What is bitter in all this is that the *Kultusgemeinde*[24] – and it alone is the administrative body which decides for the Jews – doesn't allocate a separate room to women who are alone, but simply puts them in with some stranger. So imagine, dreadful things are happening. Often the landlords and tenants can't stand each other. It's terrible how it is sometimes – few people show consideration and a willingness to meet each other half way. And when I consider that such a fate

---

[23]Historically, Czech anti-semitism was often directed against Jews as perceived Germanizers. These sentiments further increased during the occupation, when the Jews, who continued to speak German, were highly resented.

[24]The Germans tasked the *Kultusgemeinde* (the Community Office) with the implementation of all directives issued by the Nazi authorities, which led to frequent tensions between the Jews and the community leadership.

may now befall me, I would lose courage if I didn't think all the time about you. If I weigh up living with Irene, in a practical sense it is the best, but it would be at the cost of my independence.

Beloved, forgive the typing errors because of the dusk. I am ashamed that today I have only written about myself and my worries – that happens when letters don't arrive! I embrace you now very lovingly, kiss you many times in the usual way, and am

Your Mitzi

Karlín, Saturday evening, 2/8/1941

My beloved Ernstili,

Today I was hoping for news from you again; I thought there would be some but nothing came. Well, I hope perhaps on Monday. I am alone and am just very full of yearning for you.

Eman wrote today that the 'friends' send many greetings. Things are going well for them. He also wrote that both men are apparently so good and I really don't know what to think. He seems to mean Otto Reichl who is apparently giving his wife an allowance.[25] He lives only four hours away from her and it appears that he is constantly sending her money as he seems to be doing very well at his job. In a material sense it would simply be a small instalment of what he has to pay her but also a penance for the deliberate pain he gave, which was undeserved. His conscience is probably troubling him, because he was basically a good person, but he was goaded by his mother and was under her influence to an abnormal degree. God grant that he doesn't make the child unhappy again, because he is not a normal person and I can't say it doesn't matter to me, even if I can't do anything about it. But if, God forbid, my fears were to be realized, that would certainly be a misfortune. Evidence indicates that there is something psychologically wrong with him, which is how at the time he ruined the child mentally. All that appears to me now like a bad dream and I can still hardly speak about it, the memories of what we lived through are so horrific and tormenting.

---

[25]Grete's divorced husband, Otto Reichl, also fled to England where he enlisted in the Czech army.

As I take it that you will only get pleasure from reading newspapers in German, I recommend to you the weekly 'Das Reich'.[26] You will be able to get it there just like here, so please buy it some time. Have you still got work? Sunday, 3/8, evening

I have been out since 10 o'clock this morning. I was visiting my friend Olga Löwenstein in Vinohrady.[27] She was given notice to leave her nice flat last May, had to move out within three weeks and of course, according to the regulations, she had to become a sub-tenant.[28] That is particularly bitter for a single person because one usually cannot get a room of one's own but must share with some other person that the *Kultusgemeinde* has assigned. You are offered three flats (that is, three rooms) and from those you must choose one. No further offer is made. The flat is identified three days before the move and then, if you don't want it, well, then you can live on the street. So one has to get a grip if one doesn't want to be without a roof. Poor thing, she had to take a room which can't be heated and in which the landlady has dumped a large part of her own furniture which can't be used. She isn't allowed to use the kitchen or the bathroom. There is no room or any other possibility of storing coal. And then along came someone else to share the room who brought with her enough furniture for two rooms, who argues every day with the landlady and there is a constant danger that the two women will fly at each other. Horrible scenes like that are now unfortunately the order of the day among our co-religionists and the *Kultusgemeinde* is fully engaged with settling quarrels. Unfortunately most of the Prague families who have to let out part of their flats are very unreasonable and unkind and see others as intruders. Of course there are exceptions here and there, people who are humane. So now you have an idea of the daily game in our town, but also in Brno, etc.

---

[26]'*Das Reich*' (literally '*The Reich*' or '*Empire*') was a weekly newspaper founded by Nazi propaganda minister Joseph Goebbels in 1940. It mainly circulated inside Germany, but was also available to subscribers in other European countries. Reading it might give Ernst some information about laws affecting Jews in the Reich, which he should take as a warning.

[27]A district in Prague.

[28]Marie several times describes the limited options open to Jews in Prague when assigned accommodation by the *Kultusgemeinde*.

I went with my friend to the old Žižkov Cemetery, the Jewish one.[29] There one can sit down and it looks like a park. There are even sand-pits for small children to play in and this place of relaxation is much visited.

Midday at the Lípas' and in the afternoon with Mutti at Frau Neumann for our bridge party. Richard N[eumann] has married a widow with a seven-year-old girl, but his wife looks young and nice. He was designated as a Class 1 worker and although he has been an excellent gardener for a year he is now working in a brick factory. He digs clay and also works a machine. His fellow workers are apparently very nice to him and as a heavy labourer he gets double food ration cards. Of course, when he gets home in the evening he has a hearty appetite. He leaves home at 5.30 in the morning, but he gets a good wage, about 50 crowns a day, I think.

I wanted to ask you again, my good one, whether butter and fats are also rationed or if they are freely available. If you can, eat plenty of bread and butter because that would be good for you – it is especially good and healthy to eat butter. Here the sick, or those who have a doctor's certificate to show they need it, get an extra allowance.

And now, farewell. I hug and kiss you 10,000 times and am, in great longing,

Your Mitzi.

Karlín, 20/8/1941, 10 in the evening

My beloved

I really feel a bit ashamed because I sent your letter off today without a signature and ask you to forgive me.[30] This two-hour period for shopping makes one very tense, but there's nothing one can do about it. I will send the bathing caps off if they are to be had, I will let you know soon whether they are.

And now I want to answer your letter – the one of 9/8 – properly. Since the picture gave you such pleasure I will send you another soon, my golden treasure. I can offer you this harmless pleasure, it is sad enough that I can do so little else for you.

---

[29]See also the letter of 22 June 1941.
[30]The unsigned letter of 20 August is missing.

Of course I can understand that you are impatient with bridge parties and other social chit-chat with strangers. I feel just the same. The very fact that you were usually reserved and taciturn towards most people makes me all the happier at your openness towards me and I know that between the two of us a wonderful dialogue will develop. Our heads are in fact full of each other, we are two crazy lovers, it's almost scandalous, Ernstili, but what can we do about it? It makes me laugh again from sheer happiness. But you know, my treasure, you must nevertheless force yourself to mix with people, just don't become a recluse.

I am really very well now, I have a lot of work and a lot of running around to do. Everything is now fully prepared at the storage depot. If I have to move out of the flat, I have decided not to go to the Lípas under any circumstances because I would lose my independence there, I would rather content myself with somewhere else. Now I have about six weeks before the decision is made, but will in any case take precautions and be ready to move. But the main thing is that I know where I will put the furniture and all the rest, and from tomorrow that will be settled.

So now I am going to bed. Good night, my love! Now I am snuggling down under the covers and imagine to myself that you are with me, then I embrace you most lovingly in my mind, send you the most beautiful kisses and am

Your Mitzimarie

Karlín, 23/8/1941, 8.30 p.m.

My dearest

Once again the post is not quite regular – today your letter of the 12th arrived. It makes me a bit nervous, I don't know how it is that I immediately start worrying about all sorts of possible and impossible things.

On the other hand, the contents of your letter cheer me up enormously. When I read your description of the return from the vineyard and the fruit you brought back, I involuntarily thought of the biblical story of the first humans, but Eve was not there.

I am very pleased that the situation with H[ella] is bearable. So do what you want, whether you want to tell Hella something [about us] or not, just follow your instinct.

I am already looking forward to the picture. I already know that you will be much thinner than before. With that heat it couldn't be any other way. If possible, please send me a picture of the children. I would like to see the pair of them.

I will send the three caps to Herr Gustav Jurgscheit,[31] probably next Tuesday, and also if possible a box of *oblaten*[32] for you. Please tell Herr J. that they are for you. There is no need to send the money, it is only very little, there's no hurry. In any case, I don't like mentioning sums of money in letters because I don't want to give the wrong idea, so consider this trifling amount as a little gift. These things are very cheap and it is just a tiny favour. One is allowed to send things from here to the Altreich[33] and also to send and receive money, but there are a great many formalities if one wants to send money outside this area, then one has to be very careful not to make a mistake on a form. I ask you again not to stint on your food, allow yourself everything you need for a decent life.

As regards the flat, I have been told that I will not have to move out so I can keep hoping that things will remain as they are, except if the day comes when suddenly everyone here has to move out in a short time[34] – that happens and then there is nothing one can do about it. If only I knew where I would be able to put everything quickly in such an event.

Beloved, farewell, stay healthy. I hug you tenderly and kiss you with all my heart and am

Your Mitzi.
PS Eman wrote about the 'friends', they are fine. If I understand Eman correctly, Grete is in contact with Dr Reichl. I wouldn't be happy about that, but I can't prevent it and wouldn't want to.

---

[31] In her memoir *From Thessaloniki to Auschwitz and back*, Ernst's grand-daughter Erika writes that two rooms in the Cougno family house were requisitioned for a Gestapo officer and his orderly. Apparently Jurgscheit was one such officer.

[32] Wafers.

[33] The Altreich was the name given to pre-1938 Germany (before the annexation of Austria, Bohemia-Moravia, parts of Poland, etc.).

[34] Marie anticipates the possibility that there would be new restrictions on Jewish residences in individual Prague districts or even deportations.

Karlín, 31/8/1941

My beloved

I haven't had any news from you for a week now, and I am uneasy again but I am convinced this is not your fault, one has to expect such interruptions in wartime and be all the more grateful for every happy moment. When I remember the interruptions in the World War, when I often waited weeks for news, then one has to be glad that it is still a lot better now, so far.

How are things with Hella? Is there harmony between you or are you both still irritable and tense?

I haven't much time now because I want to get this letter to the post so that you don't worry, but as no post is coming from you I am going to answer more completely the letters of June/July.

Once you asked whether I go to the café. Well now, Ernstili, what do you think? Go to the café? No, I don't do that, nor do Mutti, Irene or Gustel; none of us goes to the café because we wouldn't enjoy being at Aschermann's.[35] We have enough work to do in the house and, with the shopping in the afternoon, time just flies. One has to hurry to get everything done in the two hours for the following day. There's no time for walks. And where would one go?[36] At the most a visit from us to you and from you to us, as we say. But that is very nice, there is always someone one knows there, one has a little chat and then one hurries home because I am always home before eight o'clock.

A while ago you offered to send me anything I needed. Even if I haven't got any coupons I don't need anything now. I am provided for, my beloved. No doubt you'll be getting coupons too, who knows? You still seem to have all sorts of things, there are still enough clothes etc. here, but it is controlled by ration cards. The rationing system works brilliantly here, its organization is quite exemplary.

---

[35] A former Jewish-owned café in Prague at Dlouhá ulice which continued to serve Jews when others were no longer allowed.

[36] An indirect reference to the edict prohibiting Jews from entering any of Prague's public parks and gardens.

Now I must stop, I have a guilty conscience again about the Herr Censor – he must forgive me just once more. I hug and kiss you lovingly many times, keep healthy and cheerful and content.

With deepest love from your Mitzimarie.

Karlín, 2/9/1941

My dearest

From your letter of 15/6 [*sic*] it does indeed really seem as if you have been gone from us for a very, very long time, beloved. Sometimes I think you are living on Mars. And I am glad, and grateful to fate, for this feeling. I do know, thank God, that things are all right for you. But for us too. The papers I named were often of interest to me because they kept me informed of events in far-away lands.[37] I was always greatly interested in the stories of [people's] journeys etc., but I couldn't discuss things with you in any other way because I never do anything at all which could give the slightest impression that I am interested in some other matter.

I note what you write about your papers. From them it is clear you are a citizen of the Protectorate, that is sufficient. The passport would not be valid here any more, you would get another if you were here but there it is sufficient.

Recently Frau Vacek asked me to rinse her back in the bath. I did so, I took the brush and gave her a good hard scrub because she had already annoyed me several times. Then she squealed and I said to her 'You know, I must practise on you before my Ernstili comes, then I will wash him from head to toe, that's my speciality.' She said 'He's got something to look forward to, poor thing.' 'You don't imagine', I said, 'that I will scrub him like I scrubbed your back!' There was a lot of laughter, she means to get her revenge, the Madam.

And now! A kiss and another one and another, and then farewell.

Lovingly, Mitzimarie.

---

[37]Marie is possibly hinting that she is following the situation in Greece.

Karlín, 3/9/1941

My sweet merry little boy

This salutation is the answer to your letter of 17/6, to complete it. In that letter you called me 'Mother'. My love, do you still remember your mother's love, when you were a child? I am sure your mother loved each of her children with a mother's love. Do you know how my heart lights up when I picture how I played with and cuddled my children, how often they used to argue about who was going to sit next to me. And do you know whom I could compare you with, who your gentle words remind me of? My Edithel. I can imagine so beautifully

Photo 7 *Marie with her husband Emil, before 1936.*

how, like with my Edithel, I would stroke and cuddle you. My Edithel was such a little one for honeyed words. And she and I, we were so close to each other. She would often come and take a cushion, place her little head on my knee and then off she went. She really is a very sweet person. My God, how my heart pains me when I think about it …. But no, when I have you, you will be Edithel too.

The photo is delightful, even if the thinness cannot be disguised, and I can see that the head is quite untroubled by problems, looking completely healthy and that makes me happy. I will set about feeding up the rest of you again.

Of course, Ernst, I will love you with all your weaknesses, although I would point out that I don't know these yet, only what you have told me. Emmerl also had his weaknesses, but I liked them too, I mean I got used to them. Often in his absentmindedness he would take the office key with him and when I wanted to open up I had to get the locksmith. Or, in the evening, I would hunt for ages for my nightie and then my eye would fall on Emmerl and he was wearing it. Imagine, he was sleeping so peacefully and contentedly, that is how absentminded he could be. Anyway, that was in the early years – I had been given real English nighties in my dowry, which was very modern in those days, and the poor thing mixed it up with his nightshirt. But anyway, that could only happen to Emmerl! There were lots of things like that and I soon got used to it.

And now I must stop. I give you a very, very loving hug and kiss from your

Mitzimarie

Vienna, 4/9/1941

My dearest

My friend, Frau Anna Riemer, is forwarding you this letter from Vienna.[38] She is completely trustworthy and you are quite safe writing to her. I am just waiting for confirmation through her that you are getting my post regularly, then I will be able to give you further instructions about your letters. Anna

---

[38] Anna Riemer was a sister of Olga Löwenstein, Marie's very close friend in Prague.

will certainly deal with everything as you wish. She certainly will not read the letters. I will ask her on her word of honour not to do so. She really is a decent, fine person. But all the same, I know that you will be inhibited, I can understand that. I am the same but I have such wonderful old letters from you that I have to content myself with them in the meantime.

This letter is going to A. in a sealed envelope. She can then send it on. I am well, everything is in order. I have only one worry which only you can cure: that is the great longing for you. Oh God, I've got it badly!

Yesterday I sent you two long letters direct. Today I was able to write another. I hope I will get news from you that my letters have arrived.

I hug you most tenderly, send you a number of sweet kisses and am

Your Mitzimarie.

Karlín, 6/9/1941

My beloved

At the same time as this letter you will receive one from Anna; oh, it is so hard to write these. If I only knew whether you are receiving the letters which I am sending you directly, so that I could write accordingly. Treasure, I cannot thank you enough for your loving consideration and solicitude. Now every day I read your last letters in place of those which can't reach me and they fill my whole existence.

I am asking Anna or Alois to let me know whether all my letters arrived. Now I will carry on answering unanswered parts of your old letters. Your picture is just smiling so beautifully at me, as if you were sitting next to me and looking over my shoulder as I write.

As regards clothes coupons, I can tell you that for us there aren't any. Thank you for your kind offer, but for now I still have enough because one saves, and because we dress very simply when we go out and don't visit places of entertainment of any sort, we need far fewer fine stockings and all the lingerie which was dear to our feminine hearts. Anyway, I am already looking forward to the revenge I will take when I clear out my collection of stockings because I have never darned as much as now – understandable, isn't it?

My sweet, you can imagine how I suffer when you describe your walks and I can't be with you. Yes my love, we would sit down now and again – would the kisses remain restrained? I wouldn't want that! How I am already looking forward to you pointing out this and that. That is just what I have been missing so much since our separation, that generous sharing of your knowledge. I am as thirsty for this as for your kisses. Or do you think that it will be a while before we talk seriously? Sometimes it seems like it to me. It is unbelievable how, when I think of you, I can only ever have a one-sided conversation. Oh, you old sinner (and yet so young), how did you manage to change me like this?

Beloved, it has turned 12 o'clock midnight while I've been talking with you, so good night!!!

I am imagining you are with me, I am going to fall asleep in your arms. Be healthy and happy and write a lot to me as soon as you can. With great longing I kiss your eyes, cheeks, mouth and am

Your Mitzimarie.

Karlín, 8/9/1941

My beloved birthday child

Now your birthday is over and I will describe to you how this morning I lived it with you in my vivid imagination. I woke up at 4 a.m., I wanted to be the first to wake up today, of course we were together in our bedroom, you were still sleeping deeply and peacefully. I wondered: shall I, shan't I? Without waiting, still half asleep, I rolled over towards you to congratulate you and as I started to say 'Sweet birthday child, congratulations', two strong arms grasped me, the elbows were a bit pointed, and in a torrent of kisses my stammerings were lost. It was bewitching, wonderful, and then we fell asleep again, until we celebrated the birthday in the morning according to plan. In reality I prayed for you then very fervently, as I always do. All day long I thought only of you, but I was filled with great sadness, arising, in truth, from my longing for you. It was all I could do not to howl out loud.

And now, back to reality. I may soon send you the address of Miss Grete Rudolph. She is a good person, the twin sister of Edith's mother-in-law. As soon as I send you her address I will write to her too. Yesterday there was a letter from Paul,[39] saying that the 'friends' are well and that he is in correspondence with them, that everything is as Eman writes.

I showed your picture to the family and it was much admired. I can never hide how joyful and happy I look when people talk about you and the others might think it a bit ridiculous that we are burning with such young love. I don't, of course, say anything about either you or me, that we are so in love, but they just see it. It set my mother off to tell the old story that the Buxbaums (she meant you) stay young for ever, the grandfather became a father again at 70. You know my mother, when she starts on her stories about Luck,[40] she's very amusing, everybody laughed a lot, but I felt very proud of the good opinion they had of you and just nodded appreciatively. Were your ears burning?

Beloved, today I am writing more briefly, farewell. [*no signature*]

Karlín, 11/9/1941

My dear Ernst

My treasure, would it not be possible to get Alois to send you a Viennese newspaper[41] regularly, an official one, it could even be the Jewish one? It is really important that you hear something from your former homeland. I can't send you any newspapers from here but I think it is allowed from Vienna. I will have to hand in my typewriter to be mended, I think.[42] I will find it very hard to say goodbye to it because of my correspondence with you, I hope I may be able to borrow one from some business or other. Have you still got yours?

You haven't teased me about my prediction for a long time, which is why I tell you today that I am starting on it again, so that you can tease me about it again! So listen, five months from my last birthday[43] I intend to hold you in my arms, I don't wish to wait any longer, then we will celebrate one year of being engaged.

---

[39]Paul Buxbaum, see Chapter 1, footnote 26.
[40]Luka, near Karlsbad.
[41]See footnote 16.
[42]Marie is disguising the fact that she has to declare to the authorities whether she has a typewriter. She does this on 13 September and on 1 November she has to hand it in (see Introduction).
[43]12 June.

There are good reasons for me not wanting to live with the Lípas. Irene, with all her kindness, behaves towards me in a way which doesn't suit me, which makes it better that we should not be together so much. I became convinced that it is better if I remain myself and am not under Irene's influence. She knows it and it often vexes her, but there is nothing one can wish for or change in that. That's why it will be better, if I do have to move out, that I simply live with strangers rather than with the Lípas. To be constantly ordered about and corrected, laughed at or ridiculed, if she feels like it, and when I don't do things as she wants, letting me feel my dependence, getting punished like a small child – no, Ernstili, I won't ever surrender myself to that. I also believe I understand more than Irene, even if she is better off financially than I am – that doesn't matter to me at all. It is all happening because everyone is very tense. It will soon be three years that I have been rootless. They have often had worries about me and less joy than before, that is obvious. But now everyone has enough trouble and torment and therefore has only half the understanding for others, or none at all. Everything is taken amiss, as happens when things are not going well for people. Then it is best if one is not so much together, so that one doesn't get on each other's nerves. As you know, I have been through a lot and my way of thinking has changed, others just have to bite the bullet. There's nothing to be done since they didn't choose a different path. But you mustn't think that we are any less good sisters, that wouldn't be true, but we will never understand each other completely because we are quite different and because I won't ever again let myself be influenced by Irene's opinions but will stay as I am.

And if fortune allows us to have each other one day, then we will creep away and hide, at least for a time, and talk over and recount everything, heal our wounded hearts of all the pain left by these times, each healing the other. May God be merciful and grant us at last this fortune.

For now a very, very loving farewell. With a hug which will drive you senseless, and a number of sweet kisses, I say goodbye. Utterly yours,

Mitzimarie

Karlín, 13/9/1941

My dearly beloved

I am writing so often to you now because I am afraid I will soon not have a typewriter. I have been worried about this for days now. Today I was at Karel's[44] and I asked him to help me out with one and he half agreed to do so. Yes, one has endless worries. My family can't understand why I don't want to write by hand, but we can understand it, can't we? How many sheets of paper would I need? I can't ask that of Herr Censor and I wouldn't like to have to give up my conversation with you.

The picture of Erika is delightful, a real little teenager, natural and sweet.

I am very surprised that there is so much you can't get and hope you have some things stored away. The coming decision on the question of the flat, the final settling of the matter, is making me very tense, as you can imagine, but what can one do? At a time like the present all that is just immaterial and if the individual is also affected, so what? I have various plans, and even if I did have to move out, I would always take into my calculations what I would do if you suddenly came. I have just made provision for an alternative which would at least be half satisfactory – I hope so anyway – but let God take care of a little too, my treasure!

I remember the storms at the seaside very well. It is interesting how they really stirred me. This spectacle of nature has a curious effect on people from countries with no coasts, at least it was so with me. When I was at the seaside I loved getting up early and walking along the beach on my own to watch the sunrise and the return of the fishermen with their catch. Looking at the sea when it was calm always had a most powerful effect on me. I could have sat for hours studying it, musing and thinking. But the storm stirred me above all because I thought of how many people might again be losing their lives at that moment.

You are right to take up your studies again, that is a good distraction. I myself always enjoyed learning and broadening my knowledge very much, so you can imagine how happy I am if you also look for diversion in studying.

---

[44]Karel Struzi.

Unfortunately I can't do anything for my mind now, time and circumstance don't permit it.

Would it not be possible for you to have a warmer room? On no account should you, heaven forbid, get ill.

My sweet, I too have no patience for anything, wherever I am I long to be at home so that I can be alone with you, writing to you and reading one of your letters. It is always the same and will be so until we are together.

It is late again. I am going to go to sleep and dream most beautifully of you. I kiss you lovingly, good night, be healthy and happy.

Your Mitzimarie.

Karlín, 15/9/1941

My dearly beloved sinful one

Today I ate at the Lípas', which was fine. One has to realize that they lost all their provisions yet everything is still very respectable there. Irene now cooks for herself as her maid can't do it. One has to be glad if one can get a maid who is decent, because the majority won't go to Jews. There are also plenty of Jewish domestics but they have all been snapped up.

Afterwards we went to Frau Louise Neumann. [Her son] Richard has got married to a widow with an eight-year-old child, a nice little woman. They live with Frau N. but she is expecting to lose her flat any minute. Richard had an accident while doing heavy labour because a J[ewish] colleague dropped a 150 kg heavy metal plate on his foot, breaking some of his toes. He says that if it weren't for the pain he'd be glad to be able to be at home for a bit. Frau N. has other worries too: today she handed in her inventory.[45] Her son Karl and his wife are in Split, which they like, but they don't know whether they can stay there.[46] They have abandoned everything to make this journey.

---

[45]In the course of the autumn all Jews were required to hand in to the authorities an inventory of all their possessions.
[46]Split, in what is now Croatia, was occupied by Italy since April 1941.

And then it is evening and I am sitting here with you. On my left is your picture, which is smiling at me. It is the most beautiful present for me, as if I were talking to you.

Do you know that in a few days it will be New Year?[47] I think you don't bother about the festivals any more, but I don't want to miss this opportunity to tell you my dearest wishes: my love, you know what I want for you and for me: our happy reunion very soon, in health and peace. Like you, I hope that all the great suffering may make people gentle, that everyone may once more be able to behave well towards each other, that for us too there may be a quiet little place in the sun. During the festival I will spend some time in the synagogue and will pray fervently even though I know already that I will get very worked up. It is very strange, as soon as I enter a place of worship, I listen for a while to the service, then I see at once before my eyes, in all vividness, the synagogue of my home town with all its ceremony. All the long years I went there pass before my eyes, all my memories are so powerful, going right back to my youth, and then when I see the beautiful building in ruins and ashes,[48] I am seized by a pain I can't put a name to. I feel so alone and miserable, so without any support, so broken. That is why I only rarely go to a service. One Friday evening recently I went past the building in the Geistgasse[49] where even today the service is like an opera. I went there with Irene, there wasn't a seat left in the great building. When I heard the good music, deep and solemn, I was overcome and it felt as if a great worm was burrowing and gnawing in my breast and the tears streamed down my cheeks. I was upset, too, to see the distress in faces I knew, everyone is so serious and anxious.

During the days of the festival we will wear our own badge.[50] I won't mind it at all, but some people are very unhappy about it. I have nothing to hide, I am not breaking any rules, so I can happily wear it. I will not do anything

---

[47]Rosh Hashana was on 22 and 23 September.

[48]The synagogue in Karlsbad was burnt down on Kristallnacht in November 1938.

[49]Dušní ulice. The synagogue is known today as the Spanish Synagogue. It had an organ and choir and was known for encouraging congregational singing.

[50]On 1 September 1941 it was announced that Jews in the German Reich, including the Protectorate, in future had to wear the yellow Star of David in public. Distribution of the stars commenced on 17 September and wearing them was compulsory from the 19th onwards.

forbidden, either with or without the badge. In a few days one will have got used to it.

My letter today is a report, not a love letter, but the report is necessary this time. So farewell, be healthy and happy.

Your Mitzimarie

Karlín, 18/9/1941

My dearly beloved boy

It is a load off my mind that my letters are reaching you and also that the parcel and the pictures reached the people they were addressed to and gave such pleasure. I was a bit anxious that I might have changed a lot and that my picture might disappoint.

I'm so glad that the *bäckerei*[51] tasted good and gave so much pleasure and that they arrived undamaged. If I had known whether I was allowed to or not, I would have sent more, and now I ask you to let me have, if possible, another address to which I could send you a further parcel. That would be a great pleasure for me.

I thank you many times for the photo of Bubi. What a joy to have two such happy healthy youngsters.

I received a verbal assurance that I can stay in the flat, but I don't feel it is completely reliable. In any case, at the end of the month I will call in at the *Kultusgemeinde*, which has taken over the handling of my notice, and wait to hear more.

Tomorrow I will move the paper things. I will do that together with the removal man because everything is well prepared. Then everything in the warehouse will be neatly organized. I won't move the rest yet, I'll wait until after 1 October. Now that I know where everything will go I am more at ease.

But of course I will often give you a scrub, I'm good at that, don't be afraid. Then I will wrap you well in your bathrobe, rub you down and into bed. Then

---

[51]Pastries.

I'll accept a tip, but not too measly a one. Hmm, what do you think? Will the gentleman be 'magnanimous'? Hopefully he'll behave like a nobleman.

I am wondering a great deal about how it came about that I love you so passionately and have such a burning desire to give so much love. In my whole life I was rarely asked whether I wanted to give as much as to receive. It is quite different with you. You are an absolute master, you know how to reach my weakest points and that is why you will get further. I feel as if there was some unopened reservoir there which you discovered and which belongs only to you. You have enticed another secret out of me, you bad one, but enough for now!

I kiss your beloved eyes, your cheeks, your forehead and then five times your mouth, hug you warmly and lovingly and am

Your Mitzimarie.

P.S. Treasure, it is lovely of you to want to send me nuts. I haven't had raisins for a long time, there aren't any here. In any case, I thank you with all my heart for thinking of it.

Karlín, 19/9/1941

My dearly beloved

Now I am going to try to answer the old letters in order. So, number 100. As I now know that my letters are arriving I am much calmer and am therefore very grateful to Anna and Marie[52] for their kindness. You can hardly imagine how happy your pleasure at the modest little gifts made me. I am very glad that you immediately noticed my new hairstyle that I thought up and requested especially for you. People here like it too, they say it suits me well. The dress in the photo is in a deep red material, a good colour for me. You bad one, I deliberately ignored your remark about getting a podium and there you go and mention it again, just wait! If you make fun of me any more because I am small, then I will think of a way to tease you. After all, I can stand on tip-toe.

---

[52]Marie, like Anna Riemer, is a friend in Vienna.

We have received delightful greetings from our 'friends', heart-warming. You can imagine what a joy that was. Apparently they are all getting on wonderfully. Yes, America is a land of boundless possibilities, but only for young people. Older ones have no place there, on the whole they are less well appreciated, according to what one hears and reads. The couple have apparently set up a delightful home and the others too are busy and content. They have a lot of good friends and have settled in wonderfully in that distant country.

Now I'm coming to a serious bit. It is about your views on respect and my thoughts about Emmerl. Oh Ernstili, don't you see from everything that I already belong entirely to you? You have always known me, you know that I was a serious person with a great sense of duty and high ideals about morals, etc. Do you think, my beloved, that if I hadn't freed myself from many things I would be able to love you so very, very deeply? You yourself showed me the way, I want to tell you that now I am more or less a part of you. Don't you see how we are woven together? There is such an understanding between us in our way of thinking that no more assurance is needed. I admit freely that I feel a lasting respectful reverence for Emmerl, and for you a passionate love, which knows no bounds or limits, and I long ago cast away all caution and misgivings. And you alone taught me this.

It is now 11.30 at night. In the room next door the married couple are sleeping sweetly but I had to laugh out loud about you, you old-young rascal, just wait. What would Gretel and Edithel say? They know that I always said yes to real, true life. It was with Edithel in particular, and only her – neither mother, nor sister, nor any other woman or female friend – that I spoke about my feelings and my marriage. When Edithel became a wife she came to me in her sweet way and asked me all sorts of things. She was trying to work out the right way to make her Franz happy. I immediately recognized how the child was thinking.

I did out of love what I had never been able to do in my life, in order to help her not to make mistakes, I told her about many things from my own life that I thought were important for her. There is no one else, and never has been, to whom I ever spoke in this way. Already when I was at school my friends and fellow pupils knew that I never joined in their conversations and they stopped talking when I came near saying 'The child is coming, you must be quiet.' And that is how it remained with our marriage too, there was an understanding between us that we would not talk with anyone about our marriage, neither with my mother nor my sister; neither I nor Emmerl wanted that. He was extremely touchy about that and would have been deeply offended and I felt just the same. And to discuss it with other women? I would never have dreamt of it. Why should it interest other women? I don't really know how it was that no other woman ever told me her story, but I didn't want it and never encouraged it, but also nobody asked it of me.

Today is New Year's Eve, do you know that? The service was cancelled.[53] We had got a little used to wearing the badge. The first day, the 19th, I had to leave the house at 7.30 a.m. and I admit I had a ringing in my ears and felt dizzy when I took my first steps in the street. I was filled with an indescribable feeling of humiliation. But only for a few moments. Then I lifted my head high and looked everyone I met full in the eye. Thank goodness the public is on the whole humane and nice.[54] They are yellow Stars of David, the size of a hand, with the word 'JUDE' [Jew] written in black in the centre. I don't know yet whether there will be a service at all tomorrow morning. I don't think I will go but I will eat at Irene's anyway.

I have already moved part of the goods into storage. It was pretty tiring but I managed to do it on my own. Today I was told again that I am not allowed to give up my flat. I must get hold of the official at the *Kultusgemeinde* and get him to inform the court that the notice is invalid and then the business will be over for now. Do you know what they call Pařížská?[55] The Milky Way! Because that is where most of the Jews with stars live, and there are plenty more such jokes now.[56] Today, following the old custom, I was at the cemetery. I always

---

[53]This could be as a result of the tensions after the introduction of the compulsory Star of David.
[54]Other sources confirm the positive response in the Czech population. The Czechoslovak BBC Service from London broadcast a speech in support of the Jews.
[55]Pařížská třída (= Paris Avenue), the main and very elegant thoroughfare through the Old City of Prague. Irene and Gustav's flat faced this street across a small park.
[56]The German intelligence agency in the Protectorate (the *Sicherheitsdienst*) recorded the circulation of similar jokes in Prague.

look for the grave of Franz's first mother there.[57] She would be exactly as old as me. I didn't know her but that is where I always make my prayers. Franz is Edith's husband.

Before I run out of space I want to tell you, my love, that I am so utterly and completely happy with you. I am no longer capable of answering your sweet letters adequately, I lack the words but in my mind I turn the words into actions, I take you in my arms and say to you that I love you dearly and

Photo 8 *Edith.*

---

[57]In a letter to her daughters, Grete and Edith, dated 6 June 1939, Marie describes how she chanced upon Ada Sternschuss's grave. 'Yesterday was Papa's *jahrzeit*, I lit a candle for him on your behalf at the cemetery. I wanted to look for Onkel Vogel's grave and as I was looking my gaze fell on a grave: Ada Sternschuss. She was Franz's mother. So I prayed there and took a few flowers which I will send to Edith.'

passionately and that I long immeasurably for you. God protect you, keep well and cheerful and happy.

And now, good night, my sweet boy. I am falling asleep beside you. 1000 loving kisses,

All yours, Mitzimarie

Karlín, 22/9/1941

My most dearly beloved

Today I have at last, as you wished, told the friends [through Eman] as you wanted. In my heart I am not too happy about the friends, I can't say that to anyone here but it upsets me that I haven't seen a single line from them in 1½ years. I know, of course, that there will be reasons for their silence, perhaps it is also not to endanger us, but still, I'm just not happy about it.

Do you know what I am reading at the moment? Joseph Roth's 'Radetzky March'.

Anna Riemer wrote me such a nice, kind letter today. She will deal with everything as wished, assures me of her utmost discretion, so if necessary please do use her to make your arrangements, my love. I don't need to, touch wood. It's only because of you that I smile, my sweet treasure, who else could I ascribe it to? Oh, the thought of you is so wonderful and so beautiful. When I sometimes imagine our future life together this is what happens to me: first, I feel a trickle of cold down my back, like a shiver, then I become burning hot and then I am swept up in a delirium of happiness unlike anything I have ever known. Then I rummage about for scraps of the songs I knew when I was young and a sort of song comes out, all of a jumble, yes it wasn't the Lorelei who made me do that but Ernstimann!

Am I to ignore our love's past? What a question, how could I? No, my love, these will be my most beautiful memories, together with my gratitude that you called me back to life, yes truly it was you alone. If it hadn't happened I don't know whether I would not have done away with my life. You won't be surprised when you hear all that I went through for a few years.

We spent the festival days as weekdays. I only had 10 minutes in the synagogue, yes, it has never been like that before. We wouldn't have been able to feel any sense of devotion so it was pointless. Do you know what nickname they have given to the Jewish Town Hall? 'U Flecků'.[58]

Now the weather is fine again, warm during the day but quite cool in the early morning and in the evening, quite autumnal. Autumn in the country around Prague is very beautiful, it is just a pity we aren't able to enjoy it.[59] I did a lot of running around today and now I am off again. One gets very angry when one goes to the Jewish office, where I was just now about the business with the flat.[60] One has to wait for hours with a number and then watch as a lot of people who haven't registered go in first. Then, when it's finally one's turn, one is told by the official on some pretext to come back another day when it suits him better.

And now, I embrace you, kiss you warmly in my own way (which you know) and say goodbye. Keep well and cheerful.

Your Mitzimarie

Karlín, 25/9/1941

My most dearly beloved Ernstili

As if I had guessed that I would get a letter today from Anna-Sarah, I decided not to go out because I had some more to do in the flat. Although it was a beautiful day the yellow mark spoils going out for me and I stayed at home. Lo and behold, Anna's letter 108 arrived in the afternoon. I am still waiting for 107, which hasn't arrived yet. Anna is very good, she sends me her originals and even sends them by airmail. In the meantime I hope all my letters arrived, that you get news from me regularly. I will carry on reading and answering old letters from you – if you can't write to me what else can one do?

You told me about a visit to a little wood. Oh my treasure, do you know how I long for the smell of a wood, for the smell of fresh air, but I could bear

---

[58] U Flekň is one of the Prague's oldest pubs and breweries, dating back about 500 years. Giving its name to the Jewish Town Hall was an ironic play on the German word 'Fleck', meaning a mark or stain, which was also the word people used to denote the yellow Star of David: 'der gelbe Fleck'.

[59] According to a new regulation, introduced in September 1941, Jews were not allowed to leave their residential area without permission.

[60] See footnote 24 (letter sent on 25 July 1941).

everything easily if you were with me! When we can go walking in our woods again I'll give you a little kiss now and then, but otherwise one must behave properly in the woods, that is only decent. I am just saying that to myself because I know you wouldn't do anything else, hmm hmm!

I have already written to you about the problem of the flat [but] it seems you didn't understand me, so I will explain it to you in detail now. Thus: if anybody is given notice – and that can only be by the *Zentralstelle*[61] in Střešovice, so not the landlord – he must go to the *Kultusgemeinde* with the notice and get himself registered. That means his name is recorded and he will then be told to come back in about 14 days, i.e. about 8 days before he has to leave. He then gets about three addresses from the *Kultusgemeinde* from which he must choose one. Of course, there are a lot of people who have acquaintances. If they think they will be able to live with an acquaintance they go to the *KG* and ask 'Could I take a room in such and such a place?' Jews are now allowed to rent in only 3 districts, Prague 2, 5 or Vinohrady, but they can never have their own flat, only a subtenancy. In Vinohrady, not in the main street, only in the side streets. So for me it would be normal not to get a room to myself because it is calculated that one person gets 4 square metres. If I had to rely on the *Gemeinde* they would put me up with some stranger, which is pretty bad. It can happen to anyone, even those who have had a room of their own for a long time and they just have to take in another one or two people. It happens frequently that two couples have to live in a large room and they say it is still better than barracks. In the long run one needs to have sympathy and feeling for one's fellow human beings.

You have to understand that notice to leave one's own flat is given all the time and that people may then not take another flat of their own. All, without exception, can only become subtenants. But it is the *Kultusgemeinde* which

---

[61]Full name: *Zentralstelle für jüdische Auswanderung* (= Central Office for Jewish Emigration; in August 1942 the name changed to *Zentralamt für die Regelung der Judenfrage in Böhmen und Mähren* = Central Office for the Solution of the Jewish Question in Bohemia and Moravia). This was a Nazi organization, which held the central authority in Jewish affairs in the Protectorate (another similar office existed in Vienna and in Berlin). Established in July 1939 by Adolf Eichmann and Walter Stahlecker, it was initially created with the aim to centralize and speed up the process of Jewish emigration, whilst at the same time to confiscate most of the Jewish émigrés' property. Later the *Zentralstelle* directed the deportations of the Jews.

allocates the subtenancy, as it is the authority considered to be in constant contact with the *Zentralstelle*, and as there is a great shortage of rooms it is rather difficult to find accommodation for all the people. That is why they are constantly measuring up space and the families who still have their own flats within the three permitted areas – only Jews, of course – are forced by the *Kultusgemeinde* to give up as much as possible. No matter how many rooms they have, they have to surrender it all and are allowed to keep for themselves only their few square metres for sleeping and living. They are still better off in that they do have the bathroom, kitchen, dining room etc., and they have to offer the tenants the use of these rooms. Now, you can hardly imagine how much irritation that causes. There are several offices and a whole lot of officials at the *KG* who have nothing to do but to settle people's arguments and squabbles. It's dreadful, what's going on, but one also finds the opposite: individual families who are still civilized, who get on with each other and are considerate.

I have written all that to give you a general idea. As for my case, the Lípas have six people in their two largest rooms, not counting Mutti. They have one room for themselves, their former bedroom, Mutti has the former office. Up to now Mutti has not had to share. I am registered there and that is why Mutti hasn't yet got anyone with her, and also because she is old and very unwell (the doctor certified this). But there is a possibility that she might suddenly get someone. Now, as you know, the landlady's notice is not valid, so I can stay here, but it is quite a new house, something could happen and we could all have to leave and then fate would have caught up with me.

Tante Lidi still has a room free. If it came to it and I was ordered to share a place to sleep with another person, I would allow myself the luxury and rent a room at Tante L's. I would have, in any case, to sleep where I was registered. That would be one possibility or I could do something with some other of my acquaintances if I am not afraid of spending a bit of money (that would be if my treasure came).

The second possibility would be the Lípas. They have been saying up to now that I can come any time to them but you are right, my love, I would be 'looked after' as far as food and everything else goes, but my freedom would be gone. Irene is far more kind and loving, a truly good sister and yet as long as I can I want to be independent. If I have to move out some time I will only go to them if it is in their interest, not mine, out of consideration for Mutti, so that she doesn't have to share with a stranger. And if I have to be with someone else I will always arrange things so that I have a room somewhere else, that is what I hope.

So, my love, don't worry, I know how to make sure there will be a little nest for us. Trust me, let me take care of it. I will make sure everything works out.

And now, where am I sitting? And then? Then most loving kisses, your Mitzimarie

Photo 9 *Irene Lípa.*

Karlín, 25/9/1941

My beloved

I feel a need to explain yesterday's letter about the question of the flat and my relations with Irene, so that you can judge things properly. If it didn't suit me at the Lípas' it would be very difficult to get anything else, because I would be in the bad books of the *Kultusgemeinde*. They would be annoyed with me in view of the present situation and would punish me by giving me some very unpleasant accommodation, if anything at all, or even threaten me with mass accommodation. They would say one can't be so choosy today.

I mentioned Tante Lidi because her area is unrestricted, the *Kultusgemeinde* isn't allowed to send people there. I couldn't be registered there, but my aunt could happily let me use her flat during the day and I could sleep where I have rented, it would just cost me a bit more. You will be shaking your head and thinking 'Why doesn't she want to go to her sister's, when they were always so close?' Quite right, we still are. I have been here for three years already and during that time the Lípas have been very kind to me. They still are but the times have made them very tense and people around them feel it. Nobody, including their nearest and dearest, ever felt and understood our lot as refugees,[62] until it happened to the people of Prague. Then they began to moan, but they still don't understand what we have already lived through. On the one hand, Irene would like to give me as much as she can, but on the other, she wants to keep me completely under her wing, to tell me off if she feels like it, to force her opinions on me, and her style of living. In short, she is so domineering and thinks that what she does is so well done that there can be no discussion and that everyone else could learn from her. But I won't take that. The giving doesn't matter, it is quite unimportant, I can be content with little if necessary, but I must always be handled nicely and kindly, not be scolded by others or have my supposed faults laughed at in public in order to be witty so that others can be entertained at my expense. I find that tactless. I could easily take my revenge, but I don't because I am who I am.

---

[62] People who were expelled or who fled from Sudetenland.

Irene can very well sense my awkwardness towards her in various matters, she senses the complete harmony between you and me which she has never been able to have herself because she is too restless and too house-proud and never has time to devote herself to her husband. She suspects and knows that I am a woman who belongs 100% to her man; for example, she can't understand why I have so much to write to you or you to me. Recently she said to me, when she saw your letter in my pocket, 'Gusti hasn't written to me as much in our whole marriage as Ernst writes to you in one go.' She was making fun of me in a superior way, as if it was the most stupid thing. And why? Because they didn't do it. I could easily have answered her back but I love her too much to hurt her or offend her. The result is that inwardly I move further and further away from her. So, because she hasn't got enough to discuss with her husband, others shouldn't have either. And what she dislikes even more than our discussions is our constant effort, due to our enforced separation, to live our marriage through our letters.

Let me explain better: it had already been decided a good while ago that I would eventually live there in Mutti's room. We talked about what I would need to bring, such as a bed, wardrobe, etc., and I said I would like to bring my long mirror, at which Irene said it wouldn't suit the room. That's not true, it belongs with the things I mentioned. I replied that I wouldn't leave it behind. She: 'Since when have you been so vain? You just can't take orders from others.' This last made me resolve under no circumstances to go there. And to repeat, if she gets a stranger there she will have to let them bring three times as much, let them cook with her, etc. I have immaculate, new, beautiful things that I am bringing. A stranger might bring the most horrible rubbish and she wouldn't be able to grumble. And they have six strangers, to whom they permitted, in the most humane way, more than would happen anywhere else.

Farewell, I will write to you again tomorrow. Now I am sitting down in my favourite place and then a kiss and another and then? That's all! Tenderly,

Your Mitzimarie

Karlín, 28/9/1941

My dearest

All your many suggestions give me occasion to talk about things that I would have loved to discuss with you long ago if, out of consideration for Herr Censor, I weren't anxious about the letters being too long. You claim that my letters are more beautifully written and better composed than yours, but that's not true. Haven't you noticed how in a few words you can usually deal with a matter, whereas I need so many?

I can't send my letters any more from the Karlín post office as all mail has to be sent from the post office in Ostrovní [Insel] Street.[63] You know that we have to hand in all mail destined for abroad and registered letters open and unstamped at the counter. Here in Karlín it was only three minutes away but now I have to travel for ten minutes on the [tram] number 5.

How did you spend the new year? Do they celebrate the festival there at all, I mean in your family? Next Wednesday is the Day of Atonement but it is hardly being celebrated here.[64] They are working at the *Kultusgemeinde* and everywhere because that is more important.

Christmas was almost always a beautiful, happy time for me; oh, if only we could see each other by then, what would I give to be able to!

Good night. I love you and am completely your

Mitzimarie

---

[63]This decree was issued on 24 September 1941.
[64]Marie alludes to the tense situation after the arrival of Heydrich in Prague.

3

September 1941–January 1942: Heydrich arrives

*O*n 24 September 1941 Hitler appointed SS Obergruppenführer Reinhard Heydrich, formerly head of the Gestapo and later in charge of the Einsatzgruppen murdering Jews in Poland and the Soviet Union, as Acting Reichsprotektor of Bohemia and Moravia. This 'man with the iron heart', as Livia Rothkirchen calls him, who was to become known as 'the Butcher of Prague', had since 31 July 1941 been responsible for preparations necessary to 'bring about a complete solution to the Jewish question in the German sphere of influence in Europe'. He was therefore well prepared to carry out Hitler's demand that 'the Reich and the Protectorate, from west to east, be liberated from the Jews as soon as possible'.[i] Heydrich arrived in Prague on 27 September and by the 29th had ordered the closure of all synagogues and other Jewish places of worship. The compulsory Star of David had been introduced for all Jews in the Reich, including the Protectorate, shortly before Heydrich's arrival, signalling the radicalization of the German anti-Jewish policies. On 10 October a meeting was held at which the first deportations of 5,000 Jews to occupied Poland were planned. Heydrich announced the deportation plans at a meeting with Protectorate journalists. Plans were also made for a ghetto, with the first Jews arriving in the fortress town of Theresienstadt on 24 November 1941. These heightened tensions explain Marie's agitation in her letters at that time. On 12 October she warned Ernst she might have to 'emigrate' in a fortnight. By the next letter on 17 October the first transport had already left. Although the ultimate purpose of the deportations to Łódź and Minsk was not known, the atmosphere of powerlessness and terror *was tangible and it took Marie a good while to come to terms with her fear. Amongst her co-religionists, suicide was frequent and was an option Marie herself considered in her letter of 27 October 1941. Martial law tribunals were established on Heydrich's arrival with the intention of intimidating the Czech population and the Czech Prime Minister General Alois Eliáš, accused of cooperating with the Czech resistance, was imprisoned and sentenced to death. He was executed nine months later in late June 1942. During the martial law, which was finally lifted on 20 January 1942, 486 people, both Czechs and those considered Jewish, were sentenced to death and another 2,242 people sent to concentration camps where most perished.[ii]*

Photo 10 *Reinhard Heydrich, acting Reichsprotektor.* (*Courtesy of German Federal Archives*)

Karlín, 30/9/1941

My dearest

It could be, given the circumstances, that my letter doesn't arrive. In that case, I ask you not to worry about me because I will always try and keep at least the postal connection going. At the moment there is no cause but something could suddenly happen and then, please just don't worry about me.

Your observation about religious concepts is interesting but my clever master is a bit mistaken about me and my opinions. I myself have some sort of faith but my respect for people of every kind is so great that I put them all in one pot and say that each one will find spirituality in his own way. All religions have the same goal; they all lead to a higher morality when adhered to. I think religion is a means to an end, it is meant to give people direction and support and everyone who follows his religion in every way is to be congratulated. But anyone who figures out his own religion for himself is just as well off and at least as worthwhile.

Each religion can only claim to be one if it elevates and improves mankind, no matter which religion it is. Indeed, in the last few years and to the annoyance of my family, I have very often expressed the opinion which you mentioned in your letter, that it is pointless to keep making sacrifices as a minority and that if I knew that it might be useful to my descendants I would change my religion without further ado. Just as I could never blame my children if they did so, if by so doing they could make their lives easier, because how is it that one has to suffer so much and that it keeps on being repeated? Why should it be us? Life is so short and every creature has the same right to life. And if people are good and sound they can be so anywhere, it has nothing to do with religion. Well, now it is too late for it all. I will stay as I am [stick to my religion], but for me all people are dear and precious. No individual can help me [now] in my suffering, but this is my opinion drawn from my life's experience. If I liked to keep to the old ways and customs – it is now not possible to practise them – it was out of respect because they were often connected with lovely memories, and not from piety.[1] But that will not be allowed to burden you in our life together.

---

[1] Marie's relationship with her religion did not conform with conventional norms. Furthermore, she believed that conversion to Christianity could save Jews from persecution. See also the following letters on 1/10/1941 and 18/4/1942.

Tomorrow is the Day of Atonement but I don't think there'll be any service. It is wonderful autumn weather, but there is no question any more of walks, one doesn't walk any further than one has to with the star, although nobody has yet upset me, even by a look, thank goodness. But now I can only go to the allotted post office between 1 p.m. and 5 p.m., and during this time it is also shopping time (3 p.m. to 5 p.m.). In the morning there is work to do in the house and at 8 p.m. I have to be home. One has to watch the time carefully, it makes one nervous.

You mention my smile; yes, thank God, however serious and worrying the thoughts that come into my head, if I look at your picture or think of you, the smile is there. This love for you keeps me alive. Tenderly,

Your loving Mitzimarie.

Footnote in Ernst's hand: 'Religion is not church. E.L.'

Karlín, 1/10/1941

My dearest

Today is the Day of Atonement but there is no service. I will stay at home, pray a little and fast until the afternoon. And what will happen then? What more beautiful thing could I do than commune with you, that is after all the most beautiful prayer. God will surely forgive me that I have to write to you on this holy day. Is it surprising if, after communing with my heavenly God, I then commune with my earthly one? I woke up at 5 a.m., I read letters from you and see that I could still find plenty to answer.

In one of your letters there was a sentence I want to come back to: you said that what the majority generally do is the right thing. Well, I share that view, based on my own bitter experiences. So if we Jews had previously gone over to Christianity we would now be able to enjoy life like other people.

2/10

I was told again today that I may not move out of the flat but I won't know for certain until 20/10 because Frau Hnátek[2] seems to go her own way. I have

---

[2]Marie's landlady.

no wish to go to court, that would be too stressful and the effort would be too much for me, I have already overstretched my nerves about this affair and I've had enough of it. You will shake your head and think 'I don't understand any of it'. My precious one, neither do I. These are just different times and I can't explain everything to you as I would like.

I daren't make any more predictions [about our reunion], they are just hopes. One keeps on comforting oneself in order to keep the longing at bay. But it is so blissful to feel, even though you are so far away, that you are still close to me. Just keep nice and healthy and cheerful.

Undated
received 9 October

My dearest,

I am so surprised how you, with your loving tenderness and consideration, think of so many lovely things which I will be given. Saul[3] has still not been in touch but I hope to hear from him soon because I would dearly love to *******
obliterated by the censor) **** to him too. I would be so very glad if he came here as I would have all sorts of things to tell him.

The happy laugh in the picture I sent must indeed be new and due to you, my beloved. I was, of course, thinking of you at that moment and [when I do that] I am immediately filled with joy and happiness which are reflected in my face.

You are right as always, my treasure, it was a fire glowing beneath the ashes. I didn't understand what was happening in me. It is only now that I can understand why I was so unhappy when poor Thesa withdrew her friendship. For days, despite my deep mourning, I was unable to calm down, it was like a blow to the face. And it was the realization that I had lost you, which I did not admit to myself, which existed nevertheless.

Your thinness will not diminish my love for you; I can picture it very well. It will surely move me painfully when I first see it because I remember you

---

[3]Saul is one of several people, including Hans Bartl and a certain Jan, who seem to be able to travel and take things from Prague to Greece or vice versa. He appears to be married to Frau Marie in Vienna.

as a man brimming over with strength, but as soon as I hear your dear voice, feel your handshake, I will know that that is my Ernstili in whom nothing has changed. Ernstili, do you realize that we have never kissed each other? Which of us will be the more courageous in that first moment of seeing each other again?

Dearest, I am going to go to sleep now – it is late again. I have had some very vivid dreams about you these last nights, they were very real and beautiful.

Your Mitzimarie

P.S. I hope that the respected Herr Censor will forgive me the long letters. I have to take the letter to Ostrovní Street as it is the only way to send it. It takes me an hour to go there and back. People who want to get to the counter stand in a giant queue, right out into the street. I am lucky if I can get to the counter. Kisses again!

7/10/1941

My most beloved

I beg you not to worry if no post comes because it could be that I write less or that my post is held up. Whatever the case, don't worry, my treasure, if, as you always warn, it happens. These are simply extraordinary times, so if there is an interruption you should know it is not my fault and that it just can't be any other way. I will always write to you regularly, as long as it is allowed. I do hope that with my unobtrusive, modest existence I will not annoy anyone because I try very hard to behave correctly everywhere.

The landlady wrote to me just now that she is putting the flat on the market although I have already paid the rent and insists I move out on the 14th, but the *Zentralstelle* won't allow me to move out and it is the highest authority in matters of accommodation. The landlady will certainly demand that my removal is carried out – it could be lively! If I moved out voluntarily I would get no certificate of departure and no registration certificate from the police and also no permit to live elsewhere.

Here the bitter winter is arriving, the days are still quite fine but it is already getting very cold. How would that suit you? I am dreading this winter with its cold, the short days, etc. I am also very glad that our 'friends' have such a mild climate in their country. I haven't heard anything from Frau Marie and her husband hasn't been in touch either.

Tell me, my treasure, do you speak good French? Do you have a gift for languages? I once spoke it well and have always liked the language very much. Do you speak a bit of Czech?[4] What a pity I can't be with you, or with our 'friends', or we would surely all be together now. Sometimes I am so very afraid and the moment when we will see each other seems to have withdrawn into the distant future.

I am curious *whether Hans will get in touch*;[5] I'm worried, time is passing and I won't get another chance, which I would be very sorry about.

Beloved, I take my leave from you with a heavy heart. I press myself in your arms, take your head in my hands and cover it with loving gentle kisses. Then I am going to go to bed and will dream wonderful dreams of you. Farewell, keep healthy, cheerful and happy.

With dearest love, your
Olly-Mitzimarie

10/10/1941

My dearest

Yesterday was a heavenly, beautiful day because I had such lovely news from my name-sake [Marie in Vienna]. And do you know, she sent me a parcel of love too. Oh, my treasure, the things that were in it! Don't be cross if I don't detail everything but I am still so ecstatically happy, it's just fantastic, all good lovely things that I really need. I simply don't know how I can thank my dear friend. And she wrote such a lovely letter too.

The warehouse move has been successfully completed and I am not worrying at all about the flat because all these things have lost their importance today.

---

[4]See Chapter 2, footnote 6.
[5]The censor has tried to obliterate the *shaded* words but they are nevertheless just legible. Hans is probably Hans Bartl, Ernst's batman during the First World War. After the war, Hella Cougno wrote 'During the occupation he helped us a lot.'

My treasure, my good one, today's letter will not be a love letter because I have all sorts of things to tell you first of all, and with whom could I speak of it all better than with you?

Yesterday I was reading your old letters until 12 o'clock at night and feasting on them. I am so happy and thank God again and again for bringing us together. Jan is a good person, I really must say. It is only a pity that he doesn't want to visit me – I would very much have wished to speak with him. I am amazed that it is summer again for you. Here the weather is already miserably wet and cold and on top of this the atmosphere in general is sad.[6] I am terribly sorry I can't tell you anything better but you are my beloved man and I must tell you all my cares as well as my joys.

Gusti's sister in Vienna is going on a journey with many others, so I know to whom I should now send my parcels.[7] And sadly, 1,050 people are also leaving from here on Monday; there will be many sad partings. We don't know yet who is to go, but it could happen to anyone, as I must regretfully tell you. So far it hasn't happened to me. Don't be shocked, my good one, but we must be prepared. I was afraid the whole time that this would happen and now that it has become a certainty I am resigned. Why should I not be when I know that wherever I am, I am yours alone? After all, one can take all sorts of things with one in a 50 kg rucksack and the parcels which are sent are not bad, and one always has three days in which to get ready. One can organize a journey in that time. You have been to the Lichtmanns and the Ashkenazis[8] in the past, and Emmerl too. I remember that you both quite liked them, apart from the cold.

So far there has been no mention of me and my family, but now that the post is so slow I have to say what a terrible pity it is that I didn't try to come to you, but God be thanked a thousand times that you are spared these worries for now. How long for, nobody knows. So, my beloved, whatever may come, I am resigned and beg you not to worry more than is absolutely necessary.

---

[6]The martial law imposed by Heydrich and the anticipation of deportations.
[7]Pauline Juckerová was deported to Łódź on 19 October 1941. Gustav's other sister Olga Doležalová was deported from Prague to Łódź a week later.
[8]Marie uses people's names to indicate possible destinations, see Chapter 1, footnote 59.

Let's hope that it will take a good while. There are 45,000 people here and I don't have to be one of the first. In the end, if it happens, I can write to you from there just as I can from here. Whether I will eat a little better or worse, until we are reunited, is of no matter to me. Without you life is in any case no life. One must just not imagine that it couldn't happen to us. That is why I am preparing you in good time. It would hurt me unspeakably if I were to make you more anxious than necessary because I myself am resigned and calm and have resolved to remain so. One must keep reminding oneself that matters of great world historical significance are being played out. The fate of the individual is unimportant and looked at from this angle it is a matter of making the best of it, whatever happens. If one thinks of the misery and suffering of those who are experiencing the war directly, such an outcome would be nothing, don't you think, my love? And the main thing is that one is alive. Then things will change again. In spite of everything, life is still worth living.

Then I just think of you and my shining smile and laugh are there. I am not allowed to be worried because my Ernstili doesn't want me to be – that is a holy command. It makes my heart ache to have to say all this to you but how can I keep quiet about it?

Although we are not yet affected, others here are. And if it did happen to us, then be as calm as I am. I promise you I will stay as I am, my love for you and my aim to live for you will remain the same, wherever I am. Perhaps the 'action' will be put off – that is what happened before in Vienna,[9] but as it has begun every individual must expect it and prepare himself for it. And I am writing it to you now so as not to surprise you too much.

I want to get this letter off, so I will stop for now. I'll write again in the evening.

Your Mitzimarie

---

[9] There were deportations from Vienna to occupied Poland in February and March 1941. The next wave of deportations started in October 1941.

Karlín, 12/10/1941

My dearly beloved

It is Sunday morning and I can't make up my mind whether to go to the Lípas. I'll go later. I must collect myself a little because wherever one looks one sees troubled faces, every one filled with thoughts of suicide. It is a dreadful atmosphere. I myself have adapted to the new situation quite well because I tell myself that I have no cause yet to fear and each new day may bring new hope. I am feeling guilty, my beloved, that I am having to worry you so much from far away and beg of you one thing: take everything I tell you about myself as genuine and true. Don't look for other, inapplicable reasons to be fearful and then you will have no grounds for anxiety about me at present. It is better that you hear the truth from me rather than garbled snatches from others. The most important thing about this is that one gets used to the new situation and then prepares oneself early enough. From tomorrow I will set about putting my house in order; slowly I am coming to terms with the latest developments, my family too, the worst is with Mutti because they leave the old people behind and we don't want that.[10] She says she won't leave, that she will take her own life. Well, as I said, it isn't our turn yet. We'll see when the time comes.

I have read your old letters so often and am not in a position to answer everything you ask, as I want and should. My head is in such a turmoil, what wouldn't I give to be able to lay it on your chest and rest myself there! If I could only hear a few soothing words from you! I am sure you are not taking all this too tragically – as a former front line soldier you are no stranger to such a situation.

My flat is centrally heated. I don't need any coal, but warmest thanks for your kind concern. The only question is how long I will be here.

My treasure, I am unspeakably distressed that I have to give you such worries. For myself I am not very much worried because I have lived through and seen a lot which was much worse in recent years (even if it didn't happen to me). But when I look at my Irene and Gusti and think that this or that will happen to them and then think of my mother and that I might have to leave the little old lady without protection or help, then I think I will shrivel up inside; my heart breaks at the thought. Irene says if it comes to it Mutti must

---

[10]Marie assumes that old people will not be deported, at least for the time being.

come too and we could go together, if it was allowed. But I don't know whether one can ask that of the old lady. I think it would be even worse and she would certainly reproach us when we were there.

Do you know that Jan wants to go into the country for 8 days?[11] I did my baking for him yesterday in the midst of the turmoil, now I will see what happens next.

We have received two stars, 1 crown each – workers receive one more. Of course that is too few because one has to keep sewing them on again whenever one changes one's coat, or one has to wear the same one all the time, which doesn't matter now. With all my heart I don't wish for you to wear one now or hopefully, ever. God save you from all that!??[12]

And now your description, if you were suddenly here with me, what would I do? It would surely be you who would have to open the doors. I wouldn't be able to find any of the keys for sheer excitement. I would enjoy all your caresses at first, like a doll, and submit to everything with quiet delight, not forgetting to observe carefully in what way you quench your hunger. I would gladly let myself be drawn into an earthly paradise and if you wanted to flee after the Fall I would stammer out 'No, stay here and don't ever go away again!'

As I promised I want to try now to answer you about the worries you have thanks to what you have been reading. I too will be frank. If you have read my earlier letters thoroughly and not misunderstood them, you must have gathered from them that the woman has exactly the same joy in a passionate love life as a man. Why should a healthy woman be 'spared' from the age of 50? I can't understand it at all! I translate 'spared' as 'punished'. For my part I could not contemplate married life without a love life, that is no love, and without love a marriage is not a marriage. For me, from the age of 50 was the time of my saddest experiences and my greatest physical and bodily torment. That was the time when the most strenuous demands were made on my whole person. In August 1938 I became so ill here in Prague, where I was staying because of the move, that for 10 days I had to remain in my bed in a boarding house through overexertion as a result of great agitation. Scarcely was I home again when in September it started

---

[11]She means Jan wants to go to Greece and could take things for Ernst.
[12]Note the question marks. Marie seems to be asking whether Jews in Thessaloniki now also have to wear the star. The Nuremberg laws, including the compulsory wearing of the Star of David, were not introduced there until February 1943.

again when I was involved in extreme changes in K[arlsbad], against the wishes of the family. I even had to get the doctor to examine me as a precaution and calm me down. I had the most thorough check-up and I was and remain healthy and when, now and again, I missed my period, I still did not need to be 'spared'. And now listen – this will interest you – because I am going to admit to you that doctors can make mistakes. In the spring, at the time we confessed our love to each other, I began to have strong pains again, after a long pause. The doctor couldn't understand it, nor could the second, medication didn't help. I was the only one who knew [the real reason]. I laughed to myself … Then I had proper regular periods again until a few months ago and that is how my change of life has gone up to now.

So good night, fare well, stay healthy and don't worry. In deepest love,

Your Mitzi.

P.S. Treasure, I just got the summons to register.[13] Perhaps I may have to emigrate in a fortnight.

Photo 11 *Irene and Gustav Lípa in Marienbad.*

---

[13]The new registration was ordered on 1 October 1941. 88,105 Jews lived in the Protectorate.

Karlín, 15/10/1941

My dearest,

Although I have already written to you today,[14] I am taking the opportunity to add a few lines. I am all right so far and am now much calmer and more composed. I think we still have eight days left, it could be called off again in that time – one always hopes. Well, as God wills! I will give you my friend's address again – she is an American – you should send your next letters to her, until I tell you not to. She will forward them to me and keep you informed too, as I don't know whether I will be able to have direct contact with you. Mrs Eisenberg is a lady with a very big heart and sympathetic to our situation. She will do everything promptly and conscientiously. She herself, however, is not at any risk.[15]

You can't have any idea of the upsets and worries we have been living through in recent days, before we got used to new prospects and then to the preparations. Now you can't look forward to the lovely home, that is over and who knows what I will look like then? Yes, my beloved, you must think things over afresh now because I don't want [you to make] any sacrifices. I wanted to make you happy, to bring you life and joy. But what will become of me now? I certainly do not want to drag you down with me, not at any price, because you are far too sacred to me and too precious and have already been tried quite hard enough by fate. You deserve a comfortable, beautiful life and it mustn't be disturbed by anyone, including me. It is my own fault that I did not shape my fate of my own free will, but that is no reason to drag others along with me.

My treasure, learn from this and take your fate into your own hands, because otherwise it will happen to you and yours. People never believe me, as far as they are concerned it is out of the question, but history turns out differently from how we expect [and] therefore one should take charge of one's future. It is no good hiding one's head in the sand.

---

[14]This other letter is missing, presumably withheld by the censor because it was too explicit about the current situation.

[15]Being the holder of an American passport, Mrs Eisenberg would have been exempt from some of the laws imposed by the German occupiers. Letters to Britain in 1939 indicate that Mrs Eisenberg escorted several *Kindertransports* from Prague to London and that she helped Grete Reichl, Marie's daughter to reach Britain as an assistant on one of these.

As the letter must go I will stop. I kiss you in my mind in the usual way, sit in my favourite place, embrace you warmly and now farewell. You are a man, keep a clear head, don't worry any more than you need at present, things haven't reached that point yet,

With dearest love, Your M.

Karlín, 17/10/1941

My dearest

I haven't heard anything from you for a long time; that was to be expected, so I am not worrying about it. As you see, I am still here.[16] I am still hoping to be able to stay a bit longer because of my 80-year-old mother and one must be grateful to God for everything. If only I had some news from you so that I could hear your opinion. Write to your brother Alois as quickly as possible that he should visit Marie and send you instructions *via* her. If he is such a lazybones about writing, his wife certainly won't be. I have a lot to do all the time, at the moment Emil is here, which is why this letter will be only a shadow of my usual ones. If it comes to it that we leave, then make sure to send me something for stamps because we will not have any money, so that, at least in the beginning, I will [otherwise] not be able to write to you from the place we arrive at. The *Kultusgemeinde* here will know our address and be able to give information. Your two friends will be able to deal with the information … (words deleted) I've just made a mess again.

Now, my sweet, how will you get on? Did you even get my last letters? In any case I will send Marie news for you. Parting from our good friends is very hard, believe me. Please also write to Eman. If he gets Mrs Eisenberg's cable with my address, he should send us money and provisions, but he would have to do it quickly. I have already written to him myself. It is just a question of whose letter will get to him first, if any. If you contact the *Kultusgemeinde*, write to Herr Abraham Fixler, Jewish Town Hall, Philipp de Montegasse. He

---

[16]The first deportation of 1000 persons left Prague for the ghetto in Łódź on 16 October. Four more transports left within the next few weeks.

is the most trustworthy official and will certainly answer you.[17] Ask him for news about airmail. Don't offer him money for postage, he is not so petty. It is Prague V.

I will also give you the address of my American friend again, to whom you could eventually send your letters: Mrs Henriette Eisenberg, Prague, Berlínská 25.

I hope I will be able to write a few more letters to you from here. Perhaps then they [the deportations] will be stopped. That is how it was in the spring in Vienna.

Utterly yours, Mitzimarie
P.S. Send your letters here until I tell you otherwise.

Karlín, 18/10/1941

My dearly beloved

A year ago I was *soooo* happy, I imagined the next year so differently. If you don't hear anything from me for a long time, if I have to leave, then contact Abraham Fixler at the *Kultusgemeinde* who knows me well. He will give you an answer at once.

We are still here, thank God, we are hoping that we won't have to leave too quickly. I have now prepared a lot and I have had my hair cut in a bob again because those being sent on a journey must do that and I won't wait to be told.

My good dear one, my treasure, what will you do? I am so longing for you at this moment when I would like to cuddle up to you and when I could so do with your comfort and help, how hard it feels to be so far from each other, yes, fate is hard and cruel. They say there is already news from one transport, that they are in Łódź lodging with kind Jewish people, but one doesn't know if everything is true, so much untruth is spoken. Apparently the second transport

---

[17]Abraham Fixler (*1911) held a prominent position in the *Kultusgemeinde*, where he worked as a liaison officer with the Prague *Zentralstelle*. He was deported to Theresienstadt in January 1943 and was murdered after his deportation to Auschwitz in October 1944.

went to Minsk.[18] This morning the third one left; again there were many people I knew on it including the gentleman from the house who was always offering me cigarettes. I am smoking my good ones with pleasure and love, each time I inhale I imagine a kiss from you. I am keeping the raisins for the journey. I hope they will still keep for a long time or can they be preserved?

Tenderly, your Mitzimarie.

20/10/1941

My dearest

Today I was really hoping to hear from Anna, but in vain. What is holding things up? Did you get my letter of the 10th? And then the other SOS letters? I hope you are in good health, my sweet. I am, even if I am extremely tense and from time to time also very depressed. Now everyone is concerned only with himself, or with those nearest to him, so I am very much alone. But I am not helpless and I do hope that my good sense and correct behaviour will continue to help me follow the right path. At present my dearest wish would be to have news from you; the break in correspondence is harder for me than ever. Yesterday somebody suggested to me that we should have a proxy marriage, which probably could be done by the colleague of your acquaintance with the prim wife – I mean the colleague here. Only I don't know if you have your papers here and what you think of it. Apparently it would then mean it would soon be possible for us to find ourselves together again. Please think it over before it is too late.

You once wrote to me that you had friends in Turkey. Is that still the case? Then you could all visit them some time, or is that not possible now? You probably can't travel. Perhaps we might have been able to work there which would have been the main purpose for us.

The recent upsets have affected my poor mother very badly. At the last consultation three days ago with Prof. Kubík it turned out that her better eye

---

[18]Marie was wrong, the transport went to Łódź; the first direct transport to Minsk went from Brno in November 1941. Marie's letter confirms the febrile atmosphere at the beginning of the deportations when rumours about the destinations of the departing transports spread in Prague. The second transport left Prague on 21 October and the third on 26 October. We are unable to explain how it was possible that Marie mentioned that three transports had left by 18 October.

has deteriorated so much that it will have to be operated on in four weeks. She is in despair about it and looks terrible. If Gustav and Irene had to leave now, I would have to remain with her, which would probably be permitted. I would rather that I came to you and that Irene had to stay here. These last items of news of mine are not decided, depending on whether things turn out well or ill, but are simply speculation. You see now what worries I am giving you. I'm so sorry but what can I do?

A card just arrived from Emil saying that Lidi and Hulda cabled Oskar for visas for a passage to Cuba – a lot of people who have relatives in the USA are doing that. I can't since I don't have such close relatives there who would put themselves to so much cost and trouble for me.[19] In any case, it is likely that permits would come too late. It is possible that anyone who has one will have their journey postponed – that's what people think.

When I read your last letters, dearest, I can smile and still feel the happy, confident and hopeful life in myself. Isn't that wonderful? Or can you also understand how much we are suffering so that you can measure what my assurance means today?

Photo 12 *A family gathering in happier times.*

---

[19]Other documents confirm these unsuccessful desperate efforts to escape the Protectorate to the Caribbean and Latin America in October 1941, when the Germans began the preparations for deportation.

Your Mitzimarie

P.S. Beloved! Forgive me, I am not in a state to write long letters. But my heart and thoughts are with you alone, surrounding you day and night. Kisses, Mitzimarie.

Karlín, 20/10/1941

My dearly beloved

This afternoon, at last, your letter of the 15th arrived. It is written in a sad tone; my love, I understand; it is exactly the same for me. Everything you tell me I feel just as you do. The longing, that certain loneliness from which nobody but ourselves and the fulfilment of our love can rescue us. Oh yes, this time of separation is hard to bear. How beautiful it could be if we at last belonged to each other, I mean in reality, not just, as now, in our imagination. Mine is very vivid but it is still not a reality. I am sitting here this evening after taking a bath. There is no hot water in the morning this year so I wash in the evening. I have made myself beautiful and am thinking how lovely it would be if you were here. Perhaps whilst I was absent you might have fallen asleep, it is so warm here in the flat. Do you know what I would have done then? I would have gazed at you until you woke up. And instead I am with you in my thoughts and am going to answer your letter at once.

I am very sorry that it is cold in your house because you haven't got enough wood. That is an ordeal. Of course, here too it is the same for a lot of people. For me it has been nice and warm up to now. But anyway, it is not cold on the whole at the moment; it is raining here too. You must just all help Hella with getting hold of food; she can't do it all on her own and people mustn't grumble either. It doesn't help. It is difficult for the housewife now, one must realize that. I am sure you know that parcels can be sent to you from here, but we [the Jews] can only send them within the country. Please, what is your houseguest's full name?[20] Frau Vacková would like to know in case she wants to send you a few samples some time.

---

[20]The soldier, son of a German friend of Salvator Cougno, was stationed in Thessaloniki and was a regular visitor at the Cougno's house. A non-Jew in Prague would have been able to send parcels through him.

Ernstili, my sweet, we are just so tiny, we humans, I believe in a kindly fate so it is pointless to worry too far ahead. Everything will be as it has to be. Please will you keep my recipes safely with my papers.[21] I wanted to know they were with you because I wouldn't have been able to keep them safely here.

My poor mother is very broken. She can't recover from all the distress she has experienced and unfortunately she is very low physically. Sadly, we can't provide her with her usual life-style although, as an old person, she has an extra allowance, but that helps only a little. On 25/11 it will be her 80th birthday. That will be a sad day. Apart from a few flowers we can't give her anything this time because we have no possibility of buying anything for her. Not even sweets. She often complains and moans like a small child; it makes us sad because we can't help. And above all she longs for the 'friends'. Gusti smoked his last cigar today; he will miss them very much but what can one do? Nothing.[22]

On Saturday I was, of course, with my family but, you won't believe it, I don't feel 100% comfortable there either. It is ungrateful of me but I just belong only to you and everything else is secondary. I don't care if I have to eat grass, I won't mind at all, but I want to be yours, to feel your closeness, feel your breath, hear your heart beating, feel the pressure of your hands. When the documents I asked you for arrive, nothing will stand in the way of the wedding any more. Next Monday I will give Karel my papers – he asked for them.

Here in the building a mother and daughter were supposed to leave on the 19th. She rang my doorbell at 10.30 in the evening. What went on there for two days I really can't tell you. Then she came in beaming with delight: postponed for 8 or perhaps 14 days. A lot can happen. Playing such games with people's nerves is the order of the day, wherever one looks. Well, God be thanked a thousand times that it is so, one keeps hoping for something good, so you too, in particular, keep hoping! If I could tell you everything, that would be a very

---

[21]Recipes for EBE products.
[22]On 1 October 1941, Jews were excluded from any allocation of tobacco. This regulation was introduced by the (Czech) Protectorate finance ministry.

long chat! Unfortunately that isn't possible. You have to imagine more than I can tell you. Be calm and stay calm, hope and believe, as I do, in our kindly fate which will guide us and make us happy.

Emil is coming to see me tomorrow. Who knows whether Rackermann[23] will travel earlier? Who knows, who knows? What do you think? Thank God you write of your security, that makes me so happy, my love, my good one, that does me good.

Is it very difficult for you to read my letters now? Or have you got used to my handwriting already? Please be honest! Then I am going to fall asleep in your arms. Good night. With dearest love,

Your Mitzimarie

Karlín, 22/10/1941

My most dearly beloved

I had news from Anna today and was very glad at what she told me. Unfortunately I haven't got time to pass it on to you but I will do so soon. Anyway, she is, thank goodness, well and everything is fine with her, touch wood.[24] As for myself, I can tell you that I am very glad still to be snug in my nest, each day is good and I am just hoping that kind fate will let me stay a little longer in my flat. The feverish preparations for travel are still carrying on – it has to be. Only with the large numbers the single person may with luck not be among the first.

My mother has completely collapsed as a result of the agitation, she is weary of life. I went to see Professor Kubík yesterday about my eyes because I want new glasses. He was very satisfied with my eyes. I said that I was worried my eyes might suffer because of the high blood pressure I have at the moment from all the tension and he said 'The blood pressure won't hurt you and you won't have a stroke for a very long time because you are very healthy, your eyes

---

[23]In an undated letter following that of 22 October, Marie refers to herself as 'Rackerlein' ('minx'). The underlining of 'mann' (meaning husband) in Rackermann suggests she may here be referring to Ernst and the possibility he may soon be able to travel to Prague.
[24]It means that she is not to be deported.

are wonderful.' So what more could I want? About Mutti he said she should be kept under observation and that he would make the timing of the operation dependent on further investigation. And if she had to be operated on, one of her daughters would have to be with her. We hope it would be possible. I would prefer to be with you and I would come whatever the case and forsake everything but it isn't likely to happen. There is no way you can come here. If there was any possibility for me to get food there, and if I got permission to be there, and the exit permit, I would simply go and leave everything behind, but I don't know what ideas you all have, whether it is at all possible to be put up in the house with the children, etc. Would there be enough work with the doctor?

Everyone is amazed at my calm, the huge appetite I have just now. I am very calming for the others, you can imagine. Irene would like to have me there all the time, Mutti too. Gusti is an old man, he is absolutely finished. His two sisters, one from Vienna, one from here, have gone. Many good friends as well, so much sorrow at all these partings. And I, what do I think? Whatever happens, in the end I am living with my treasure, then my smile radiates which comes whenever I think of you, because after all I don't want to get ugly, you don't want a woe-begone wife. Well, I am doing what I can. These times certainly can't fail to leave their mark on me, but I am trying to keep calm, to preserve myself as well as I can. I am alone a lot and for the most part alone in crucial matters, but I don't find it hard because I know you are thinking about me.

As you can see, I have become truly selfish in my thoughts and actions, in complete accordance with our principle that we do indeed feel and suffer with everyone else but only up to a certain point. I have often noticed that nobody looks out for me apart from the family and a few real friends and so I have also become hard and practical in my thinking. I am glad to help people if I can, but only up to a certain point.

It is good that the suits are being made, and practical too. You were always a smart dresser, at your age one can still be, just stay healthy, then everything is fine. The lady with the generous kisses may catch it from me one of these days! If, as I hope, she is pretty, then I might allow it to you, but otherwise woe to her! Would anything like that ever in my life have occurred to me? Shameless! Imagine what they are saying about me in the house where the Lípas live! You know that architect Eisler, who has lung cancer, lives on the floor below. As they are also relatives we see them quite often, sometimes I meet him in front of the house, in the lift, etc. Well, to cause a sensation, he said he had dreamed about me, that I came to his bed and importuned him so much he had difficulty defending himself. And by chance I once considered taking a room in their flat. When he recounted his dream his wife said 'And I'm supposed to take her into our flat as well!' And recently when I was in the lift again with him, knowing nothing about his dream, a friend of his wife got in, smiled and said 'Oh, I'm in the way, I'm sorry!' I looked at her with big eyes, she got out and said goodbye. And afterwards I heard about his dream, you can imagine what they are all up to, they are having fun at my expense, despite the *zores*.[25]

I could tell you a lot but I am not able to because in my present state I am not sufficiently composed to write long letters to you, which anyway don't sound so tender now because I am sending several. You are my only hope, my comfort and my trusted one; it is because of you that I remain alive. The cigarettes are very fine, I smoke one every day and feel as if I'm closer to you, breathing in your smell.

Lovingly, your Mitzimarie

Undated letter (the address and date have been cut off) but preserved between those of 22 October and 27 October 1941

My dearest

At last I am somewhat calmer, I will try to write to you again in the way I used to – people get used to all sorts of things. So far I am well and still in my flat. Mutti's condition has improved to the extent that she can again go out into the fresh air for a little, but she must be operated on in the near future and if possible I am to care for her then, that is to say be with her. We'll see. Perhaps I can come to you, then I will drop everything and just go. Yes, if I got work there, never mind whether in an office as a secretary or in a household, that is unimportant, I would only not want to cause you any burden. I would manage

---

[25]Yiddish for 'misery'.

in French, I can get by in English but I don't know Greek at all. Shorthand and typing – you know I can do them.

Would I be able to come to you as your wife by proxy marriage? It would certainly only be achieved with great difficulty, but people think it would perhaps nevertheless be possible. I will make enquiries here while I wait to have your decision or your opinion.

I was very sorry to hear that Thesa's brother died. He has no doubt lived through all sorts of things, these trying times are hastening the illness of many. I am very sorry that you are worrying and anxious about Hella's marriage, but understand that we parents see things very differently from how they are, one should just not get involved. Hella is so absolutely independent in her thinking and actions and you seem to have no meeting of minds with her, so you are suffering without being able to help, that is a lot to bear and I regret it very much. Unfortunately you can do nothing in this case since she won't take any advice from you.

I gave Jan the notes and the measurements and am curious whether everything will meet with approval.

Dearest, don't be afraid that I will be too submissive. No fear! I will make it hot for you sometimes, this way or that, just as the fancy takes me, Sir! I only become pliable when treated with great kindness, but one look, one gesture can make the opposite happen! So there will be plenty of variety for us! Yesterday I saw the gynaecologist, as usual, I have myself examined once a year. He found everything in good order and when I told him I wanted to get married again he said 'Yes, why not?'

I would not be happy with keeping things secret, my sweet treasure. I won't ever press you, you must come of your own free will and speak openly with me. I am never indiscreet, or even curious, but I must be able to be your comrade, your equal, in joy and in sorrow, as it should be. I will treat you in such a way that you will not hide anything from me and you know anyway that I believe in you. Just don't be so vain, even if strange, ill-mannered ladies want to kiss you. What women! Was she at least pretty? Then I would have allowed it. The southern sun seems to arouse the spirits particularly.

You absolutely cannot come with me to the Lichtmanns, I am telling you now. If I have to go, I will make the visit alone, but I hope that I can leave it for the present. You know I was never keen on relations with them.[26] And anyway, I know from you that you were not keen on the whole family and so I reject in advance any prospective visit together. It would be better to go to Eman if it were possible.[27]

My thoughts are with you constantly, and although I have plenty to keep me busy I can only concentrate when I express myself in writing, then I feel as if you are near me. I say farewell to you now, stay brave and firm and believe in me. I will do everything to let us live to see our happiness. With this thought I am finishing, praying God to bless you, keep well and take care of yourself with the patience of a mature man who knows that difficult times too will pass.

27/10/1941

Frau Henriette Eisenberg[28]
Prague I, Berlinerstrasse 25

My dearest

I have just received your letters of the 15th and 16th, you can imagine with how much yearning. In the meantime we have become a little accustomed to the great worries but these have not diminished one iota. I have therefore decided to send you a telegram on the advice of other, more experienced people, and also of my brother-in-law. The moment it was possible for me to come to you I would make my decision to leave my family, perhaps, even probably, for ever. But I wrote to you recently that at present I too have become selfish. Nobody would blame me for it, but it would be the most tremendous burden for my poor sister because in me she has a support and with her husband, who has grown old, and our little mother who has completely collapsed, she has nothing but duties. But she is healthy and in good condition and I hope she would be able to hold out, because what I have been living for years she

---

[26]This reference suggests that 'Lichtmanns' is Marie's a code word for Eastern Jews. Did Ernst propose to join Marie?
[27]To the United States.
[28]Without explanation, Marie uses the name and address of the American woman referred to earlier. This could be a way of reminding Ernst of this potentially useful contact.

has been spared. I see that you do have an idea, but unfortunately you can't picture how things really are, particularly as I weigh every word I write to you concerning the exceptional situation, because I don't want to do anything at all which is not permitted. Thank God I haven't let myself be guilty of the least offence up to now and I will not knowingly be so in the future. It isn't always easy and now especially one has to be doubly cautious.

But if I tell you that I want to come to you, that is not a whim but a consequence of the situation which has developed, and if this is not possible then, like everyone else, I must expect to leave on a journey in the near future. The journey is tiring and unpleasant and so is the place where we will stay. Whether there will then be a return, who can know? Up to now I have simply not got either the courage or the strength actually to undertake this journey alone or with the family, and my store of V.[29] tempts me very much. Don't be angry, my sweet, if these thoughts creep into my mind, but it will also help you to see how I feel. This is after ripe reflection and not all at once in a moment of crisis. It is a lot for a woman who is alone because today everyone is preoccupied with himself. One can't make demands on another, that would be unfair.

I still have time, thank God and that means a lot, that is a merciful gift from heaven. There is no age limit, nobody can know. As long as I had the hope and prospect of living with you, even in the most primitive conditions, I could have borne anything, but if I am faced with the question of taking this new burden on myself with almost no prospect of a life with you then, if I am quite sure of that, I don't know whether I will find the strength to bear life any longer. All this is not meant to be a threat to you and I won't do anything without consulting you and talking it over with you because you are the dearest I have and I want you to be convinced of my point of view, so I will put my future life in your hands, and when you realise what that future will be, I know you will say 'Mitzimarie, you are right, do it'. When I know you say that, only then will I decide, or not – depending. But for the

---

[29]See Chapter 1, footnote 60 to the letter of 17 March 1941. Near the end of this letter she refers to taking her own life if she cannot be reunited with Ernst. A number of Jews committed suicide, when summoned for deportation.

moment I hope that a kind fate will still spare me and my family also, as regards the coming operation. Unfortunately I can't write anything more to you, it isn't possible.

The pain of parting from so many dear relatives, friends and acquaintances, from friends of yours too, touches me deeply. Please, beloved, don't be cross with me, I can't help my nature. But I am not the only one like this, everyone, everyone is the same. We are one single deeply grieving family, racked with sorrow and grief. I will get Čedok[30] to telegraph you, because that is what I was advised to do. I still do not know whether a journey out of the country would be allowed, nor entry to where you are, but perhaps [it will be possible] as your wife. That is why people suggested the proxy marriage to me. As I have just seen from your letter which arrived today, there would be plenty for me to do in Hella's house in the beginning and after that I could look for something else because that would be easier for a woman than for a man. But, as I said, first we must know whether it would be at all possible.

And now I beg you, love, just don't be angry about today's letter, whatever I write to you must not hurt you or make you doubt my love for you. Everything I think and do happens only through my great love for you, including the thought of ending my life if there were no prospect of a life with you. Because then life would have no sense or purpose.

I will keep hoping with great longing and wait to have a sign of life from you. Farewell, tender hugs and kisses as ever from your boundlessly longing

Henriette – Marie

Karlín, 28/10/1941

My dearest

Before I write to you about various matters I want to have a few moments cuddling up with you, at least in my mind. It is 8 o'clock in the evening, I have done all sorts of things today and now it is your time.

---

[30]The Czech national travel agency.

If my worries overcome me, I re-read yet again your old letters of the 15th and 16th July and your picture is in front of me. Then I become a changed person; yes, these letters have restored me so much in recent days.

I am curious to know whether Jan has arrived. I haven't heard anything more from him. I don't know why, but I am hoping to hear from you how he is and so on, whether everything worked out. Alois wrote to me yesterday that he had news that Hella would like me to come to her. Yes I would like to. I will hear, perhaps tomorrow, whether it can now happen. I am only afraid it won't be possible. Anyway, I will report on it very soon. I would go just as I am, if I could, with the greatest pleasure, even at the risk of experiencing everything all over again in the near future, as I very much fear. We all refuse to learn, we won't believe the others; then, when calamity befalls one it is too late.

So you are partially proficient in various languages, that is fine. Greek does seem to be the most difficult. In French there would be brilliant expressions for terms of endearment. I don't actually know them at the moment but the French are unbeatable in that. Did you get the pictures of me when I was young? Please let me know. And did you enjoy the *oblaten* again? I had to finish them and pack them up just when things were at their most worrying, it was all so rushed and couldn't be done carefully enough, otherwise I would have remembered to send something to Frau M.[31] I fear she may be a little offended.

So you are already in the rainy season. Here the weather is dreadful, yesterday it was already snowing a little and this morning the puddles were frozen. I wore my fur lining for the first time. I was at Čedok at 8 o'clock. I wanted to send you a telegram but I couldn't – there is no telegraphic connection with you. I wanted to ask you for an answer about whether it is possible to enter Greece – I mean whether I would be allowed to travel there from here. Only then would I try to get permission for an exit permit, but I fear it will not be possible, which is what everyone predicts. I would still try it nevertheless.

With us potatoes are also rationed, we get 3 kg per person a week. It's enough for me and anyone who wants them can get them now for the whole year, right up to summer, in one go, but one has to undertake to store them properly.

---

[31]Marie in Vienna.

I am very glad things are now better between you and Hella. It is in the best interests of both of you. You must not be too strict a Papa and not take offence at everything, often the child probably means nothing, she is such a natural upright person, it is not in her nature. Don't forget, treasure, that she left home very early and then got married so young, she missed a lot of what she would have picked up or learnt from her mother at the most important time in the life of a woman or girl, things that strangers can never teach a child. She is bringing the children up like Spartans. If they have to help in the house from 6 in the morning, that is fantastic, where else would you find that? I find talking with others cheers one up, at any rate now, when we have all become silent. We slink around like ghosts, we have no wish to talk much, everything is shrouded in grief, everyone is running and chasing around, looking for lightweight first aid kits, rucksacks (only there aren't any), straps, eating bowls, camping flasks, everything has been grabbed. I have pretty well all I need if necessary and what I haven't got I won't get upset about. How I would cope with my rucksack, that is a puzzle. Because one has to put a lot into the rucksack in case the suitcase, which has to be handed in, should get lost.

I hope it isn't necessary to answer your questions from the July letters, as you have now heard everything about me. You are surprised that you haven't read anything, yes my treasure, then you would have to read other newspapers, ours from the Protectorate, the German newspaper reports from the Reich, ours from here. Our largest newspaper here is called *Der Neue Tag*.[32] Do you know it? Then there is *Die Zeit*, etc. You are also mistaken about the age limit: there is none at all, it is of no consequence. Karl,[33] Lípa, they are all of no use, the men here are not strong and firm any more. Karl has collapsed, Lípa is an old man who can't cope with these times.

For myself, I have only one thing in my head, to be united with you as soon as it is possible, never mind what happens afterwards. I can make myself useful, I can earn my living anywhere because I will not be choosy in what I do. I have had absolutely enough of living without you much longer. Your wonderful calming words have brought me some peace of mind again.

---

[32]This was the official German newspaper in the Protectorate, founded in 1939.
[33]Emil Bader's brother, who lived in Brno.

I am at least in a state to be able to concentrate again, even if I am very on edge.

So, now I am going to bed, I hope it will be a quiet night, because one gets woken in the night, too, when one is summoned. I hug and kiss you warmly and passionately and then I imagine you are with me, I fall asleep in your arms. Tenderly yours,

Mitzimarie

Karlín, 30/10/1941

My dear Ernst

I am so sorry that I am giving you such worries, believe me, but in the last two days I have become much calmer and also much more confident. In the meantime you will also have heard from me through Jan and realize from him that it is not so easy to travel to you at present. In fact, at the moment nobody can leave, whoever they are. On the question of the proxy marriage, I would have to try the regional office. The most important thing is that if there were to be any question of my making a journey to you in the near future I would need to obtain an entry permit. Whether that can be done I don't know. Only then can I procure permission to leave, if I am still here. Treasure, you can take your time over finding out about everything, it won't happen in a hurry.

The first transports are said to have arrived already, although there is no news from the people themselves – they are not allowed to write yet – but they are supposed to be in a big textile manufacturing town[34] and to have work there. That is important as it means there are living conditions which allow one to hope that things will be all right for the people. If my turn comes and I have a similar fate, I will be quite content because apparently in the administration they are glad to make use of people who can do clerical work, so if I drew that lot, I would be very content because first of all I would be happy to be occupied and secondly if it was also a job which I enjoy, then my life until I am able to come to you would be bearable.

---

[34]Łódź was the centre of the Polish textile industry and was known as the Manchester of Poland.

You ask what my family is doing. Lady Worry [*Frau Sorge*] is of course a constant visitor there. Every ring at the door makes them anxious, but everywhere people are always thinking the summons has come. Irene is sick with worry about me but she has to think about herself in the first place, yes, it is everyone for himself, God for us all. Well, I have prepared everything in such a way that nothing can surprise me any more. I am at least half fitted out, if not as well as possible, then at least not too badly. I have weighed everything so that the weight is correct and believe I have done everything according to instructions. Emil would probably not be called but their names have been taken and what will happen to them, who can know?[35]

Unfortunately you can't imagine how it is any more. I am not able to explain more precisely why, neither will I tell you why not, as in any case there is no room to do so. I am also sending you the address of my relatives whom I am still supporting – unfortunately I can't send them any more now. They are called Max and Ida Kammermann, in Modliborzyce, Kreis [district] Janov, Lublin, Poland.[36] I write to them often. In the event of my departure they would soon have my new address, so you could get news of me through them more quickly if circumstances demand, because if I do leave, two months will probably pass before you get anything from me.

And now I want to tell you that as a result of the recent proof of your true love and devotion I am standing tall again. I have pulled myself out of my state of despair and misery and I believe I am armed, all thanks to you. I will hold out, so that one day we enjoy the happiness we long for. As for our loved ones, they are young, they can still build things up again, they have their lives ahead of them.

Tenderly, your Mitzimarie

P.S. Tomorrow I say farewell to my Continental [typewriter].

---

[35]This implies that Emil Löwy was still formally married to his 'Aryan' wife.

[36]Modliborzyce is a village in the Lublin district, which had a ghetto until October/November 1942. The Kammermanns had been deported there from Vienna in March 1941.

Karlín, 31/10/1941

My dearest

The letter I sent today was unfinished. As I am quite alone, I will not be disturbed when I write and I am going to settle down with you again as I used to in quieter times. My friend Olga, who so often spent a lot of time here, has decided to have the operation that she has been meaning to have for years, so I will be quite alone in the flat, but that doesn't matter as I am always very busy.

It is good that you are not with me now because, should I have to emigrate, you could more easily take measures [to protect yourself]. I have become fairly calm again but for a few days last week I was in an awful state physically. I felt utterly disorientated, weary of life, miserable. I truly believed this could not go on. Then your letter arrived and everything was good, as if all my troubles were blown away.

Anna will also be very frightened about her fate. It should already have caught up with her last spring but then her husband fell ill and so they stayed.[37]

Please add c/o Stanislav Chornbala 45 to the Kammermanns' address. He is going to accept the parcels which I can no longer send. They asked me to send the old rags that I am throwing out, and very old stockings and underwear but unfortunately I can't send them anything; it's a shame.

I won't need a baptismal certificate; but I don't have it anyway. I hope that Emil will be spared for a good while yet, nobody knows anything but at the current rate a move from his present flat to somewhere like Edersgrün[38] could happen. One knows nothing for certain, it's just what people think. The last time he was here he was very worried and had lost a lot of weight, like all of us.

Never before have I felt as alone as I do now. One simply can't describe how on edge everyone is, how each thinks and cares only for himself. And yet there

---

[37]Anna Riemer and her husband were deported in June 1942.
[38]Edersgrün (Odeř) is near Karlsbad. There was an assembly camp there in the first half of the war, where many elderly Jewish males were temporarily held.

are people who report voluntarily, but they mostly don't get permission to go. They are on the whole young people looking for work.

Tell me, my treasure, are the children studying foreign languages in depth, and which ones? What are they good at? Certainly German, grammatically as well? And how about their French? They are surely good at speaking it, and how about the grammar? You wrote a little while ago that they don't have much school, and that reminded me how during the World War, when my children also had little time in school, I got them to learn languages thoroughly in their free time and that was very good, but they were only very small then, they had to learn French from a primer. Now it is, I think, their greatest treasure that they have completely mastered some languages, that is certainly the case with Edith, how it is with Gretel I can't judge.

It was a mistake on my part to fight so hard for my home, I couldn't know it but if Irene had not sometimes been so fussy, so critical, and if I had been less sensitive, I should have lived with her and a lot would be better for me and for her, because now it is not at all nice not being together. In their flat there is an almost unbearable atmosphere, especially Gustav, and then dear Mother have completely given up, but Irene would just be glad if I were with her, Mutti too and Gustav as well. You know, at such times it is good to huddle up together, but now it is no longer possible. I have to keep ringing them and going there, but I also have to keep my home in order and [at the same time] prepare myself for all eventualities. I have done most of it. One has to weigh everything exactly so that one doesn't exceed the prescribed limit. That is a real headache because one would like to have one's most important things among one's luggage.

I have two suitcases, each weighs about 18 kg gross, and a medical kit. Then a rucksack, about 14 kg gross. Then I have a sort of bundle of blankets, a flannel blanket, a quilt, a knitted blanket, a little cushion to sit on. Then a large bag for food for the journey. All sorts of good things from you are packed in there and I will always be thinking they are kisses from you and everything will seem fine to me, that's what I hope.

And now, farewell, beloved, be confident; I am too.

Your Mitzimarie.

Karlín, 1/11/1941

My dear Ernst

Will I manage to make my dreadful handwriting legible for Herr Censor and for you?[39] I very much fear I won't. Today there is a rumour of a two-week halt [in deportations]. I hope it isn't just a rumour. Numbers 127 and 128 from Anna did not arrive. I am worried about those good people. I am not happy with their silence. It is Saturday evening, I am alone again, but not really because in my thoughts I am living completely intertwined with you. I have been so disappointed in everyone just now, so from now on I am going to be thoroughly selfish. I haven't been so up to now, but I am going to change utterly, you will see. There are reasons why I did not arrange for the proxy marriage as intended, my good one. You will find out why in good time.

There is, of course, no sign from the friends and Eman. My brother-in-law no longer collects stamps;[40] it's a pity he hasn't this pleasant distraction any more as it gave him a lot of enjoyment, just as typing did for me.

Can't you get our German newspaper, *Der Neue Tag*, there? You should read it every day, then you would be much better informed; try it. My bridge games have stopped too, because one can't keep one's mind on it, can you understand that? When I was taking your letter to the post the day before yesterday I happened to meet the family of Director Brod as they were walking to the assembly point.[41] Gallus, his wife and daughter and many other people from our home area left a long time ago.

How are you for provisions now? Is Hella having a very hard time getting hold of everything for you all? Or are you men also giving a hand in the house? That is mostly what is happening now, that the men are helping.

---

[39] A receipt issued by the *Kultusgemeinde* dated 1 November confirms that this is the day Marie handed in her typewriter.

[40] In February 1941 the Protectorate ministry ordered that Jews had to hand in their collections of stamps to the banks for safekeeping by 15 March 1941.

[41] The assembly point for those summoned for transportation, and where Marie was in due course ordered to report, was at the Radiomarkt at the Trade Fair grounds in Prague-Holešovice.

Monday, 3/11.

I waited for your little letter of 29/10 and was very glad that the misunderstanding has been cleared up. I wish to follow all your suggestions but unfortunately I have seen, my beloved, that you picture things quite differently and wish for things which are unthinkable. I am not reproaching you for that but I have one request to make of you: please, please, treasure, don't think that I don't want, when I can't. And please remember that I must be careful above all to obey the regulations to the letter. I would go today, without anything but the clothes I am wearing, if I only could. Ruthlessly I would leave behind my mother, my sister and all I possess if I could only finally rest in your arms free from all the worries that oppress me. You have always believed me, continue to do so. I can't tell you more today.

Your photo, lit up by the midday sun, is smiling at me. I take your head in my hands and kiss you with deepest love and say farewell, keep well, stay confident, as I am.

All yours, Mitzimarie

Karlín, 8/11/1941

My beloved

I've just received your letter of three weeks ago. Regarding my preparations to come to you, the following is the long and the short of it: our homeland is being run, as you will soon hear, in a way which allows no obstacles. The journey itself will not easily be possible because traffic is so very tightly controlled, as you may have read in the last October issue of *Der Neue Tag*. None of that will stop me from getting on with my preparations. With regard to the marriage: I have to send you the document on the basis of which you will get me the entry permit from the German authorities. Only then will I be able to set about getting a travel permit.

My love, are you in the picture now? I wrote to you that, at a time when people are standing in crowds outside the office of the *Kultusgemeinde* and waiting for hours before they are seen, I couldn't see anyone about this business. People would have resented that, at a time like this, I seemed to have nothing else to worry about, because I was told specifically that it was completely pointless to try to do anything about it. Nevertheless, your sweet words have lifted me again. I am pulling myself together and hope and believe in our happy future.

Tenderly, your Mitzimarie

First page missing, filed after 8/11/41

Today I have been requested, like everyone else in the house, to go to the *Kultusgemeinde* where we will be given forms on which we have to write down in detail all our possessions, furniture, linen, etc.[42] It has to be done within eight days. Another nice job. I have packed two cases, a rucksack, a bundle of bedding for the eventual journey to the Lichtmanns, and now I have to unpack everything again and indicate what I was keeping for the journey, so I am well provided with work for the moment, and there is also the warehouse to think about. There is no help at all, nobody will help no matter what one offers to pay. Everyone is watching everyone else, the woman who used to help in the house won't and neither will anyone else. So the motto is 'help yourself'. I am not writing this to complain, but because I know Hella will also have to work hard one day, so that she doesn't get caught by surprise then.[43] Well, she will let the children and you men help her. It is better if one has no unnecessary stuff, then it is less trouble, that is what experience teaches. The greatest art of living is and will always be to adapt to changing circumstances in good time, not to stand still. I don't mean to preach, I just don't want those near to me to make the same serious mistakes I made. I should quite simply have packed my bags and gone either with the children or to Palestine. Then we two would soon have been reunited and busy starting a new life. I didn't do it, but I don't want to make excuses. I recognize my mistakes and others should take it to heart.

So you've got pickpockets in the house. That sort of thing rarely happens here. Everybody is on the lookout, things have got much better. Theft etc. is almost never heard of. Everyone is trying to observe the law and respect

---

[42]On 2 November 1941 it was announced that the Jews could not dispose of their personal belongings without official permission. It is likely that this registration was linked to the new regulation.
[43]Marie believes that the Jews in Thessaloniki may also face deportation in the near future.

it, not to get into conflict with it.[44] That is my dearest wish too, so as not unintentionally to break a rule.

My sweet, I must stop. I will write to you again soon, because I would still like to tell you an enormous lot. Above all that I have a huge and terrible longing for you.

Most lovingly, your Mitzimarie.

Karlín, 9/11/1941

My dearest

Today, a Saturday, was a sad day for me, although a bit better than the rest of the days of the week. I believe and hope that my worst worries for the immediate future are now over;[45] God help me that I am proved right. But there are plenty more worries, life is a constant battle. One's dearest wish would be that for us, too, better, happier times should come again. For the moment my mother is a little better, she has grown a little calmer, as have Gustav and Irene, and if they all still look miserable, they are no exception to the rule.

Today, when I was supposed to take a nap with Irene after the meal, I couldn't. I closed my eyes and I was immediately with you. You had your right arm around me, your left hand was being a naughty tease and I grabbed it when it got too naughty and tried to pin it down. No, it didn't work because then I went on to the attack and it got so lively that it turned into a delightful bit of canoodling, until in the end we fell deeply asleep.

My love, you must be having a very hard time with provisions. I am worried about you all, you can imagine. But we, too, have to live very modestly, today nothing else is possible. We get enough bread and potatoes, which is important. Nobody is allowed to keep much in store and nobody does, one has to divide things up carefully and be frugal in one's housekeeping. One

---

[44] Around this time *Der Neue Tag* published daily lists of the severe punishments meted out to lawbreakers during the martial law introduced by Heydrich.

[45] The first wave of deportations ended on 3 November 1941. Marie hoped there would be a longer break before the deportations resume.

can eat a small portion of meat twice a week, the same for sausage, otherwise one just has vegetables, potatoes and side dishes, but desserts, as we once used to have, are not possible because one could not make them when one only gets four eggs a month. Shopping is only with ration cards, and one also needs those for rolls and other things. Paraffin is in short supply here at the moment.

Your Mitzimarie.

Karlín, 19/11/1941

My beloved

You were no doubt surprised to get news from Karel [Struzi] which you should have had from me. And you thought the little rascal is as irresponsible as ever! Perhaps! At the present time one does not always get a chance to get a letter for abroad to the Jewish post office [in Ostrovní Street] between the hours of 12 and 5; during that time hundreds of people crowd into the little street in front of the post office and when 10 are allowed in, the pressure of pushing and shoving is so bad that I cannot compete. I am neither tall enough nor strong enough to compete with the big men. But, as I wanted you to hear soon how it is about the wedding, I asked Karel to write to you. For him it is a 15-minute job because he is very near the post office and can go in at any time. So I repeat to you: we can marry when Thesa's death certificate has been translated into German and sent back by you with the completed legal declaration. Then it would all be plain sailing once I know that the authorities there will let me in – and that only you can tell me. And before all that happens the wedding must take place.

You will be surprised that I have written so little to you about myself but in the last few weeks I have seen so many sad things happening around me and amongst people I was close to that I am not in a state to talk about trivialities, when so much more important things are going on around us. I am healthy and my morale has picked up a bit. For weeks I fell asleep at night fearing that there would be a ring at the door, that the man with the summons would come. I kept thinking about my childhood when we sang: 'Don't turn around, the *plumpsack*[46] is coming'. Now things are supposed to have stopped for a bit (for how long?) and we are recovering a little. For myself I am not so afraid, but the whole affair has had a big effect on me and when I think of all the good friends who have gone, it makes my heart turn over. Not one has written yet and the 'friends' are silent and Eman is silent. But I hope and trust that they are well and I believe that we will be united soon.

The post to you is now working, please write down the address for me, the whole name of your friend so that Frau Vacek can send something to him when she wants to. Write down what you need urgently. Please don't send me anything because I am well provided for and am still nibbling at my provisions.

Farewell and keep healthy. All yours, Mitzimarie.

First page missing, filed after 19/11/1941

Today the family brought up all their misgivings at the Sternschuss', all sorts of worries. I rejected them all emphatically and never again will anyone have the slightest influence on me. I explained that I consider myself already married and that I will go to my husband as soon as ever I can. Sadly I fear that won't be so easy or simple, but for my part I will make every effort to come to you. In any case it is possible that you may eventually be allowed to come to me, who knows?

Treasure, I don't get upset when you reproach me, just tell me everything you think. What is hard is that I can't just tell you everything that is in my heart as I would love to do and then misunderstandings can so easily arise. It is so dear of you to like my smile so much, but it is your own special skill: whenever I just think of you, it is there at once and I am very lucky because it keeps my spirits up. Sometimes when I am walking about I think about you and then I realize I am smiling that smile, my beloved magician.

---

[46]The *plumpsack* is a German children's game (very similar to the game *Duck, Duck, Goose*), where children stand shoulder to shoulder in a circle, facing inwards, while another, the *plumpsack*, runs round outside the circle and inconspicuously drops an object behind one of the players (the victim), and continues to run round the outside. None of the participants in the circle can know who will be the next victim. Marie uses the term *plumpsack* man to refer to the summons to report for deportation.

It would be ungrateful of me to suggest that my mother or sister don't want the best for me, but they don't accept the necessary limits to what they are entitled to decide about our fate or our future. The 'friends' can't do anything else; their silence must just be borne with patience. And finally the day will come when one can say: all people should be brothers and sisters, then I will certainly be resting in your arms and then we will be endlessly happy.

Your Mitzimarie

Photo 13 *The portrait of herself which Marie sent to Ernst.*

Karlín, 25/11/1941

My dear Ernst

Today I spoke with the head of the department for emigration at the *Kultusgemeinde*.[47] He said that when we are married you can get the entry permit on the basis of the marriage certificate and, when I have that, I shall ask for the exit permit. At present I am still waiting for the death certificate and the legal declaration.

I don't intend to waste any time because I am serious about coming to you. Tomorrow two women acquaintances from the house are leaving and many people we know are going too. We were hoping for a pause, but unfortunately there isn't one. Perhaps their journey will be shorter, that would at least be one advantage.[48] Yesterday I slept at the Lípas' because it was Mutti's birthday today. She was showered with flowers and even with sweets, so hard to come by, and other good things. We ourselves didn't give her anything, in view of the difficult times. A nice breakfast and a better lunch, that was all. I stayed there till the afternoon, a lot of people came to visit, then I went back to my quiet retreat. There I refreshed myself with a bath, washed my hair, then sewed, darned, mended and now, before I go to bed, I am totally with you.

Just imagine, my landlady who has been wanting to have my flat for a year now and who initiated the notice, came to my flat and suggested I should go to the *Kultusgemeinde* and the *Zentralstelle* and say that I can't pay the rent, because she is determined to have the flat. I answered her very politely but firmly that when I get the order from the authorities I will leave the flat at once, but that I could not accept her suggestion because it didn't correspond with my wishes. Then she said 'You could save your furniture,' but I said 'I am not aiming for that either, I have put everything in my declaration of possessions and it is my habit always to be strictly honest and correct. I don't care what happens, I'll accept anything.' You must understand, in fact, that she apparently wanted to lay a trap for me, but she was to be disappointed in that.

---

[47]Possibly Dr Hanuš (Hans) Aschermann (1914–44). In July 1943 he was deported to Theresienstadt. He was murdered in the Small Fortress of Theresienstadt shortly before the end of the war.
[48]Marie seems to be aware that the transports will now go to Theresienstadt in the Protectorate and not to Poland. The first, the so-called AK transport, left one day before, on 24 November.

The things one experiences! How happy I would be if I could shake off all these harassments. What I go through for the sake of the flat isn't worth it any more.

I am going to bed, I am really tired, in my mind I lay my head on your chest, I hug you and fall asleep smiling blissfully.

Letter continued next day

Gusti has now lost three of his best friends; he is very sad and monosyllabic and he has no more cigars and the meals we once had are a thing of the past. He never complains, but he always sits in a corner and is irritable. He particularly misses the friends he had known well for many years, the ones he played cards with. Two of the best friends of Irene and myself have also gone, the third is dead, you know about that. Herr and Frau Bass' sister received a card from Litzmannstadt.[49] On it was written: '*Artur and Paula Bass have arrived here, they live at Hanseatenstrasse 37. (Signed) The Elder of the Jewish Council.*' Now one will be able to send them a little money and letters weighing 100 g with biscuits etc. Their family will do that. They themselves have still not written after 6 weeks. Now I have told you all sorts of things, but nothing about what is going on in my heart. Farewell, warmest love and kisses from

Your Mitzimarie.

Karlín, 27/11/1941

My dear Ernst

Your letter of the 20th did indeed restore me and from it I can see clearly that you are feeling well. I thought Karel wrote to you that he needs to have the death certificate, translated into German and notarized, but perhaps the declaration where you are entered as a widower will suffice.

Just imagine, yesterday Frau Clara Reichl, Otto's mother, visited Irene! I was quite dumbstruck by it! My wounds from those times have not yet healed; I will not offer anything to encourage frequenting each other or even being friends. I have no anger or hatred, but I want my peace. Irene received her nicely, she

---

[49]The name given by Germany to Łódź after the occupation of Poland. Artur and Paula Bass died in the ghetto.

wanted to hear about Otto, whom she apparently has not heard from for a long time. She is apparently terribly surprised that we are getting married, for her that is sensational. I don't care. I was completely honest and decent to this woman, but she could not conquer her inborn nature and with her intrigues succeeded in destroying the marriage. Probably her bad conscience is troubling her and they would like to make friends but I am not interested any more because I feel that I always come off worst in dealing with such people, I don't understand that sort at all. God grant that Greterl does the right thing.

Dearest, of course I believe that everything will turn out well for us, but we must adapt ourselves to the changed times and not expect miracles which will not happen. Don't you agree? One has to accept the facts before it is too late. Recent events taught me a lot – the fate of many of the people I know. Today a good acquaintance of mine left the house, the parting was sad and hard.[50]

I am rushing to the post, so I will stop. Thinking of you I radiate happiness. Farewell, keep healthy. Most lovingly,

Your Mitzimarie

Karlín, 29/11/1941

My dearest

Your letter of the 22nd came today and I am awfully sorry that you had so much running around and trouble, my sweet, and that, despite it all, you didn't have any success. I rang Karel immediately.

It doesn't matter if the food is not as good as it was, there's no harm, just keep healthy, winter will pass and when you can enjoy the beauties of nature again in spring time, the hardships will all be forgotten, since there are far, far worse things which I hope you will be spared. I am happy with your lot, so long as I just know you are in good health. You have no idea how much better it is for you than for Gallus [in Łódź], so just be content, go on taking care of yourself, and, if one day we are reunited, we will enjoy everything as much and as well as we possibly can. I will do everything I can to provide the comforts you miss.

---

[50]She was deported.

Continued two days later

Now it is December again, it is quite cold here, there is a bit of frost. Month after month goes by, I am glad when another week is over. Yesterday, Sunday, I was at the Lípas' again. I was there already on Saturday evening, because in the afternoon there was a family gathering at the Sternschuss', it is always very nice there. In the evening it is usually quite lively at the Lípas' because of their lodgers Robert and Stein but yesterday we were all feeling low because the *plumpsack* man was on his rounds again, but this time the journey is to Theresienstadt and that is only a short journey and people cheer each other up with that. Many people from Karlsbad have already gone, you would be amazed.

Your winter will soon take its leave, in two months it will be spring again. If only I could experience that with you there. I very much fear that the difficulties will grow, sadly, sadly! It is wartime. In spite of everything, if we can just stay healthy, we will come through; the sun will have to shine again one day for us too. So you just keep being confident and don't let yourself be dragged down by the little discomforts of everyday. Here old and young, the youngest and the oldest, are all getting married, recently a cousin of Emmerl married a 73-year-old man, that's a good one, isn't it? That means she doesn't have to leave because he is old.[51]

Don't worry about Hella and Salvator, things happen in a marriage, all the more so with such hotheads who are so temperamental and in these times, when life is making the hardest demands on everyone, people get very irritable then and it is often not surprising if two people momentarily find it hard to put up with each other. Just don't make any judgments or get involved. They will make it up again.

Your oranges are unbelievably expensive, there are none here at that price, I wouldn't buy them. Recently I read that steps have been taken against profiteers in Athens.

A sweet kiss, your Mitzimarie

---

[51] At the beginning of the deportations, the elderly and sick were not deported. They shared the fate of the rest of the community later.

Karlín, 3/12/1941

My most dearly beloved

That you and Hella are already worrying about how to make our home cosy is sweet and dear and thoughtful and touches me deeply. If I were there I wouldn't be able to offer much help at first, not knowing the conditions and the language, where even the script is a total mystery to me. That, and the thought that I would have to come penniless, put a damper on my anticipated happiness, even if only partially. Never in my life have I been a burden, ever since my childhood I could always offer some useful service in our daily life, but what the future holds for me nobody knows. I beg of you, Ernstili, don't buy anything in advance for setting up our home, because we want to be modest in the beginning and to help as much as we can.

What you wrote to me about Salvator surprises me less, all sons-in-law are like that or similar. You mustn't be angry or hurt. You have offered plenty and you should not feel you are in the way. What you have cost him he will one day not need to lament, if he has to give it up, which is not at all out of the question. He should remember that, even though I don't wish it on him.

And the day will come for you when you will be able to settle your debt to him. I had a similar experience with Gustav who apparently also sometimes said bitter things to Irene when we all appeared there and he had a lot of extra material expense.[52] Now we have reached a point where I am quits with him. I think I have made it up to him, if in different ways.

Look, my treasure, you have been a bit unfair in your thoughts about Hella; I'm glad your relations are again as they should be. She needs you and you need her. You can tell her what you like about me and my letters. I very much hope I will get on well with Hella, as I was so fond of her children and was looking forward to being with them.

At the moment things are going quite well for me, I have regained my mental equilibrium; you can see that from the letters. In recent days my acquaintances have only gone to Theresienstadt, that is good in many ways, and it soothes the nerves. Now there will be a long break before the festivities, one is grateful for that. And so people live for the moment and are glad to know that the greatest worries are hopefully averted for a time.[53]

---

[52]After Marie, Louise and Grete escaped from the Sudetenland in 1938.
[53]There was a break in deportations from Prague between 17 December 1941 and 30 January 1942.

We have had a bit of snow for two days, good, healthy weather. But just have patience, my love, in two months it will be spring again. And now I am stopping. I am rushing to the post.

Lovingly
Mitzimarie

Unknown date. Page 3. Earlier pages missing.

I am living on my own, quite alone in the flat. Tomorrow morning the third family from the house is leaving me, all my acquaintances have gone so that I have no one else to talk to here. In the afternoon I am always with Irene and Mutti but – don't think badly of me – the atmosphere there sometimes puts me on edge. Yesterday we were at the Sternschuss', we also meet the few other acquaintances who remain. Gustav is a bit calmer, my dear mother has become a frail little old woman and Irene is now Gustav's mouthpiece. I am not always happy with that. Gustav has not treated me particularly nicely since I have been living in Prague. I don't find his surly, grumpy behaviour easy to put up with and I think he knows that I don't care much for him. Anyway, he lets himself go in the way he behaves towards me. Over time he has made unfair allegations about me but I have never behaved badly towards him. I won't go into all that.

As I was always anxious not to cause my sister any hurt, I swallowed many a bitter word, many an impoliteness, because she would have been the pig in the middle: here the husband, there the sister. But now a lot has changed so much that I am not going to accept it any more. When he spoke to me roughly again recently, I declared that I would not be coming there again because I would not accept such treatment. He said: 'I won't change any more', to which I replied 'And neither will I.' I took my leave of my mother and sister and disappeared, ignoring him. Next day they were both there at 10 a.m. and I was polite to him in a formal way, gave him my hand, etc. But when we are together again he will surely often be glad to enjoy the company, and then he will be paid back a little. He is a decent, good person, but sometimes he is just very unpleasant to me and

I won't lie down in front of him like silly Irene does. So you can imagine how I sometimes feel and, when you describe to me the happy future we so long for, then I toss my head proudly and think: 'So what? Let's wait and struggle on and hope.'

I am always gazing at your picture and then my face lights up and shines with joy. In the morning when I wake up and in the evening when I lie down my first thoughts are always dedicated to you. Today a card came from Gusti's sister [Olga] in Litzmannstadt; she has been gone for two months already. We are glad to know that she is still alive. In any case, she received the money that was sent on the off chance, without our knowing her address. The sister from Vienna [Pauline] is also there.

And now, my sweet, *auf wieder, wiedersehen.* Tenderly,

your Mitzimarie

Photo 14 *Hitler inspecting troops outside Prague Castle. (Courtesy of German Federal Archives)*

Karlín, 12/12/1941

My most dearly beloved!

I'm still not comfortable writing by hand, which is why I am always changing my equipment: paper, pens etc. Yesterday the *plumpsack* man was on his rounds again, hearts thumped when there was a ringing at the door. Now, thank God, we have a few weeks' holiday, let's hope it really is. And everyone is looking forward to this period of quiet. I have prepared everything for Jan and am glad it was all available. It was the last of the medicine so he should keep it for his own use. I am greatly looking forward to talking things over with him, it is enormously important to me.

I wonder what you are doing now: it is 9.30 in the evening here. I came back from the Lípas at 7.30, cooked something for tomorrow and this next little hour is for whiling away with you. It is mousey-quiet in the house, one can hear the muffled sound of a radio coming from the 1st floor. At the moment the weather is mild and fine, although the sun is not shining, but there is no frost or snow either. The climate in Prague is a good healthy one; the city is well protected, much better than Karlsbad. One sees Christmas trees being sold already and things are more lively, as they always are at this season.

Soon it will be the anniversary of poor Thesa's death. You know Tante Lidi really is a spiteful woman. When she was at Irene's a week ago for afternoon tea, she argued with me, declaring that it had only been one year, even though my argument against was well substantiated.[54] She always has to pick a quarrel, but she won't get away with it with me; I feel far too indifferent about her, as I do mostly about people in general.

Treasure, how glad I am that this year will soon be over because I am sure that our reunion must be in sight, with every week that passes, with every month, we must be getting closer to each other. Oh my God, if only it was already here! Sometimes I am rude and grumpy to Irene, when she provokes me in some way, and it's no wonder, the constant yearning and hoping, other people can't really understand it, but I know you can.

---

[54]Ten months after Thesa's death Ernst and Marie expressed their love.

Recently Frau Paula Klein and Herr [Vítězslav] Rosner got married in order that, should they get summoned, they can go together.[55] I could tell you endless stories, and if I don't it is out of consideration, so as not to give trouble to the most esteemed Herr Censor. I write only about personal things to you, because, after all, neither of us wants, or is allowed, to be much interested in other people. So my letters will not be very interesting for a time, but it can't be any other way, I will omit everything so as to keep the correspondence going. You must be content if I only tell you about myself. And my life is exceedingly monotonous, lonely, but I don't want to have it any other way, I don't even walk in the street if I don't have to. The longest stretch is from my place to Irene.

I am still making preparations for the departure. Now I am worried where I will get the right fabric for a sack for straw; we are supposed to take one with us, but without the straw, only the covering. Well, by 6 January, when it is supposed to begin again, I shall have found something, I think I already have something in mind.

Continued three days later.

15/12/1941 evening

Today I stood for two hours at the post office and had to bring my letters back home. It has never been like that before, such a pushing on one side and such slowness on the other. So I am writing some more this evening and will try again tomorrow. Have you got enough milk? If I were there we would soon move to the vineyard, get ourselves some hens, a cock, a goat and we would work hard, get up at 4 a.m., grow vegetables. But our reunion will happen soon, I firmly believe it. Go on, laugh, I can see you smiling, yes, and yet Ernstili, I will come to you, or you to me, since you have a pass, so that would also be possible, if necessary, wouldn't it? That feeling of being understood by you makes it possible for me to be open and free with you. With you I see myself as quite a different person to what I am with others; they have not the patience and don't take the trouble to listen to me, they are all so busy with their own affairs and so preoccupied with themselves. Then, when times get difficult, they reach out for me, and then I am supposed to be with them all the time.

---

[55]The Yad Vashem database records both as having died in Theresienstadt in 1944. They got married on 19 November 1941 (http://www.holocaust.cz/databaze-dokumentu/dokument/354799-rosner-vitezslav-nezpracovano/).

I have never forgotten the journey we made together to Leipzig, how lovely those few hours were, your attention and kindness. My God, how stupid we were! I had no suspicions, didn't suspect anything, but I was happy with you then and sorry when it was over. Why didn't you carry on with me to Berlin? You must have felt often in Karlsbad how I loved to discuss all sorts of things with you. Even if it wasn't clear to me then, I realize now what always drew me so powerfully towards you. It was the feeling that you understood me.

It is late again. I am going to bed and will be with you in my dreams. Keep well, my love, be healthy and cheerful and content.

Your Mitzimarie

Karlín, 15/12/1941

My beloved

Your explanation of why you are so worried – that it is because I am – I quite understand; I would be just the same. But you must not let yourself get depressed again and must stand up tall just as I too would. In recent times I have met two kinds of people. Some, broken and bent, go under in different ways. Others take everything on themselves, help their fellow men with word and deed and, when it is their turn, they begin their new life composed and clear headed. At first, when I was faced with the question and considered that I would have to begin a new life quite alone, there were moments when I thought to myself that perhaps it wouldn't be possible. The future loomed like an insurmountable mountain before me, but now I have got used to the idea and tell myself that what others can handle, so can I. I am determined to be in control of my life. So, my sweet, be calm and confident about me; I can hardly bear the thought that you should be anxious and worried about me. In any case you know that fate has been merciful to me and why should I not hope it will continue to be so? Out of 40,000 people I'm only one single person. My [business] experience won't be of great use and [in any case], there are still plenty of young people here who would surely be considered first.[56]

---

[56]Marie believes that those who are deported are sent to manual work assignments.

Yes, my sweet, Clara Reichl is a weird woman, I have never got used to her, I have to keep out of her way.

Evening, 15/12/1941

You are quite wrong, my sweet, if you think we are living well. Oh no, we are not. We have enough to fill ourselves but every housewife has worries and trouble. Of course, for me on my own it isn't a problem. Anyway, it is a catastrophe that bread and potatoes are so expensive for you, because one needs those first and foremost.

Beloved, if I could come to you I'd be with you in a flash, because the peace of being by your side would make up for everything. But we must be content, we have the prospect of three weeks' peace ahead of us and that is a heavenly gift. Of course I will write to you as often as possible for as long as I can, because now in particular I really don't want to get you worried and because I know how many worries I have already given you.

Two days ago the mediator, Krebs,[57] wrote to me from Karlsbad that I should sell Haus Lanner for 75,000 Marks. Interesting. I am not going to answer; I think it's pointless, particularly as there is an administrator there.[58]

There's no point now in thinking about our union, the two of us aren't able to leave our skins behind, it is as if a magnet is pulling us in two different directions. I believe and hope that we will be able to hold out and that we will live to experience our longed for reunion. But each of us must take care of his body so that we are capable of dealing with future trials. I am watching at the moment how people with a weak will and a feeble constitution go under, sometimes willingly, sometimes unintentionally. That is why, my love, I am always warning you to sacrifice everything for your wellbeing and your health.

In my heart I am with you.

Your Mitzimarie

---

[57]Josef Krebs was the director of the Union Bank of Bohemia. This Bank held the property of the Jewish population 'in trust'. Selling the house was pointless as Jews could only access a very limited amount of their money. A single or widowed person could only draw 2,000 Czech crowns a month.
[58]Treuhänder.

Probably 17/12/41. Page 1 missing.

A stay with the Ashkenazis would not appeal to you because you would not get on with many of the people, God protect any decent person from them![59] Work is certainly the best way to get through all sorts of things. My intention was and is, if I am called, to present myself at once for any work, whether in the kitchen or in the factory, whatever there is, just trying to forget by working.

Unfortunately, we are all talking too much about the *plumpsack* man, that is what makes my brother-in-law so tense, people have little good to look forward to. But, thank God, we have a break for a little while.

I am very glad that you are happy with the food, I'm pleased to hear it. Here vegetables are apparently going to be rationed too, we don't know yet whether it is true. In any case I cannot buy onions, lemons and garlic,[60] but I still have some stored away. One sees beautiful apples which are only for children. What is good with me is that I have no hankering for impossible things. I hardly miss sweet things like sweets, not even fruit. I always think to myself that for so many years I have had an excess of everything so why should it not be different for a change?

Yesterday I received a long letter from Else Auerbach in Hilversum (Holland).[61] They have had a lot of sadness in their family. Their children have been living for years quite near to the 'friends'. She was, of course, absolutely amazed about us and very interested and pleased.

I think, my love, that worrying about me depresses you very much. You know that I am open and honest with you. So I am telling you that at the moment you need not worry. From now until 6 January it is holiday, and as for what happens next, one must keep hoping. Even if my life was not a bed of roses, God has always taken care of me. When I see how others have been housed for years while I still have my home, isn't that a blessing from God?

---

[59] Ashkenazi and Lichtmann were Marie's code names for the *Ostjuden*, the Jews of the East, who were seen as alien and primitive by the assimilated and integrated German Jews.

[60] Marie is not writing here about mere shortages. From 8 November 1941, Jews were no longer allowed to buy these items.

[61] This letter has survived.

If you feel like it and if it suits you, then write one day to Ulli,[62] but only if it does not bring you any trouble. Ask him to tell the 'friends' that we are still alive and still have the same address. They must be very worried, poor things.

By the time this letter reaches you the year will be turning. God grant that we can at last, and soon, find happiness together. I am confident in my hopes.

A most loving embrace, deeply longing, from

Your Mitzimarie.

Karlín, 18/12/1941

My most dearly beloved

Your letter of the 12th came this morning and as I want to go to the post office I will answer it as much as I can before I go. I understood the newspaper cutting. One cannot get the transit permit they mention. You will hear the whole story in person from Jan. I can well believe that I don't understand the conditions there and I feel very sorry that I can't help at all, although here too, and particularly for us, everything is in short supply. But we can fill ourselves, we don't suffer from hunger. There is no question of roast meat etc., as you know it, for 'us'. That is not possible and we don't want it either. We are happy for things to remain as they are. It is wartime after all and everyone has to accept that. Food is the least of our problems, my love. If only people were not weighed down by other troubles. I can imagine how much irritability there is amongst your people, as among all those who were used to happy carefree times. I experienced it here for two years before those here also got their own heavy worries. Before that they only partially understood the troubles of the others. That is why the irritation is so objectionable to me and for you too, because we went through a lot long before.[63]

If you don't feel like describing your childhood to me, then leave it till later. But I beg you, pull yourself together and don't be miserable like an old maid,

---

[62]Fritz Ullmann.

[63]Marie again refers to her experience after 1938 (possibly also her personal trauma), and to the increasingly threatening behaviour of Konrad Henlein's followers in the years leading up to Munich.

that's not the real you. Everything will turn out well, that is what we both hope, we must just have a little patience. We can't do anything about it.

I strongly recommend '*Martin Salander*' by Gottfried Keller to you, and as often as you can buy a copy, please read '*Der Neue Tag*', so that you know everything important about the situation here.

I completely share your opinion that one is largely in control of one's own destiny. Your view that here too one can be in control of a great deal I will not answer for now. It is always a question how a person copes with this and that, how he deals with life, whether more easily or with more difficulty, how he interprets different things. One person will just cling to the past, to 'how things used to be', another takes a look into the future, deals with the present, weighs things up and reflects, braces himself, accepts things as they are and fits in with the situation as it is and then, naturally, he lives more agreeably. When all is said and done every single person is hoping that there will one day be peace again for all. But those who think they can't bear life are obliged, willingly or unwillingly, to submit. [*blacked out section censored*] you will find out why.

I hug and kiss you in warm and passionate love and am

Your Mitzimarie

21/12/1941

My most dearly beloved

It seems strange to me that I have not written to you for almost 3 days. I had various things to do this last week: on Saturday I had my bridge ladies here and today I was at the Lípas' again. But not overnight this time, because the *plumpsack* man is not doing his rounds so Irene can be 'without worries' for the moment. I partly enjoy being there but on the other hand I prefer to be at home. Gusti, who is altogether very morose, silent and shut off, certainly doesn't like me much and doesn't want to see me, I think. The overnight visits upset him. Often I wouldn't go, but I don't want to cause any annoyance and I also don't want to offend my sister. So I play the sad bit of theatre with a happy face, but when I can find a good excuse to get out of it I am happy to do so.

I wonder whether you will celebrate Christmas this year. I know you always had visitors there. Here there is a great throng in the streets, as there is every year at this time. There are still plenty of people who are happy and content and one could easily envy them if one went and stood there as a solitary observer. Well, perhaps our time of happiness and contentment will come soon too. We are mostly together with good friends, sometimes in one place, sometimes in another. We never go for walks.

Keep healthy and happy as much as you can. Till our *wieder-wiedersehen*. Most lovingly,

Your Mitzimarie

Karlín, 24/12/1941

My most dearly beloved

Your two letters of the 15th and 17th came today, so a little later than usual and I was very glad to get them because I was beginning to be a bit anxious. My God, the things one thinks when one doesn't have news of one's loved one! Treasure, I could give many answers to your reflections, but I won't because I don't want to risk saying anything incorrect. I believe there will always be wars because what has been going on for thousands of years always repeats itself. The world and its people do not improve and change for the better. It is almost as if there has to be destruction so that then there can be reconstruction. In the last three years I have lived through and seen so much. If I think of the luxurious life of so many of our co-religionists and their abrupt fall, one could certainly make reflections on that! We who have on the whole led a life of risk and worry, and many others like us, aren't so easily shocked by the various privations. I always think of my Greterl, when we were living for a year in Bubeneč[64] in a dreadful flat and had plenty of other troubles and suffering as well. The clever child often said 'Oh never mind, Mummy, nothing much more can happen to us, we are already as low as can be.' Yes, she was right, for us[65] it all happened quickly, but nobody wanted to listen to us.

At the moment I am all right. Today I am sitting alone in my flat, because Olga L. was going to come and spend the night. But she hasn't come, she is

---

[64] A Prague suburb, where Marie and Grete stayed after their escape from the Sudetenland.
[65] By 'us' she means those who were driven out of the Sudetenland in 1938.

always unpunctual. I refused the Lípas' invitation tonight because of her. But I am not alone, because I am with you! I am imagining that you are sitting there, that it is peace time and you are feeling happy and content after a good supper. I am busy doing some household task or other while you read and every now and again twinkle at me over the top of your reading matter. Then I get myself ready, I want to make myself look really nice, to give you a surprise. I disappear, taking advantage of your preoccupation, and watch how you suddenly miss me. I enjoy it when you at last see how I have tricked you.

I am very sorry that where you are you have such worries about food due to transport problems. That is no fun and it is hard to imagine it from here. I am sorry for poor Hella. I hope you are all being very helpful. I can well imagine that it is the main talking point. It would be good if the prices were regulated, that is a good thing. You will read in *Der Neue Tag* how severely black marketeers are punished here.[66]

I use the electric tram a lot because I don't often have the patience to walk alone, only if I have a lot of time, and that doesn't happen. God grant that we will still be allowed to use it in the New Year; otherwise I would have to give up many errands.

… … … (*name indecipherable*) left everything to his wife. Like most people, he was hardly allowed to keep anything. Everyone is working out how long he has to live and is hoping that their savings will last. Nobody has any wealth today but it is absolutely wonderful how everyone knows how to apportion their finances. Most people have had to sublet their flats or become sub-lessees themselves. Many have left, others have taken lodgers in. There is no way in which one can make one's own arrangements. Nobody can go out for entertainment, nor does anybody want to, and that saves a lot of expense. Some earn money when snow needs to be cleared or by working in the Labour Service.[67] All that is quite well paid. Some are employed in manual work, women work as servants and so everyone gets by as best he can.[iii]

---

[66] A large number of those sentenced to death during the martial law, introduced by Heydrich, were those punished for economic transgressions against the German law.

[67] Marie uses the term *Arbeitsdienst*. This was a compulsory labour assignment demanded by the German authorities. In September 1941 over 7,000 Jews in the Protectorate were engaged in some form of forced labour; in December 1941 already 13,030 Jews worked as forced labourers.

You mustn't be upset about Gusti. He isn't happy with himself, it seems. He has plenty of reasons to be annoyed with himself. He knows my opinion of him is fair, and that will certainly annoy him. He insists on remaining silent, except that when I ask him something he usually snaps and shows his displeasure towards me or that he is not pleased to see me. Perhaps I am over-sensitive. I am sure that if it were important he would take responsibility for me but I have absolutely no intention of letting myself become dependent.

Apparently Gusti has always been like this, Irene says. He is often unfriendly to her too but thank goodness I have no need to let myself be treated like that. For example, for the last six weeks he hasn't had any cigars. I found one of inferior quality and gave it to him. The next day he said 'You think that was a cigar, that rubbish?' So you see how obnoxious he is. First he was delighted and reached out for it greedily but then he wanted to poison my pleasure at giving him pleasure. Wasn't I silly? Why do I repay nastiness with kindness? I keep seeing him be loathsome to me. And even if it was a bad cigar he shouldn't say so to me, because he could see that I wanted to make him happy. Surely his sense of tact should have told him that. I can't help it; it hurts me so much that I understand from his whole attitude what his opinion of me is.

Don't torment yourself, my sweet, let it be. Just don't write to him, please. I wouldn't want that, it would just make trouble! When we are together there will be plenty of opportunity and then, at the right moment, you can impose your will. I know already how nice he will be to you – he is indeed a highly respectable, decent person – but we will see how we will deal with it all. Let's wait until the time comes. I don't want to make life difficult for Irene, although recently I often oppose her and don't agree with everything the way she wants. She gets upset but I am firm.

As to your opinions of Mutti, yes, my love, unfortunately that is how it is, old age is hard and cruel, and the difficult times which are gnawing away at her life are even more so. She keeps worrying what is going to happen to her if we have to leave. And even if we tell her a hundred times to just wait and see and not to think so far ahead, it is always the same song. But before, when there weren't yet any transports, she behaved differently, she was just very unhappy, without any reason. I think it is her nature, there isn't much one can do. And I don't want to become like that one day.

Ernstili, my good one, I am really not afraid. I don't know how it comes about that, although I have experienced life's harshness, I am incapable of worrying seriously about our future. Today I handed in the form with my details at the employment bureau so that I can get an employment book. Many people were turned away. When the official looked at my form and read that I worked from 1906 to 1938 he asked me (I had put myself down as bookkeeper and manufacturer of pudding and baking mixes) whether that was correct. Then he said 'Come on the 30th for the book.' Who knows, perhaps I will get some work. That would be nice – I would very much like to practise my profession. And if I came to you the employment book could only be helpful.

With all this chatter it is half past one now! Oh, and now I must go to my rest alone, what wouldn't I give to be able to curl up with you! Keep well, my beloved. Good night!

Continued the next day

25/12/1941

Now the first day of Christmas is over. I am very glad because, strangely, festival days put me in a very sad frame of mind. I am quite filled with torment; nothing cheers me up any more without you. At midday I was at the Lípas'. Fixler was also there and it was nice. And in the afternoon we were at the Sternschuss' and that was nice too. I was firm and did not go back to the Lípas', but went home and now I am with you, my love. That is the most beautiful of all.

Don't worry at all about Gustav. There will never be any trouble because neither of us will let it come to that. I must take some blame for my oversensitivity. So, my sweet, let's leave it. Of course, I am susceptible to tenderness, but only yours. I am not at all nice to my former family circle. They have crushed everything in me. I simply cannot put up with a blow on one cheek and a kiss on the other. I like a nice, calm, cultivated way of behaving, not comments which are untrue and always intended as a put-down. I don't like that and in my heart I don't forgive it. I don't quarrel about it, I think my own thoughts and my inner self shuts itself off completely. Like a snail I creep back into my shell, I can't do anything else and I just keep quiet. Their mood changes, they don't remember that they were bad tempered but I draw my own conclusions from it. A dear, kind, nice Jan is worth more to me than a good meal and they still don't understand that.

If we are finally reunited then I too will once more be a completely happy person. Mankind has long since learned new ways of thinking, there will be quite different ideas about possessions. I am confident that we will then spend our allotted years without rushing about chasing money and wealth. Let's hope it will be enough to earn our living decently and with dignity. I am quite certain that I will have very little part in the children's lives, at most I will see them from time to time. One could hardly expect them to change where they live, that is out of the question. So I cling to you all the more fervently, you will stand for everything and I know that our deep, ardent love can do that.

And I am going to bed again, I will dream of you as if you were really beside me. Most lovingly,

Your Mitzimarie.

Karlín, 28/12/1941

My dearest

Yesterday, at the post office, I had to take page 4 of the present letter out of the envelope. An official declared that the letter was too heavy. Now the Christmas festival is over and New Year is almost upon us. So the years pass. I spent three quite pleasant days but I am glad to have them behind me because festivals without you are a torment for me, which I don't show but inside I feel tearful and miserable.

Yesterday I was with Frau Louise Neumann and Frau Paula Klein-Rosner at Frau Fischer's for bridge. Herr Rosner was there too. He declared that the only one who looked unchanged and as she used to be in Karlsbad, was me.[68] I wondered whether he was shortsighted. Frau Neumann sends you her greetings. Richard is in Theresienstadt, her sister and the whole family are in Łódź. She is living with her daughter-in-law now. Today we were at the Lípas' with good friends, it was nice. I am supposed to go there for New Year's Eve too, to spend the evening with the Robert and Lípa families, but I will not be

---

[68]Marie's social circle in Prague included many previous acquaintances from Karlsbad.

going as I don't feel like it. I would rather be at home. Olga L. wants to come here and we will talk as we like.

I am very curious whether Jan will be in touch. Perhaps I will have news from him tomorrow, and you too. In last week's edition of *Das Reich* there is also an article on your food situation. Did you see it?

I am pretty well too, although the cold at present keeps reminding me of the old rheumatic condition. I am lucky to have a warm flat. Touch wood, God grant that I can stay on here.

Soon it will be six years since misfortune entered our family when, in January 1936, Dr. Reichl began his dance about the divorce. How quickly time passes. What a pity about 'our time' and that we have to spend it apart. How happy I would be if you were with me!

With deepest love,

Your Mitzimarie

Prague, 1/1/1942

My dear Ernst

I was a little, just a very little, bit hurt, for some reason – whether at my unkind lot, a bit of bad luck or something else – in any case, I found it hard not to receive your longed for news this week and I could not rid myself, against all good reason, of a certain anxiety. That is how I entered the New Year, and fell asleep thinking of you. And this morning (my friend Olga was here and so it was cosy) I broke a glass plate and was glad about all the broken pieces![69] At eleven I was getting ready to set off to the Lípas when there was a ring at the door and what was it? A letter, a big fat one, from you. What a joy that was and what a relief and ray of hope. The first thing in the New Year, a letter from you! Only you could be so clever!

I am glad to know you are well. I was thankful to receive the documents, but dearest, don't imagine it will be so easily possible for me to make the journey. I did write and tell you I can't travel now, or didn't that letter reach you? That

---

[69] A sign of good luck.

means we must just wait, but I will do everything I can do to prepare things so that when it is possible to travel I will be ready. If the time came I'd easily be able to put up with a night on the train – if only we were at that point!

What has Hella done wrong that you are not speaking to her? Please don't be so severe with her, please, please!

Can you believe our mutual acquaintance, Siegfried Löbl, died yesterday, and so many good acquaintances from back home? Do you remember my friends Emil and Käthe Taussig? The gentleman who, when Emmerl died, brought my family to Karlsbad that same night? He has become a clever gardener, putting himself heart and soul into his new career, his wife is an assistant dressmaker. Here in the house there is a Herr Löwy from Neudeck.[70] He had a fashion shop there. Now he is a very skilful bookbinder and I could name many others to you.

I can see that the declaration gave you a lot of trouble. At the moment the difficulties seem insuperable. There would be nothing to prevent a wedding but the journey, that is to say the travel permit, won't happen.

I also only talk to others about your problems with getting food, nothing else from your letters and even then only when people ask. Did they steal many potatoes? What a dreadful shame! I don't believe your prices will drop. Circumstances would have to be quite different there to what they are elsewhere. It is possible but unlikely.

Towards the end of the month the worries are supposed to begin again and one looks forward to that time with dread but one has to keep hoping. I agree with you and believe that we will soon be reunited, and for always.

Lovingly, your Mitzimarie

P.S. Imagine, dearest, this morning, on my way to the Lípas, a chimney sweep in his best outfit, with a basket on his arms with a piglet in it, crossed my path!! That made me pleased. Aren't sweeps supposed to bring good luck?

---

[70]Nejdek, 10 km north-west of Karslbad.

Karlín, 4/1/1942

My dearest

Another Saturday is over but today I am not alone. Olga has been here for a few days because her room-mate is so cross and unbearable and she must recuperate here. She is tense after the operation and can't put up with nastiness. As soon as Olga enters the room the wretch sings and whistles for hours on end, any old tune, hideously, and that is followed by all sorts of other unpleasant tricks. It is unbelievable what people can do out of petty spite. I said to her 'Now I am going to write and so are you. We won't have anything to do with each other until 11 o'clock.' She agrees to this and where am I? Beside you, of course.

You recently wrote to me that I could clink glasses with you on New Year's Eve at midnight precisely. I was up, my love, and thinking only of you, quite obviously.

Today a New Year greeting arrived from Jan with an enclosure. It is out of the question to deal with the latter. I hope he won't send me any more but in any case, I'll write him a few lines. It seems the visit will not happen, since there is no mention of it. In any case his wife still needs to recover and be looked after and he can't do anything else, just like me.

Tomorrow morning I am going to the cremation of Frau Sadler.[71] I will probably see many people from our home town. It is always a bitter thing when a mother like that dies, completely alone, when her children are scattered about in the world and she is alone and unloved in her illness and her death. And for the children too, it is very bitter. Sadly there are many such cases.

I too think that there will be an enormous amount of work to do but there is a lot I can't picture any more. Each of us has lived these times in a completely different way and there is a lot that one cannot judge which to the other is obvious because a great deal remains unexplained between us since the writing paper is not a suitable place for it (that is to say, there's not enough space). But we must keep up our mutual trust so that misunderstandings don't arise. I will stop for today.

With this thought in my mind I hug you tenderly and am

Your Mitzlmarie

---

[71]In a letter in the spring of 1940 Marie wrote to her daughters in England saying that Mrs Sadler was still considering whether to join her daughter in Ecuador. Sadly she never managed to.

Karlín, 6/1/1942

As I am off to the post, where I usually stand around for 1½–2 hours, I will write you another letter, my sweet. Don't worry about the *plumpsack* man. Who knows what he may decide next – one must keep hoping. And if it happens one will be able to cope with what has happened to others, one will just have to.

I see you had a nice Christmas, and that everything is terribly expensive for you. I certainly hope, with you, my treasure, for our happiness, if Hans[72] just leaves me in peace, otherwise he will destroy our happiness (God forbid). After all I have lived through, I will definitely not allow everyday troubles and worries to get the upper hand.

It doesn't matter if you have to give money to Hella. Today, every housewife has certainly too little money, I can understand that very, very well. My *mishpoche*[73] reproaches me at every opportunity that I care about nobody but you and that my thoughts are only with you. I give everyone their due but they always find something to criticize. But I don't care.

My recipes seem to annoy you. Why did I do it? To give myself some kind of role, as housewives often do? And because I am racking my brain how I can make your life a little better even from a distance, but unfortunately … The art of cooking has adapted itself completely to the unusual conditions and every day new recipes are shared.

You comment that I write so much to you even though I have no typewriter. Well yes, I think to myself, my sweet, that it would be cruel of me not to write to you now when I have described so clearly the reality, but I mustn't cause you any unnecessary worry, as long as it is possible for me to be able to write to you. Only when I feared that through silence I might cause more anxiety did I come out with the facts. That is how it was when I wrote at that most serious

---

[72]This 'Hans' is apparently Marie's code word for the German occupiers.
[73]Yiddish word for family.

Photo 15 *Hede and Rudolf Sternschuss.*

moment and informed you. Now they say that the reprieve has been prolonged until the end of January.

Nothing more will come from the friends, that is crystal clear. Who would ever have thought that would be possible! But I am not alone and must accept my fate. Strangely enough, I often find myself thinking about them just now and sometimes the tears come. It happens quite suddenly at some memory or other.

(The end of the letter is missing)

Karlín, 9/1/1942

My dearest

I will give the address of Edith's mother-in-law which you wanted. If ever I were not able to write to you for a time she would give you information: Frau Hede Sternschuss, Prague II, Beethovenstr. 33. We see each other two or three times a week and she knows everything about me. She is an utterly correct and decent person and also the only one who, if we had to leave, could still write.[74] It has been very important up to now that those left behind could regularly send something. For example, one can send money to Gallus, but no parcels.[75] On the other hand, until a few days ago one could send parcels to Theresienstadt. We are hoping that permission for this will be granted again. Imagine that we – my family and I – will leave no relatives here who could send us something, so Hede will do it. She could also pass on my correspondence with you. In any case, months would pass before you received even a card. But none of that may happen for a long time because it may not necessarily be me that they choose from among 35,000 people, I who have already endured such a lot. Up to now, thank goodness, I have not committed any offences or incurred any penalties and I live very quietly and unobtrusively.[76]

Your assumption that you will be able to enter the homeland before the papers are in order is not correct, my sweet; that can't be done now. I already wrote to you that there is a prejudice against proxy marriages and that one has to stick precisely to the rules. But even if I were married that wouldn't alter anything as regards the likelihood of my journey to Theresienstadt. Unfortunately that idea too is wrong. The advantage of marrying now is that if travel permits are again issued I would already have everything ready for coming to you. Unfortunately there is no question of it at the moment but there is no other way I can make it happen. There is no point speculating and wondering, one must just have patience and not lose courage or hope.

Now we are having a proper winter – a little snow and frost – and one must dress really warmly, but the air is pure and fresh. It would be wonderful to go walking together, I don't have much patience for walking alone. I usually go on foot to Irene's, and back again, that is the [only] exercise I get. This way I have lately put on weight again and Irene criticizes me. I laugh at it because I know how quickly the extra can disappear again. These days it is completely

---

[74]Hede Sternschuss was German by birth and not Jewish, thus not subject to the same postal restrictions as Marie.
[75]To the Łódź ghetto.
[76]Deportation to Theresienstadt was often a form of punishment for those who were caught breaking any of the anti-Jewish regulations and laws.

unimportant. It is true one feels healthier when one is lighter but weight loss has its dark side too.

Here I sit in my cell and wonder what you are doing at this moment. I wonder whether you are also thinking of me. Isn't it a crying shame that we have to spend so much time in yearning? Sometimes I get very discouraged. When I am alone and have had no news from you for quite a while, then I get despondent. I am also thinking a lot about the friends, how they will be worried to death, poor things. I can picture how Edithel will shed tears of fear and worry about us. Uncertainty is particularly distressing. And yet it is a great puzzle to me why they, of all people, have never written me a line for more than two years. I ponder a lot about that too.

My letters to you, my beloved, are really very uninteresting, that is my own verdict. I am not trying to excuse myself out of some sort of vanity. On the contrary, I wouldn't wish to keep from you the reason why they are boring. It is purely great caution which makes me write only about completely personal matters. It is not from ignorance either, that I don't reply to the light or profound philosophical comments you sometimes make. I just don't want to give cause for annoyance with even one word, or know that I have hindered our correspondence, and that is why I sometimes don't answer something. I am indeed very grateful to the most esteemed Herr Censor for his great patience, particularly with my scribble (touch wood).[77] I hope for your understanding about this. Sometimes I have the feeling that there is a great mass of unspoken words between us which here and there threatens to rear itself into a wall between us. That worries me only because I know that for that reason you can't always understand all my activities and behaviour. May I one day have the chance to give you a complete explanation of everything. Until then you must give me your trust, as I give you mine.

Farewell, my sweet. Keep healthy and happy. I hug you warmly and lovingly, kiss you in my own way and am

Your Mitzimarie

---

[77]Despite Marie's caution, she once again incurs the displeasure of the 'esteemed Herr Censor' who removes more than half of the next letter.

No date. Filed after the letter of 9/1/42. The first four sheets are missing

I don't say I am any different from my sisters but I don't want to be one of those who use this longing as a pawn in order to get this or that from my beloved. No, that isn't at all what I want to do. I would like my everyday behaviour, the way I handle things and my whole appearance to be the reason that, without any deliberate intention on my part, my beloved keeps longing for me. I need to be able to get my love to forget his everyday worries when he is with me and to give himself up to me with joy and pleasure, to confide in me and tell me everything and no unpleasantnesses are to stop him from offering me a kind word and a kind look. It will be the height of pride for me to know that he is at peace; that is as important to me as knowing that I give my love pleasure in bed.

The emigration from Karlbad was the hard school of life which first opened my eyes, when, in near isolation, I had to take stock of myself. I think it broadened my views of people and at the same time I no longer accept being influenced by anyone. Of course, the general change in circumstances is also responsible for that. Then, when I allowed myself be swept away by your love, nobody could any longer change my mind. They already know that and that suits me fine. I know, of course, that everyone wants the best for me but it makes no difference, I am old enough and from now on I remain 'me'. I will not let myself be sucked under; no, my treasure, that is over. Gustav has been making an effort these last few days to be nicer – but so what? I ignore it, just as I ignored his unpleasant behaviour earlier on. You are so wise when you say that one must think how much his changed circumstances have made him suffer. You are right, he is just no exception to so many. Unfortunately he has a lot to reproach himself with. He had always steered his own course in life so well and at the age of 66 life has disappointed him so utterly. And yet often I have felt such enormous pity for him; he is in fact a thoroughly honest, correct and decent person. When I saw him three months ago so upset and crying, I felt as though my heart were torn apart, even though he didn't deserve it from me after his, at times, horrible behaviour. Inside he has a good heart but that is not always enough. If men are inconsistent they lose their halo because nothing shows what a man is more than real, sincere, gracious and constant courtesy, not gallantry and flattery but the politeness that is due to every female, whether she is a lady or a servant. It is a woman's due because she is less strong and in some ways more vulnerable.

Well, I am satisfied with how things are, I am happy if everything is peaceful and without strife. They can all three stand on their heads, I am not going to go so often to the Lípas any more, I won't sleep there, unless it is unavoidable, and I think it is better so. I seek out the company of good friends and I find it. Then my sister always misses me a lot, but she shouldn't get too used to me, so that when you and I are together it won't be too difficult for her to get *un*used to me, don't you agree? Irene has a heart of gold and is good but she has disappointed me because she is not wise and because any stranger is her friend and their opinion is more important to her than mine, which is never asked. That is why she has paid dearly and I am very, very sorry about that. But in the end that doesn't matter to me either because, as I said, I am not important to her in all sorts of things. But even now I don't reproach her with anything, why should I make her sad? I don't have the urge to judge people, which is unfortunately such a prominent feature in my family. I think to myself 'I have got my treasure and he understands me completely, nothing else matters.'

A loving embrace, farewell, keep healthy and cheerful and happy.

Your Mitzimarie

Prague, 14/1/1942

My dear Ernst

Today, at last, your letter of 7/1 arrived and I'm a human being again, after days of worry and anxiety. I don't know why but this time I was particularly worried about you. Anyway, until today, the last letter I had received from you was your letter of 26/12. What happened to the letters you sent in between? And you, too, don't seem to be receiving everything from me because I always write at least twice a week, sometimes three times. If Jan had come I would gladly have been able to fulfil various of your wishes but to send things to him would have been impossible.

My treasure, I have such an enormous longing for you and sometimes I don't know how to deal with it and burst into tears. It is horrible. I would so love to cuddle up with you and forget everything around me. And yet I am so happy that at least I have your letters which keep reviving me.

Everything is horrendously expensive for you – I hope you are able to earn money. I am glad you have light and water again, it isn't easy to do without them. I can imagine how hard it is. But still, there is far worse, sadly. May fate protect you and all of us from it.

Your back will certainly get its turn, just you wait, I'll be happy for the whole man to be scrubbed with the brush, from shoulder to toe, it will be a gentle or rough scrub, depending on whether he was good or bad, until his skin turns red. I am pretty well too, although the cold at present keeps reminding me of the old rheumatic condition. I am lucky to have a warm flat. Touch wood, God grant that I can stay on here.

This afternoon Frau Salz, Frau Schultz, Frau Neumann and three other ladies are coming here. Then your ears will be burning! I shall enjoy it when they praise you, especially in front of Irene and Mutti.

Beloved, I kiss you very, very lovingly and sweetly. Just stay calm. I hug you warmly and am your own

Mitzimarie.

P.S. Hede's sister is called Grete Rudolph. She lives in Dresden. An acquaintance of hers is coming soon to Jurgo's birthplace.[78]

Karlín, 22/1/1942

My dear Ernst

Of course I hope we will soon be together, even if I still don't know how it will be made possible. I've been looking forward so long to your little speeches

---

[78]Jurgo, the Löwys' dog, was perhaps born in Prague. The acquaintance would be a German, probably in the military, and is referred to twice in March as possibly coming to Thessaloniki, but that if he does, he should be treated with caution.

about all sorts of things, we will have such an inexhaustible lot to talk about and we'll do it as we go for beautiful walks. It was always a pleasure for me to listen to you, especially when you were talking with Emmerl. I gleaned a lot then. It's strange: even though I am only averagely musical I react intensely to the voice and the way people speak. And yours always attracted me so strongly. I can't tell whether it was my liking for you which made your voice so beloved, or vice versa. In any case I could have listened to you for hours, and what a shame, my sweet, that I wasn't able to.

Next Tuesday, on the 27th, Gustav and Irene have to report. It's a bitter time and there will be a lot to worry about if we are not able to write to each other for weeks. I will not attempt to describe my pain to you. I am trying, even at the risk of appearing unfeeling again, to look brave. I won't describe all that is involved because, as you know, in certain matters I avoid all superfluous words. The worst thing is the parting from Mutti. My heart could burst when I think about Irene and Mutti. That is terribly hard and bitter. But I am going to devote myself entirely to Mutti and do all I can to care for her and take over Irene's duties. God grant that I succeed. Gustav too makes me feel deepest pity. Despite everything, my philosophy is and will remain: keep healthy, don't look either forwards or backwards, surrender yourself to fate – who knows what lies ahead. They are both very sensible and I hope we will meet again in good health. I hope they will let me stay on here. What I would do with Mutti, if I had to leave, is a tricky question. Take her with me in this bitter cold? Could hardly be done. Leave her alone here, then the little woman would collapse altogether. Well, one mustn't look too far ahead, there's no point.

23/1 The atmosphere at the Lípas' is terrible now. Nerves are at breaking point. You can hardly imagine such a situation, but it is the same for everyone. Today in *Der Neue Tag* it says that travel on the trams is restricted and off limits altogether to Jews without work and Jews under 60. I am going to get myself a doctor's note because this ban would be very hard for me.

My treasure, I must stop for today, I will write in more detail soon. I embrace you and kiss you with all my heart, my good love! Have no worries about me, I will keep living for you.

Your Mitzimarie.

4

January 1942–April 1942: Reporting for deportation

*M*arie had been preparing for her eventual deportation since October 1941. The day so long dreaded, when the first family members had to report for 'emigration', finally arrived on 27 January and Marie sketches briefly her farewell to Irene and Gustav, dwelling particularly on the kindness of young helpers from the Kultusgemeinde. It is only in a later letter that she confesses her fears for them in the little wooden shacks of the Trade Fair grounds in the Prague disctrict of Holešovice. At a temperature of minus 17, that would indeed be a shocking hardship.

Although Marie would not have been able to go beyond the entrance to this assembly point, it is possible to construct some kind of a picture of what really awaited them – and will await Marie herself in three months' time – from a vivid description given by Melissa Müller and Reinhard Piechocki. They recount what happened to Alice Herz-Sommer and her family when they were summoned to report to the Trade Fair grounds nearly fifteen months after Marie, in July 1943. The system may have been fine-tuned by then but it is likely that the processing to which Irene and Gustav, followed by Marie and finally by her mother, were subject was in all essentials very similar. With their transport and deportee numbers hanging round their necks they entered the building: 'The hall was a wooden exhibition shack, gloomy, ramshackle and unheated. Rain seeped through the ceiling. [They] stood in a long queue *which had formed before the "registry". This consisted of five tables behind which officials from the Jewish Community Organisation* [i.e. the Kultusgemeinde] *were sitting dealing with bureaucratic formalities under the watchful eyes of SS guards.' They were allocated beds with 'filthy, worn-out, dusty straw-filled sacks' which in due course turned out to be filled with fleas, bed-bugs or lice. Then began the long process of queueing at each of the five registry tables. At the first of these the key to their flat, duly recorded and labelled with their unique numbers, was confiscated, at the second ration cards were taken in, at the third an eight-page declaration of possessions had to be handed over, while at the fourth table valuables – gold, silver and jewellery – had to be surrendered and people's possessions were searched, resulting in a beating for anyone caught trying to hide anything of value. At the final table their certificate of citizenship – something Marie said she was so proud to possess – was cancelled, thus making a reality of their expulsion from normal civil society.*

Early on the third day they were lined up and had to

stand up straight for hours in the courtyard of the exhibition complex, and several old people collapsed and were carried away on stretchers. At last the order was given to move forwards to the nearby suburban railway station [Praha-Bubny] *under the watchful eyes of Czech policemen and members of the SS. In the order of their code numbers, fifty to sixty people at a time crammed into each of the railway trucks. It was almost three hours before the train was ready to depart.*[i]

At Bohušovice, three kilometres from Theresienstadt, the train stopped and the prisoners, with up to 50 kilos of luggage, had to struggle the rest of the way on foot.

Heda Margolius offers a very personal description of this introduction to Hell:

The scene in the Trade Fair Hall overwhelmed us. Our nerves were stretched to breaking point. Several of the severely ill, brought there on stretchers, died that morning. There were women screaming in sheer hysteria – a Mrs Taussig tore her dentures from her mouth and threw them at our lord and master,

Obersturmbannführer Fiedler.[1] *She raved for several hours until the sounds she made were no longer human. There were small children and babies, too, weeping ceaselessly, while next to us a short, fat man with a shiny bald head sat on his suitcase as if it did not concern him at all, playing Beethoven's concerto in D major on a violin, practising the difficult passages over and over again.*[ii]

Karlín, Tuesday 27/1/1942

My dearest

Yesterday your letters of the 16th and 19th arrived and they came at the right moment. Today I accompanied my good Irene and Gusti. Their numbers are 135 and 136Y.[2] Oh Ernstili, the last eight days, which I have spent entirely at the Lípas', were hard and difficult and the immediate future won't be nice. We must now grit our teeth and continue to deal with life firmly and with courage. I must now concentrate on supporting my poor old mother as best I can; it is particularly hard for her. Irene was the best and most gentle child to her, I don't think I will be able to take her place completely in everything. I can only be very gentle and loving when people don't hurt me. If they do, it frightens me off and I withdraw into myself. My intentions are good and I will truly try to give her everything. But in no way will I stay here all the time. I will stay at home now and again, that will definitely have some good sides to it. There are two families renting here and then there is a 52-year-old cook. Besides, nobody knows what will happen next. Now that Irene has gone I don't mind at all if I have to leave, it's only the question of Mother that would be complicated. In any case, one should never plan for what will happen in the near future, it usually turns out differently from what one thinks.

---

[1]Johann (Hans) Fidler (or Fiedler) (*1913) was a member of the Prague *Zentralstelle* in charge of organizing deportations from Prague and from the provinces. He escaped from Prague before the end of the war.

[2]These are the numbers which they were allocated on the transport to Theresienstadt and which remained their detainee numbers while they were there.

It has been very cold, we had a lot of snow and 25 degrees of frost. Today it is −17, the electricity was cut off, with all that follows, but it is now partially restored. I'm not allowed to use the tram any more, but I'm going to get myself a doctor's note and I hope I will get permission then. The gaping hole in the family is an open wound, I need not say more. I can't describe my pain to you today, I will do it when I am alone with you in my flat. But I will tell you one thing, my sweet, not for one moment, even in my greatest pain, do I forget that I am yours and will be and I shall look after myself for your sake. So don't be anxious, I will cope and I am at the same time confident and hopeful that I will see them again. They have the wish and courage to live, they are healthy and strong, they wish to work and to hold out, so let's hope we will see each other again soon. How happy I am that you have been spared many things, the restrictions you describe are unimportant compared with other troubles and torments. The main thing is for things to stay as they are, life has become 'boring' everywhere, but boredom is better than fear, horror and uncertainty. Irene and Gustav sent you warmest greetings, those were almost their last words when we parted.

Ernstili, you would have been so delighted if you had seen how kind and good friends were at this sad time, what sacrifices and friendships they offered. And the young people too. The *Kultusgemeinde* has organized an emergency service.[3] Young men, youths from 14 to 30 years, girls too, from every level of society, work day and night to make life easier for those affected and all for free. They fetch the luggage and the things one would have to carry oneself and carry it on their back. So this morning at five o'clock there were three men and a 20-year-old girl at the door. As if it was quite a matter of course the young woman, wearing a headscarf against the heavy drizzle, carried off a heavy rucksack and suitcase and when they arrived others were doing the same work. I was amazed when I saw the helpfulness and humanity and thought to myself: really, if there are young people such as these growing up, the older generation has nothing to fear for the future. Friend Taussig and his wife were there; in the last week they came

---

[3]The *Kultusgemeinde* was tasked with the smooth execution of the deportation, including the securing of the Jews' property.

every day and sat for hours and helped and worked. They did so much for my family, almost everything. Herr Robert too and also a woman from the neighbourhood called Neugeboren.

I can hardly describe to you how kind people have been, it is really a great comfort for people in distress and balm on the open wound. About three-quarters of a year ago Taussig was in a bad way. Gustav could have done a lot for him but he was mean spirited and didn't do it, although he had always been a good friend to him before. Taussig was very bitter about it and told me about it and I shared his opinion. But now Taussig rewarded his friend for this meanness with the most generous loyalty and friendship. I will always just tell you the naked truth, never more nor less than is true. I think I will have things sorted in two months and [you] will be here in my home where it is lovely and warm and cosy.

In my next letter I will answer some more points from your last one. I kiss you tenderly and am your

Mitzimarie

Karlín, 28/1/1942

My dearest

My letter yesterday was incomplete. I know that there is a lot I didn't answer so today I will continue. We're having a hard, cold winter. Snow, hard frost and everywhere it is very cold, often in homes too. It is no joke for my poor Irene in her shed. My heart bleeds for them both. They will not be leaving until Saturday. Mutti and I are in deep sadness, almost as if, God save us, there had been a death. You can just imagine. Mutti moans and groans half the night, waking up is dreadful. Unfortunately Gustav is much to blame because he created this fate for himself and my sister through his obstinacy. Pray God nothing happens to him, he has suffered terribly. The last days were a heartbreaking sight. Nobody can change that, now it is a matter of bearing one's fate with wisdom and dignity. Given his financial situation, G. could have undertaken to emigrate, which people on all sides were recommending in 1938–9, but he didn't want to be parted from his money[4] and then there he was, with a rucksack, two suitcases of underwear and clothes, a roll of bedding and a suitcase of food. And that's when I got your letter about money and love of money and the way money corrupts. As you say, most people love money for its own sake and that is a mistake. One should aim to have enough to be provided for in case of illness or inability to work, so that one isn't dependent on others, but in no way should one try to take care of generations to come, that is pointless.

Continued 29/1/42

One can't finish any letter here, there's always someone coming. Today it is much warmer but none the less it is a real harsh winter. In reply to your description of black-marketeering I say the whole world seems to be one single town. Of course such a state of affairs will have to be cleaned up one of these days but who will be the victims? Punishment does not always catch up with the perpetrators of crime, often quite innocent people are the victims. Today I am asking the Red Cross in Berlin for forms so that I can write to Eman.[5]

The plan to work on the clinic must please you very much. I am proud that your doctor friend gives you the recognition you deserve and acknowledges that you are an expert in your field.

I am at the Lípas' all the time now, I don't go to [my apartment in] Karlín every day as I haven't yet got a permit to use the tram. But I will get it. I don't always have time to go on foot.

Yesterday I heard that through the *Kultusgemeinde* one can send parcels and unsealed letters to one's family who have been at the Exhibition Hall for three days. So today we sent another little parcel with rolls and sardine pâté and a little note. As I can't buy anything in the morning I had to ask other people to buy the rolls and the time went quickly.[6] But Olga is sleeping in my flat and brings me your letters the moment they arrive.

I do believe, my love, that you long to have your own home and all that that means. I do too, and above all I long for you. How good it would be if I could cry my eyes out on your chest, my heart is so sore. I could cry out like a wounded

---

[4]Marie refers to the reluctance of many Jews to emigrate at the time when it was still possible.
[5]In December 1941 USA entered the war against Germany and letters could only be sent through the Red Cross.
[6]Czech people.

animal, I feel so torn and full of pain. All day and all night I see before me the picture of my family. No, I can't do it, I can't describe it to you, it is just too painful and I think I am not allowed to either. Now my poor mother is trembling with fear that the *plumpsack* man will come for me, apparently he is going to do his rounds twice more. But I hope that he won't visit me, that he won't be particularly interested in me. And if he did, I wouldn't mind very much now that Irene has already gone. I would take Mutti with me and I tell myself everything ends some time. Despite all the sorrow it brings, there are worse things: death, incurable diseases, etc. Yes, it has happened that people have spent years in prison and then lived on as happy people, so it's a matter of being strong minded. As far as I am concerned I don't mind spending a few months in discomfort, but for my relatives, who tumbled so suddenly out of their warm nest, people who were always helpful and good, I am bitterly sad, and especially for my good Irene. I tell myself that she is healthy, she has already experienced plenty of good and beautiful things in her life, she will, she must survive this period of trial which fate has landed on her, and he too, I hope. May God help and preserve them. In all events, it is a heavy blow, and an evil stroke for me, but it is not against any one individual but against a whole mass of people. So I can't ask for any special favours but must just say to myself that what happens to others I too must put up with.

30/1/42

So today they left and my poor little mother cries and wails so that a stone would take pity on her. I am rushing around, there is always a lot to do. You must not worry about me in any sort of way, my dearest. I am always careful to make myself look as good as I can, remembering your wishes, and keep trying to do all I can. I can't put right the wrongs done by others, I can only try to ease I. and G.'s lot and get some relief through that. Now I am doing all I can to keep Mutti going. Will I succeed?

I am thinking about your week. We will keep being selfish and live for each other, our life together and our future. I keep imagining our reunion and seeing each other again, and then I am as strong as iron, I stretch up tall and say 'And yet, despite everything, the day of our reunion will come.' A thousand sweet loving kisses.

Utterly, utterly yours,

Mitzimarie

Karlín, 3/2/1942

My most dearly beloved

Today, Tuesday, I was sure I would have news from you because it is already eight days since your last letters arrived. But we know there are hold-ups and we must be patient. I am writing to you again just so as to give you a sign of life at this particular time. It is already a week since our loved ones left us. A bitter, anxious time. The grief that has settled on us is impossible to describe, tormenting Mutti especially. I do all I can, am patient and forbearing, and give myself up to her as much as possible. Thank God I feel myself strong enough to control my nerves, only occasionally, exceptionally, I too am shaken by deepest grief and by fear for my good sister.

It is still proper winter, a lot of snow and frost, the temperature has already dropped. The smell of snow is in the air, fresh and healthy and I remember how lovely the walk to Leonhard[7] was on days like this. Where has the time gone? And will it ever come again?

How are you dealing with the food problem? I can't help it, I am worried and very much afraid that you are suffering deprivation. A little while ago I read that order had been restored with you and that food distribution was under control.

It is two years now since our correspondence began, Ernstili. Do you realize? My thoughts are with you all the time too now, especially when I can gather them together in the evening and at night. Then I am entirely with you. During the day I can't live my own life much. There are always errands to do, and I can no longer put together a letter like I used to send you. I am constantly being interrupted and disturbed. I can only concentrate in my flat, when I am alone.

The Lípas' room has been closed off, the key handed in.[8] It is in darkness and feels strange. I am living with Mutti in one room, we put a camp bed up in the evening. Every other day I go to my flat, where Olga is living. She has

---

[7]Leonhard was a café in the woods near Karlsbad.
[8]They handed it over in the Radiomarkt at the Trade Fair Grounds near the exhibition hall when reporting to the transport.

promised to bring me your letters as soon as they come. As one doesn't know how things will be in the near future, I won't change the address for my letters for now. We share the use of the bathroom, sitting room and kitchen with the other occupants of the flat.

Is it warmer for you now? The milder weather must be beginning for you by now. I remember how we used to look for wild daffodils already at this time of year.

Oh my treasure, what would I give to be able to curl up in your arms at last! Now especially I could really do with that. I will stop for today, because I keep being interrupted. I will write to you again from my flat.

Farewell good, dear love, greet your loved ones for me, a loving embrace and a thousand kisses from

Your Mitzimarie.

Karlín, 5/2/1942

My dearest

Today I can draw breath and I want to use the free time while I am alone (Mutti is out visiting) to chat with you. So, I can give you the good news that the *plumpsack* man ignored me and that now he is going to take a rest for about six weeks and go to the provinces.[9] I forgive him for not paying me a visit but now I am going to get busy preparing finally for the time after the six weeks, because I think that then he will come to see me too. Then I will take Mutti with me. She looks so bad, I can't imagine leaving her with strangers and I think to myself that it makes no difference. She would be better doing without various things with us and just sharing our life, even at the risk of it not suiting her, which is indeed very likely. But for now it is better not to plan and worry about what is still two months away, because today two months is a very long time.

---

[9]Deportation from Pilsen (Plzeň) took place in January 1942 and from Kladno in February 1942. Deportation from the second largest community in the Protectorate, Brno in Moravia, started already in November 1941 and continued, with minor breaks, until April 1942.

If I could describe to you everybody's agitation your hair would stand on end. (Have you still got some? Don't be cross, I would like a bald head too!) Everyone is worrying about their present fate and that of their family, friends and acquaintances. And when it is the turn of a family, then friends come but also strangers and help with packing and baking and give presents and advice and try to get through the difficult time. I would also like to help others now, in what free time I have. A service to help people has been set up which, if necessary, works night and day, and then there are individuals who are always there at the right moment just when they are needed. My friends, the Taussigs, for example, are fantastic people who excel themselves in their self-denial and humanity and love for their fellow beings. When fate summons them, most people are incapable from that moment of doing anything properly. It is as if they were paralysed, one moment they are brave, the next in despair. It keeps changing. And very few stand above it and accept things as they are.

People from our home town have left: both the Schiffler couples, three Schwartz brothers, many, many more. In Karlsbad the conductor Manzer has died.[10]

The rest of the letter is missing.

No date, but filed after the letter of 5 February 1942. Earlier page(s) missing.

… … I love what you write about the children. Bubi sounds as if he is the very picture of you! I imagine Mädi as already a young lady. I would certainly devote a lot of time to them, that would be great fun.

I have a sister-in-law and two nephews in Brno. The latter are employed at the *J[üdische] K[ultus]G[gemeinde]* so it is likely that they will leave later than the rest.[11] Their address: Fredy Kessler, Brno, Adlergasse 7.

---

[10]The Schifflers were the parents and other relatives of Edith's good friend Stella. Robert Manzer, a Sudeten German, was the father of Edith's other good friend, Litti. He conducted the Karlsbad Symphony Orchestra and Edith was very fond of him. He died in Salzburg.

[11]Rosa Kessler and her sons Fredy and Walter were in fact deported to Theresienstadt on 8 April 1942, in the last major transport from Brno (as members of the *Kultusgemeinde*). Rosa died later in Treblinka, while her sons were deported to Rejowiec, a transit ghetto near the Bełżec extermination camp, on 18 April 1942. They did not survive the war.

Photo 16 *Ernst Löwy with his grand-children Erika and Heinz.*

Frau Hede Sternschuss will write to you. I've sent you her address. My friend Olga knows all about my situation. If I left and she was still here she would also write to you but who knows which one of us will go first.[12] I also have some good friends here: Emil Taussig, Prague X, Rokycanová no. 1. If they are still

---

[12]Olga Loewenstein was deported from Prague to Theresienstadt on 2 July 1942 and onwards to Maly Trostenets near Minsk (now in Belarus) on 14 July 1942.

here when I have left, Herr T. will be the best one to tell you everything that he knows.[13]

Up to now there has been no news either from Łódź or from Irene, except for one card from the Lípas with five words, that is why I am warning you to expect a break in the correspondence and not to worry. They can't make any exceptions, and those who abide by the rules will eventually return alive and well to their families.[14] I am resolutely determined to do so. Everything I have written here is all just in case. Nobody knows yet who will draw the long or the short straw in the coming weeks.

My treasure, do all you can to amuse yourself, don't ruin that life of yours which is so precious and dear to me, even if there is no news for a few days.

I say farewell, may we see each other soon and happily.

Your Mitzimarie

Karlín, 14/2/1942

My dearest

Today I am in my flat again and I am alone, so I can talk with you in peace and enjoy this time to recover. I keep re-reading your letter of the 6th. Unfortunately I can't answer everything as I would like to. Are you really so naïve, talking about coming to visit? That really makes me shake my head. It's different in the case of your hope for the peace which will come and will bring us together. Yes, I am completely of your opinion on that and it is only this hope which gives me the strength and courage to struggle on with this bleak and dismal existence.

Life with Mutti is filled with petty, trivial activities which I really detest. I would never have let myself get involved in them if things had been different. But now it means almost nothing to me, at most it irritates me now and again

---

[13]Emil and Käthe Taussig were deported on 10 June 1942 directly from Prague to Ujazdów, in the so-called punishment transport after the assassination of Heydrich by Czech and Slovak paratroopers sent from London.

[14]Did Marie know about the first executions in Theresienstadt? On 10 January 1942, nine Jewish prisoners were hanged in Theresienstadt. They were accused of breaking the ghetto laws or contacting their relatives in the Protectorate.

but nothing more. She still sees me as her child of long ago and just like Gustav and Irene, she doesn't completely trust my ideas. Only when other people who are less involved give their approval is she ready to do something or other that I suggest. You can imagine how this annoys me. But nobody is allowed to interfere in my affairs. Gustav and Irene have unfortunately had to pay dearly for many things so I am not going to abandon myself to grief, but will remain selfish. I do want to remain at least half way human, externally too, for you, my sweet, for us for when we are together one day.

The cold spell has broken but the wintry weather continues. Today I am going to talk to Hede's sister Grete, perhaps she will be able to give Jurgscheit[15] what is needed. I hope she will now make an effort because I wouldn't be in a position to do so.

I can now write to Gustav and Irene. One is allowed to write 30 words in capital letters, that's a fine task! It is sweet of you to save for Gustav but he won't be able to smoke now, as far as I know. He already had to get used to doing without.

My beloved, it will be our own special thing not to let ourselves be pulled down by everyday things and keep enough time for each other. I also intend to be loving to those around me, to all my fellow humans, as far as that is at all possible.

I wrote to you that I got the permit for the tram, it is even for an unlimited period, isn't that fine?

(The lower part of the page has been torn off)

… … … Nothing has come so far from Irene. But several families have already had cards from Theresienstadt. However, those who sent them have been there a lot longer than Irene.

I had a happy experience in the last few days, one which gave me a glimpse of hope for the future. I will tell you in due course. You know that Emmerl, and since his death, I, had good friends in our business who valued our honesty and fairness. Because I did my duty by them, even from here, they recently remembered me after a gap of 1½ years, in the nicest way. People still know about my 'competence', my 'skills', and I will receive a visit shortly. I am really

---

[15]Jurgscheit was a German soldier billetted on the Cougnos.

curious what it is about. In fact I can almost guess already. But I will remain without work, as it must be for now.

My sweet, it is so lovely of you to picture so beautifully my being together with my family again. Yes, of course, I hope that my dear children will be kind and good, as they always were but in fact I am expecting even more from you, almost my whole expectation rests on you.

There is no more room so, what now? Quick, onto your knee. I hug you till you can't breathe, press you close and with love and kiss you more and more passionately. In deepest love, your Mitzimarie.

Sheet 2, without a date. Possibly 23/02/1942

… … Despite that, my Ernstili, don't worry. I know what I owe to you, to myself and to the children. I never forget my external appearance and do all I can to keep myself presentable because I believe in our happy future which will bring us all together again. You sense (I absolutely know that) how important the fate of my loved ones is to me, I can feel that. But on the other hand, I think to myself that I am not doing any good to anyone if I make myself ill. On the contrary, if I can keep myself fit it can only be an advantage for each one of them. Of course there are hours, or moments, when the pain is very sharp but on the whole I try very hard to bear things as the times demand.

24/2

Today I am still at home, but nothing has come from you yet. And yet the channels must be open because friends of mine received a letter yesterday from Turkey. On Friday I am expecting Emil.

This afternoon I even played bridge with my ladies but I can still find no real peace, as you can imagine. Yesterday I had such a beautiful dream about you. That is always my loveliest time when I escape the constant sorrow. We were both having a rest on the sofa after the meal. I was listening to you snoring with amusement. Afterwards both of us said it was the other who had been snoring. It turned into a real physical tussle and we had great fun.

Stay healthy, keep cheerful, dearest hugs and kisses from

Your Mitzimarie

Prague, 1/3/1942

My most dearly beloved

Please forgive me this paper[16] and the less than perfect presentation. My own paper has run out and, as always when I am particularly longing for you, I want to get close by writing to you.

But, since what I now want above all is to mean something to you, meaning that I want to appear in your eyes as I really feel and think, and now that I know, since we declared our love, that you understand me as no other person does, then you too must understand how strong your love and the bond between us make me, how it is that I am able to bear the burdens of existence. It is a bit as if somebody who was drowning was being drawn towards the river bank, spurred on repeatedly to find new strength.

Hede and her mother are glad that the Rudolfs' friend comes frequently.

If you should meet our nephew (Thesa's husband[17]), then please tell him the following: he should not have any ideas about going to be near his beloved. She would not deserve such a sacrifice, nor would she want it. I myself strongly advise him against it, it would be pure madness. It makes no difference any more whether he is without work for a few more months, he should just enjoy the free time. When his beloved one day becomes his wife she will make plenty of demands on him and keep him busy, so he should just sit pretty for now and enjoy his bachelorhood. It is better than jumping into the fire or into the waiting arms of his beloved. Obviously my opinion is well considered and based on the advice of people who are well known, not only to myself, but also to our nephew. And he should not be annoyed about this; it can't be any other way. He is my favourite nephew and I have only his best interests at heart. I will bear full responsibility for my conviction and will give him a complete account of it. His beloved will know how to take care of herself in the meantime; she has good friends and advisers. It is more important that our nephew looks after himself for her and for a later time; then his wife will need him far more in all domains, I am quite sure of that.

---

[16]The letter is written on Gustav Lípa's old business notepaper.
[17]Marie is deliberately obfuscating again. She means Ernst himself.

She has an enormous amount of work to do which she will only be able to do with her husband.

Robert [Steininger] was able to stay because he had a church marriage and his children were born from that marriage. Emil, too, should it prove necessary, has the same advantage.

Your bald patch was not very big. I always wondered if I could treat it with some cream but I was careful not to mention this wish because of Thesa's jealous nature; I knew that that would be the end of our meetings. My treasure, it was beautiful, our journey to Leipzig that time, do you still think of it? I felt so safe in your care.

What you say about mortality applies entirely in our circles too, nobody takes any notice when people they know, or relatives, die, whether their death is natural or unnatural. This afternoon (Saturday) I am going with Mutti to Hulda's. Lydie is there too. The latter has a tear in her wound because she could not take a rest after the operation. She has lost a lot of weight, has no income from her shop, nor is she allowed to let it, so she is miserable. Her brothers can't send anything either now, you know that of course. Spirits are very low.

My good one! I dreamt today that we will soon be together. Be brave still and think of me when nature opens up in all her beauty. I am determined to experience that with you.

Most lovingly, your Mitzimarie.

P.S. No news yet from sister and brother-in-law. We are expecting it any minute but apparently they are well, everything has improved. Mutti is still full of trouble and torment and worry.

Karlín, 5/3/1942

My most dearly beloved

It is always my greatest joy when, as today, I spend a few hours in my cell, gathering myself together, and then, then, when I come out, I find a letter from you waiting for me.

Two days ago I asked Karel to send the application so that we can get consent for the wedding as quickly as possible. I think he will have done it already, as agreed. Of course I made enquiries beforehand and took advice and, after thinking it over, I came to the conclusion that, at present, nothing unfavourable will happen at this end either. As soon as the formalities are completed, and hopefully I will still be here – one can never be quite sure – we will get married at once.

I am very sorry that you are again without news of me. It must be because of my unclear handwriting. I don't understand Jan and his tactics; I very much regret the affair. I hope that Horst[18] will give you a full account. Unfortunately, we still have no news [from Irene and Gustav] and that worries and saddens me greatly. It is a matter of chance because the cards [from Theresienstadt] are lying here in boxloads but only 20 to 30 are delivered each day. But when one keeps hearing that this or that person has received a card you can imagine all sorts of things. Mutti has not improved at all either; sometimes it is almost impossible to put up with it, to see and to listen to her. She works off her anxiety on me, pestering and annoying me with petty matters and I find that very hard to put up with. My head is so full of big and weighty worries, why should I be tormented with bagatelles?

You are only allowed to write 30 words to Leopold,[19] in BLOCK CAPITALS. The address too, and also the name and address of the sender must be in block capitals. On the left side of the card, where the address is, enough space must be left for the censor's stamp. It is … … …

The rest of the page has been torn off by the censor

You can hardly guess, beloved, how happy I am that you are confident, and deep down, at the bottom of my heart, I firmly share that confidence. The present time, the comings and goings are hideous, my surroundings and everything connected with it. One never hears anything cheerful or happy any more. We too have miserable, slushy weather, constant snow, which turns to dirt. I am probably going to get involved here and there with the social welfare service, because I was asked to do so by some ladies. In particular for the sake of a Prague lady (Jewish),[20] who has asked me to do it and who is very nice to

---

[18]Horst's identity is not known, but he may be the person referred to in the previous letter as 'the Rudolfs' friend'.

[19]Leopold Steininger (*1856) was deported from Pilsen to Theresienstadt in January 1942. He was murdered in Treblinka in October 1942.

[20]A reference to Mrs Isa Strauss, referred to by name in the first letter of 18 April 1942. She is the mother of Grete's friend Käthe Brock-Strauss.

me. So, on Sunday I will go to a tea party for poor children and on Monday to a session of the assistance section of the social welfare service.[21] There are so many abandoned people (old) etc., then there are children, sick people and everyone should do something [to help]. I want to as well. When you talk about a visit to the café it sounds so strange, as if from another world. May God keep that all for you!

So take comfort, my good one, I have a goal unswervingly before my eyes and it is: to possess you completely. Utterly yours,

Mitzimarie

Received 9 March

An earlier page of this letter is missing, presumably removed by the censor.

Page 2

… ….Up to now, we can eat our fill of bread, we get 1.5 kg of bread a week and one roll a day on account, and 2 kg of flour a month.

The weather here is still wintry, but the blackbirds are already starting to sing and soon spring will arrive here too. Only in people's hearts no spring can enter because everywhere there dwells grief and discord, sorrow and worry.

So Jurgscheit has gone. Oh well, he's no exception to the rule. Have you found a replacement? And how is it that you have had so many guests lately? Do you have to sacrifice your comfort? I hope not. Leave Jan alone, if he is as you describe; in those circumstances let's not bother about the various bits and pieces.

On Saturday a card finally arrived from Irene with 27 words. She is well and in good spirits, asks about Mutti's eyes, and is already working. Her address is: Transport 'V', number 136, Theresienstadt, Hamburger Kaserne, room 158. Frau I. L. Gusti is number 135, Transport 'V', Ther[esienstadt]. Please to God that they can stay there and not have to move on. I would also like to see or

---

[21]The *Kultusgemeinde* was in charge of the social welfare system for the Jewish community (Reichsprotektor's decree of 5 August 1941). It is unclear whether Marie helped with the *Kultusgemeinde* welfare system, or if this was a private initiative.

hear something from Gusti. Always these frightening worries and anxieties, whether now about G. and I, or about one's own fate; yes things have changed. Thank God that I feel so in control of myself; I never used to before. And whom should I thank for that? You, of course!

You need have no worries about our provisions. We simply have meals without meat five times a week; at lunchtime a vegetable soup, then a vegetable and potatoes or, instead of vegetables, a dish made from potatoes, but all nicely prepared. We don't cook with butter at all and only a little with fat, we just use margarine, but we have a proper breakfast, teatime and a modest proper supper. We have no fruit; there is none for us and we don't miss it at all. Our meat ration is enough for two midday meals; we use our smoked meat rations to help out. So you mustn't think that we are lacking anything so far. And I have plenty of practice at being careful to stretch things out. So don't you worry either. If I could only do what I would like to do. What hurts and saddens me is that I can't send anything at all to Irene, that is what is the most urgent, but sadly I can't help.

Now I want to tell you what I was asked for. A company, quite a big one, which ignored my existence for the last year and a half, wrote to me recently. One of the bosses begged me to let him know whether he could visit me. He asked for my advice on setting up a company to manufacture EBE products. It was the firm I offered everything to three and a half years ago, but at the time they refused. And now? A letter came, larded with compliments about the quality and reputation of these products (Fox and Crow[22]) and at the end they came to the point: they were interested in getting the recipes, information, advice etc. And I? I wrote that, owing to changed family circumstances, I was unable to receive him, in his own interest. If you can't understand this please ask me, but I believe you will understand why I have behaved as I did.

Today I was at a meeting of the social welfare service. Women are doing a great deal there. I too would like to add my small contribution.

I kiss you lovingly and will write a second letter.

Your Mitzimarie.

---

[22] A reference to the Æsop fable, where the fox flatters the crow, encouraging it to sing, so that it will drop the food it holds in the beak.

Prague, 12/3/1942

My dearest

I have been carrying Emil's letter to you in my pocket for a week. In this letter he tells you about an acquaintance who, like you, was wounded in the World War and had similar honours and because of this he is able to continue his career as sales representative and perhaps may also be allowed to stay here.[23] Emil was glad to be able to let you know that, and when I had thought it over long enough and taken the advice of others, I left the letter here and thought I wouldn't send it. It was a crazy idea of Emil's and mine and we should be sensible and not crazy.[24] Now I would like to have news of Gusti. People are going from there to the Ashkenazis again and everybody is trembling once more for their loved ones.[25] One can no longer free oneself from fear and worry. And it is supposed to start again here as well but I don't care. I have become indifferent to it. Unfortunately one is not allowed to send Irene and Gusti the smallest thing. I tell you, my treasure, I am at a loss for words when I think about them. My mother is still unhappy and doesn't want to go outside any more, she only does so briefly, she doesn't play bridge either, doesn't enjoy her friends' visits at all, and you know, with her, that means a lot. Yes, she was simply a mother her whole life long and she can't cope with this blow. Well, I hope she will find a little courage. Tomorrow I am going with her to the doctor because she is complaining so much about her head, so that he can give her some medicine.

(Continued the next day) Today I had a letter from Karel and I wanted to tell you about it. When there was still no signature on the declaration, new men joined the office which deals with decisions about marriage permits and they demand all sorts of proof, how, why, etc., and also your new certificate of

---

[23]Marie believes that decorated war veterans would be treated differently from the rest of the Jewish community. According to the Nazi propaganda, those from Germany were sent to the 'model ghetto' or 'spa' in Theresienstadt.

[24]Emil appears to be suggesting that, because of his First World War record, Ernst may be able to return and remain in the Protectorate.

[25]Marie was soon aware that people were deported from Theresienstadt further to the East (to Occupied Poland).

citizenship; in a word there are difficulties now which weren't there before. I agreed with Karel that he should just do what he could.

The doctor found that Mutti weighed 59 kg unclothed and that her blood pressure was 250, so that's not very good. She is to go back in a week; he gave her bromoral. Now I really have to laugh. Mutti has given me her plan for tomorrow, what other baking she wants to do. I say to her 'Yes, you have your worries' and she: 'Everyone has their worries, you have love worries and I have hunger worries.' That is absolutely her, I had to laugh a lot, this once after so long. I am doing a lot of running around, I can't find any peace, I go here and there, look up friends and acquaintances. I also travel almost daily to Karlín to check up on things and I still have my usual shops there.

Tomorrow Grete Rudolph is coming to visit me. It was she who had the idea that her friend should visit you. I am very curious.

Treasure, my beloved, you only ever write very little about yourself now. I beg you, write to me about everything, don't spare me, because I want to be your trusted friend. And you mustn't think that I have enough [to deal with] anyway and that you have to be considerate. It isn't how you think. God made me strong, I bear a lot with a certain calm and steadfastness, see it as the fate of a multitude of people, a piece of history, even if very grave history. But history moves on and I tell myself to keep my nerve, hold out, stay strong and brave, so that I'll be able to live with the others, above all with you in happy times. That is always before me, that is why I won't let myself be so easily pushed under and it is why I should know everything about you and [help you] deal with it. It is your life, and the kind of life you have, which is uppermost in my mind.

Are you having nothing but sunshine now? This morning we had minus 15 degrees again, there was a proper frost; it is a hard, long winter this year. When will the work in the vineyard start? If I were there I would like to have hens, that would be a pleasure, because a fresh egg today is a very precious treasure. We're allowed four a month, but up to now we have only had two per person, the rest are to come. I have still got some preserved ones but they are to bring to you.

100 g parcels are now allowed through the military *feldpost* but only in the most urgent cases. Everybody wants to try it but are unsure whether things will arrive. This feeling of powerlessness all around is very bitter.

And now I am going to bed. I kiss you tenderly and fall asleep a happy woman. Most lovingly yours,

Mitzmarie

Karlín, 16/3/1942

My dearest

Again in my flat for half a day because I was expecting the maid and I also invited Emil here today. So now I am cooking here: pea soup, dumplings, that is all. I received your letter of the 6th. If I think that in a little while – four to six weeks – it is perhaps possible that our correspondence will have to cease entirely, then I feel really dreadful.

I read with great pleasure that you are always careful to eat when you are hungry. Few people have the courage to part with their money, even when they surely know that the money can't be of any use to them in the near future because they will soon have no opportunity to go shopping. Mutti is one of these and it often irritates me. That is why I sometimes regret my decision to live completely there with her but I can't change it now. I beg you, my beloved, to sacrifice the last penny for your well-being and not to think what may be later. I am quite sure we will not die of hunger, if we are allowed to work. So don't worry, don't save up for that time.

Don't offer too much to Hede Rudolph's friend, despite the friendship and family ties; it is always best to measure out one's kindness, my sweet.[26]

I very much regret that my letters sound discontented and out of sorts. I really don't want that. In the meantime a card came from Irene – did I already write that? She is well and in the place where she lives there is supposed to be running water and central heating (apparently) and once a week a bath. That makes me very, very glad. That will be all right for a while. Nothing has come from Gusti. Unfortunately one doesn't know who has travelled on in the meantime, but one must always hope for the best.

Up to now, beloved, I have done everything one can ask for my well-being. I have the basic essentials, like a healthy place to live, the ability to care for my

---

[26]Is Horst 100 per cent trustworthy?

physical needs and a decent kitchen. Nevertheless, the mental anguish which every family has, sorrow wherever one looks and listens, is unavoidable. I am still envied by everyone for how well I look. Recently I have lost a lot of weight and apparently it suits me very well. I feel fit, of course I often don't sleep for hours, falling asleep is particularly difficult. I stretch out comfortably on my bed and then I think of [Gusti and Irene]. With my lively imagination you can just picture it. Then I quickly have to think of you and of the time ahead of us, and a happy smile spreads over my face.

It must be dreadful for you, your few words say a great deal.[27] What I would want to say to you would sound as if I didn't care, because I can't explain it in a letter as I would like. Let me just say one thing to you, Ernstili. We are experiencing enough sadness with our family and friends, that is why we shouldn't let the fate of those around us touch us too nearly. You too, my sweet, must not let yourself be overcome by grief, you too must keep thinking just of yourself and then of me – think of us first of all. What use is grief if one can't help? One always helps better when one has strong nerves. Besides I have noticed that the majority of people have no interest at all in the fate of their fellow humans, they aren't interested in listening. I have sworn to myself I will likewise be indifferent.

I took it for granted, dearest, that you snore. That is a part of you. Yes, I snore sometimes, apparently. So you can look forward to that! But you can always wake me up if it disturbs you. So you be healthy, full of hope and confidence, don't worry, everything will turn out well. In deepest love,

Your Mitzimarie

Karlín, 20/3/1942

My dearest

The approaching spring has made me a gift of a nasty catarrh or flu. I am supposed to stay inside. So yesterday, assuming that the letter I was hoping for

---

[27]Probably a reference to the severe famine in Greece.

from you would be there, I lied and cheated and toddled off home on wobbly legs and lo and behold! The letter was a delight. So I read it and was happy, undressed quickly and got into my own bed. Three hours later I went back and managed all right. Today I already feel much better.

A few days ago I had a delightful dream. The reason it was so beautiful was that everything was so lifelike and I saw you before me as if you were quite real. Picture it, my sweet. First of all, I was in Karlsbad in a bank and by chance you were there too. There was a mistake and you joined in the conversation with an official. You helped me to explain the error, and then I left. After a while you followed and said to me 'I can't see why we should stand so far apart, come with me now.' Without a word I took your arm and went with you. And then – we were both very young and you were laughing, bright, merry and entertaining – you began to kiss me so lovingly and gently and I let you do it and waited for you to hug me tight. You didn't do so out of consideration and I was quite surprised (but didn't say so). The dream went no further but when I woke up I was quite radiant, the dream had made me so happy. Beautiful, isn't it?

I can imagine how scarce things are if you walk four hours to get bread. My God, how bitter it is to know this, and that one can't help each other. My love, I am really proud of you, that, touch wood, you can walk so far but you must not overstrain yourself. After a walk like that one has to have a good meal and is that what happens? And when you live in the vineyard, of course the quiet will be restful, but – don't be angry – I really wouldn't like to think of you there alone. Please, my good one, don't stay there alone overnight. One never knows what might happen, especially at present.

As you will already have read in an earlier letter, the wedding can't yet take place because they still want various things which wouldn't have been needed in November. I am waiting for news about this from Karel and will send it on to you.

Your description of the blossoming of nature is beautiful and I can imagine it all vividly. If only I could enjoy all the beauties with you! I will be almost as much deprived of them as Irene and Gustav because I must obey the regulations.

Today my brother-in-law Karl[28] and his wife are also travelling to Irene or somewhere else, who knows? And shortly also Emmerl's sister and nephews,[29] all, every one, from their town.

I hug you tightly and kiss you most lovingly.

Your Mitzimarie.

23/3/1942

Olga Löwenstein
Prague XII
Sleszká 26

My most dearly beloved

Your letter of the 16th already arrived today; it is an unexpected joy not to wait in vain. Your letter of the 11th came 2 days earlier than your card of the 11th, isn't that funny? I haven't received any other cards at all recently.[30]

Tell me, my sweet, if it won't be on my birthday, then will it be on yours that we meet again? Or not that either? Please be truthful. I don't know where I will be by then. Probably not here any more. But we won't try to look ahead because it is pointless. Emmerl's home area will be completely 'free'[31] in a week, I think. Irene will certainly be very glad to have news from you, poor thing. Are you in correspondence with Ulli? I would like to send him her address some time. Think what would be best.

The Relief Committee was supporting various people with gifts from Portugal but it doesn't seem to have been possible to find a way of reaching

---

[28]Karl Bader and his wife Frieda were deported from Brno to Theresienstadt in March 1942 and soon they continued to Lublin, and from there to Siedliszcze or Ossowa in Poland on 9 May (none of the 999 deported survived). These were transit stations for Treblinka and Sobibór. The Baders were most likely murdered in Sobibór.
[29]Rosa Kessler and her sons Fredy and Walter (see footnote 11, letter filed after 5 February).
[30]She is indicating that she has had no further communication from Irene and Gustav.
[31]Referring to Brno, Marie uses the word 'frei' (free). The Nazis used the expression 'judenfrei' meaning free of Jews.

Irene, only Ashkenazi, I believe. Ulli works with the Committee.[32] Alois and Emil are well. It is the first time that I have heard one can't write from [where Irene is], or do you know more than I do? Probably. I don't often have a newspaper. Can you buy whatever papers you want? I'm sure you can or I hope so. It would be bitter if we could not write to each other. I keep thinking about the time a year ago when it wasn't possible. In any case, you will have taken note of Hede's address, Beethovenstrasse 33, Prague II. She will know all about me and will at some point be able to tell you exactly.

When I wrote to you last time about what we get as rations, I didn't know that there was a revision on the way and it is severe. We have enough bread but only twelve rolls a month, very little flour. I'm not complaining about it, I just want to comfort you. Next month there is supposed to be less bread and meat, the latter doesn't make any difference to me! It is widely known that there is such hunger in your country, it is dreadful. One reads about it, but also that help is being given. Yes, without organization everything is much worse, very sad. Enjoy your roast lamb, buy yourself the things to go with it and eat two portions. It makes my mouth water to think of roast lamb. Eat, Ernstili, as much as you can and want, don't count pennies, not necessarily every day but now and again. The main thing is to have something good, tasty. Then drink a little glass of wine with it, go home and think of me.

Will you be able to plant something in the vineyard? I mean, will you have the seeds? That must be the most important thing. And the fruit trees, the young ones, they may already be bearing a little fruit? Have you turned the earth around them, and protected the bark from insects? Or doesn't one need to do that there? Here I always saw fruit trees in spring with a grease-band round them so that they are protected from caterpillars. We still have constant dreadful weather, winter won't go away, we keep having frost, snow, cold, etc.

Do you know, my beloved, I can hardly think? Everything is pointless. I mean everything as far as the present or the near future are concerned. We are living in such gloom and apathy you can hardly imagine what sort of a condition that is.

---

[32]This is most likely a reference to Relico.

24/3

Emil has just been here and had a card from Alois saying he was well. A. seems to have some special protection. Emil told me his family have you to thank that they are so well provided for and sends you many greetings.

Oh Ernstili, if we had just spoken to each other once, who knows how different things might have been. I beg you, allow yourself everything, don't think about later, think of yourself and your loved ones. Just don't deprive your body of the strength it needs. I am constantly battling with Mutti about that. She is pathologically miserly and penny-pinching and I tell her to live properly, as long as it is possible; we are two hard stones! I will not give in, at least not for myself, I know that. But I very much dislike having to argue about it, it depresses me and then one hasn't the energy for much more important things.

Farewell my sweet, be healthy, enjoy the sun, the light, the air and sea and vineyard and think of me.

With deepest love,

Your Mitzimarie

Karlín, 26/3/1942

My most dearly beloved treasure

I haven't had any further news from you for a week, but just now I have such a longing for you so I am writing. The sun is shining here for a few hours as well now and soon spring will make her entry. Nevertheless it is still minus 3–4 degrees in the morning,

I am glad to read what you believe about my fate; I hope you are right. At present nobody knows what the next weeks will bring. For me it is somewhat complicated as regards Mother, because she simply will not understand or digest certain things. Anything which doesn't suit her she rejects. So if it comes to it, there will be such lamenting and distress. Once again I myself can bear a lot but have to stay calm, at least outwardly, since I know that things are unalterable. And this constant nagging sometimes wears me out. Mutti has all her mental faculties, one could be amazed at her, and that is why I can't accept that she quite refuses to endure this great test which nevertheless is not without hope. So don't think I have no patience – I have. It is only regrettable that a constant undertone of discord and disharmony creeps in around me which I find difficult to bear. I always felt a need 'at home' to sense the pull of love and kindness in our family circle. Mutti still wants the best for me now, I'm sure, but a lot does not suit me here, above all, her penny-pinching for herself, for me and for others. I have already taken the law into my own hands about various things. I can only get the better of her with lies and I don't like lying. When a third person was involved there have already been fights, sometimes quite nasty. For example she gives me a 2 crown tip for the two coalmen for hauling three sacks of coal to the 5th floor when one should give 10 crowns if one doesn't want any trouble. And one could argue every day about things like that. It all depresses me very much, I find it quite repugnant. Can you understand that?

I am glad you have your room back, at least I hope you have.

Why do you think I won't be able to write to you, my love? Do you think there is going to be an interruption? It is possible but it isn't the case yet. It is only bad with parcels, they can't be sent and just only 100 grams by *feldpost*, and then only in urgent cases – I can't myself send anything by *feldpost*. Other people don't like to do it for me, or simply won't. Nowadays the situation is such that one can hardly ever ask anyone for a favour. I don't know how it is for you, but here people are preoccupied with themselves, all one's good friends have disappeared and in any case one doesn't even want to ask anything of them. Only a very few friends have remained faithful and they can't help me in this.

I could tell you all sorts about Fox and Crow, but face to face. When I came here Herr Fox was very fatherly and nice to me. He often visited me here in Prague and behaved like a well-wisher and it seemed as if he really wanted to be helpful to me. But then there came a time when, contrary to his usual custom, he didn't answer several of my letters. I could understand that looking after oneself takes precedence over being useful to others – that is what I thought and I accepted it. Then, all of a sudden, his fear has disappeared and it's now all kind words, so how is that? He's worrying about the changes which will come later and wants to have everything ready. And it has to be my advice that he must have now? I was, and am, just tiny, quite tiny next to him.

Can you still remember Waggonmüller, our former general assistant?[33] He took everything, some of the recipes, copied the brand name, stirred up and poached the staff, even before I left. He took our trade-name (Karlsbader), our customer base, which cost us a fortune, and now he is already a big man, and Herr Fox, who used to be his supplier, gets envious, it gets too much for him and that is why he has turned to me – he wants to hurt him. I shall not make any move, I am not interested in anything, as you know.

The meetings of the social welfare service interest me a lot. A large building has been set up just for the offices and mostly it is people who offer their services free for charitable work, at least the majority of them. You must know, of course, that the care of the sick, the old, including those not in hospitals and old people's homes, and of children, is organized by the welfare service, and that the poor – and there are many of them – are clothed and everything is done by allocation. There are repair and sewing rooms, home cooking, a meal for 7 crowns, soup kitchens for the very poor and children, etc., etc. And you would be amazed at who asks for help these days. For example, Irma Ullmann[34] and her husband, and many like them.

Today Emil came, he looks well and sends greetings. He is worried about our wedding. He went to see Karel who said it will happen and when the time comes he will let us know. At the moment there is talk of a longish pause 'here' and people sigh with relief. God grant that it is so. The provinces are worried that it is their turn but nobody knows anything definite.

My treasure, I am so full of grief and sorrow that once again I may not experience the spring with you. I imagine everything so vividly and could almost quarrel with destiny for trying us so hard. For me, soon nobody will be able to do anything right, I am as peevish as an old maid, nothing gives me pleasure any more. Only when I imagine your presence, then the happy smile flits over me, then I am in 'our' world. And that is how I seek out my favourite place, whisper something lovely in your ear. Then all worries are gone and all torment, I kiss and cuddle you, press you warmly to me and then say goodnight.

---

[33]Ernst Müller worked for the Baders in Karlsbad.
[34]A sister of Fritz Ullmann.

In deepest love,
Your Mitzimarie.

Karlín, 30/3/1942

My dearest

Treasure, I'm vexed that you felt my letter of the 12th sounded troubled, that is not what I want at all but it is so hard for me, people can always tell at

Photo 17 *EBE recipe book cover.*

once how I am, even in letters. But I am going to pull myself together. Besides, two days ago there was a card from Gusti; he is living in the Cavalry Barracks,[35] room no. V 67b, Transport V, no. 135 (that is his number).

Once or twice a week I meet the Taussigs and I get on brilliantly with them. They have the same views as us and it is wonderful, the conversations we have together. The following dialogue took place between Mutti and me today: She: The Taussigs must be very rich (because they help all those in need). I replied: Oh no, they don't have a fortune, but something else: a very big heart. And when we spoke about it they both laughed heartily and nodded in agreement.

Unfortunately we can't send anything at all to I. and G. and he [Gustav] wrote that salami, striezel and pumpernickel are good. They are living separately but see each other often. We are very glad that they are not in Lublin where many of their acquaintances have gone.

With regard to Karel, this is how it is: he *can* represent us, but he is not allowed to take on any new cases.

Here people are now allowed to slaughter dogs and cats but they must be 'inspected'. As for the weather, it seems to be the same all over Europe. We also had a few days with frost in the morning and it was icy cold. But nothing is in bloom, no sign of it. I love almond trees, they are enchanting, a feast for the eyes.

200 kilos of potatoes is a large quantity, you would have a lot to harvest, I hope. I wish you very good luck with it. Now I also know how one makes good fried potatoes. The potatoes must be well cleaned with a brush (perfect) then one cuts 2–3 slices from one potato, sprinkles each slice with salt and caraway and one bakes them a golden yellow, that makes a fine supper.

With heating fuel it isn't easy in other places either. It is different for everyone. I know people who had absolutely nothing, no scrap of coal, etc. We had some. Do you have more bread now? There must be vegetables there now. We've got Italian vegetables here – fennel, which I have never seen before, salad – I think you must have your own crop of that.

In two days it will be Passover Seder evening, without Seder, without matzos, without anything.

---

[35]The Magdeburg barracks.

This week I want to tidy up my flat but when I am there I feel uneasy about Mutti, and on the other hand, here at the Lípas' I don't feel good at all. Unfortunately there is an unhappy mood here which comes from a peevish, grief-stricken old lady, and I am one of those who don't like that and who always said that one should keep up a certain front for the sake of others. So I flee to you, and relax from all the sorrows with you. And I am actually going to Karlín now to my home, then to the post with my letter. It is a beautiful early spring day, the sun is shining and I am with you. I wonder if you are in the vineyard.

Farewell, beloved, be cheerful and happy and I will try to be too. In deepest love,

Your Mitzimarie.

Karlín, 2/4/1942

My dearest

I have just received your letter of the 26th. No-one knows anything, we just have no news at all. The few words tell us nothing. Irene is living separately from Gustav;[36] they see each other from time to time. For Gustav, who was, after all, so spoilt, that is doubly hard. But I am sure others will help him prepare a little food. Nowadays there are many men who can cook brilliantly and know all about all kinds of housework. I always disliked it very much when men did housework but circumstances have forced us to.

I am not pleased to hear you predict that with you too people's fates are to change. It was always my joy that you are there and have been spared all sorts of things. Well, as God decrees! Your opinion about our future may well partly come true. I will admit that I am always aware of developments there and never miss an opportunity to find out in good time about everything which matters to me. I mean by that everything which affects my fate. But nobody can know what the next day will bring. At the moment they are saying that all people capable of working will be assigned to various jobs. However, apparently there

---

[36]Men and women lived separately in Theresienstadt.

will be an age limit. And in the provinces what happens is that those capable of working are assigned to jobs, the others apparently go to Irene or to Ashkenazi. I have already got an employment record book. Whether this will be of any use there I do not know, but it is quite obvious that I would gladly work and if it is possible I would volunteer for it. At present there is no talk of any of that here because now it is the turn of the provinces. And when the time comes I hope I too will be used for work. So I think, my treasure, that you should not worry about me at the moment.

I send Erika belated good wishes for her birthday. If we live to see the day we will, one day, celebrate her birthday at 'our house' if the dear child will be our guest. People always said about me that I knew how to make something lovely of a birthday celebration. Her writing paper is still lying here and waiting for the opportunity [to be sent]. The dear child, I can still remember exactly when she was born.

Karel doesn't seem to need anything else; he hasn't made any further move. Next week I will go and see him. I deliberately don't go very often because the star horrifies everyone; one has to take care. I would never have guessed what consequences such a symbol could have.

It may be right that it is not possible to contact Irene from where you are but keep their addresses carefully and keep the most important address (Hede's) particularly safe. Her mother, Grete Rudolph, lives there too. Hede will always know where each one of us is. Unfortunately I have to answer your question whether all bonds[37] are being dissolved with a 'yes'. That is what is so very wearing. I see you are slowly beginning to understand the situation. Even if this understanding doesn't help to cheer you up, I still believe that everyone should be properly informed, because it is in everyone's own interest to know the bare truth. Hiding one's head in the sand has not proved a good policy in these times; it brought the opposite consequences. My anxiety was not only *not* exaggerated but indeed an urgent response to the times. Everyone was repeatedly urged to emigrate but many could not bring themselves to decide to leave their warm nest and their lovely bank account. They did not appreciate

---

[37]Possibly a reference to relations between Jews and non-Jews.

the situation and have themselves to thank for their present fate. All those who decided to draw a firm line beneath their life up until then and resolved in time to set off on their travels were the wise ones. They are living far from their homeland and to some extent, or even mostly, have had a difficult start, but they are living with their family and can slowly – some of them even quickly – move forwards. Have you any idea how they are all envied?

My catarrh still keeps me inside; the air is still so biting. But in the last few days I have had some urgent business. I will tell you about it soon. Now I must see that I get rid of my catarrh. I don't want to lose too much weight myself.

Now I am going to hurry back to Mutti, who always waits for me with longing and anxiety. Do not worry, enjoy the spring and imagine I am with you. Farewell, be healthy, cheerful and happy. With dearest love,

Your Mitzimarie

Karlín, 7/4/1942

My dearest

Yesterday, Easter Monday, brought me your letter of the 29th and my heart was lightened and more peaceful again. How glad I am at your comment about yourself, that you feel young and well, touch wood. Look, Ernstili, that is something nobody can take from us. How we feel closely reflects our character and disposition and will remain ours always. Because we are no longer dependent on earthly possessions and have recognized in time that there are other more precious things which make for true happiness, that is why there will be peace and sunshine in our home.

Your account of the arrival of spring with you is more dear to me than all the treasures I ever lost. The present times make demands on the entire person and anyone who can't face them, whose nerves fail, will go under. The world continues to turn and who will ask questions about them? For me, too, cheerfulness and a happy mood always win the day, surprising those around me, and I know very well that it is you I must thank for that, and your letters, in which you again and again lift me up, as a gardener restores his trees which have been bent by the storm.

I am very surprised that you can read French books. I can't compete with you in that. Since my childhood I have always adored French. The language, everything about it, was always something that delighted me, it sounded like music in my ear. I just loved it very much and always felt very proud when I was having a lesson and made progress. And then when my sweet little children at 5 or 6 years could already chatter away so happily, I was so glad. I saw in their success everything flowering so nice and easily which I never had a chance to be taught. And now you write to me about your progress in French. For me that is an unexpected, delightful surprise. I am also amazed at your memory. I'm afraid that my memory, which was once excellent, has suffered a lot.

Your account of Erika and Bubi gave me great pleasure. They must be beautiful and smart, as I imagine them. Bubi definitely looks like you and when I see him one day I will be able to imagine how you looked as a boy. Erika may look like her father. Is her character a bit complicated? 'Slovenly' isn't very nice, but can be excused in the young. That is what upbringing and education are for and if it is an unpleasant fault it is certainly not the worst. There are far worse ones among today's youth.

My 'stay': I don't want to waste too many words on it because there is something new every day. I see it as my duty to make you aware that we have to expect the journey. It is not inevitable but it could be ripe for a decision within 14 days, just according to who draws the lots. I agree with you that one just has to cope with this waiting. And even when one is there, even then there are always some individuals who, if they are lucky in the distribution of work, can bear their lot more easily than others. Everything is a matter of chance, a bit of luck etc., etc. I heard that 1,000 women were sent to Wald.[38] … (*the rest of the letter is missing*)

This letter was returned by the censor because, at six pages, it was too long. Marie then re-sent the earlier part, intending to copy out the last two sides and send them separately, but they are missing.

---

[38]Between April and June 1942, 1,000 women from Theresienstadt were sent to a work assignment in the forest near Křivoklát.

Karlín, 10/4/1942

My most dearly beloved

Until today, Friday, I have had no further news from you, but I'm hoping for some tomorrow. Emil was here today. I read him some of your letter of 29/3; he was very pleased. At the moment he is a little anxious about his future because they need his building and its occupants must leave. E. could, as the husband of his wife,[39] have a claim to remain but his future upkeep is a worry. He still has two weeks; as long as nothing definite has been decided one can keep hoping.

We haven't heard anything more from Irene. The post is often just left unsorted for a long time and one worries oneself to death. Many acquaintances have gone to Izbica[40] (Ashkenazi) and now write of 'golden Th[eresienstadt]'.[41] Alois also wrote again, he and Emil both send warmest greetings. Alois wrote that he isn't writing to you because he has little time and he has to give up writing because of the long distance to the designated post office.

Life is strange. I am doing a lot of running around, sometimes with more success, sometimes with less. I can't find peace any more at home. I have a lot on my mind which no-one can help me with, I mean I would like to help but can't. Now I have two refugees. One is Frau Ella Schwarzkopf, born Weiss (from Buchau). She lives nearby and is very poor and sick after a serious illness. I visit her 2 to 3 times a week and usually bring her something to eat. Then there is a 15-year-old girl who is not without means but is much to be pitied. She lost her father and grandfather prematurely, her [maternal] grandmother is still alive but is as if dead for her. The other grandmother (Regine Zuckermann, daughter of mother's cousin) took her own life. I was very good friends with her and she recently wrote me a letter begging me to take care of her granddaughter, because the child's mother was in Palestine and

---

[39]Married to a non-Jewish person.

[40]In March 1942 there were two deportations from Theresienstadt to Izbica. Almost none of the 2,000 deportees survived the war.

[41]The deportees were allowed to send cards with short messages from Izbica to the Protectorate.

the father (they were separated) had died. I exchanged a few letters with her and then the child came: her Grandmama was dead. The road to Ashkenazi was too hard for her and she made an end of it. A smart, elegant, likeable woman, a good person.

Now I am looking after the young lady; she needs advice and to know that she is not entirely abandoned. My mother Louise blames me for it a little because she thinks I have enough to do for myself but I do it discreetly. I do what I think is possible and appropriate. In any case, I am making further preparations to equip us [for the transport]. I need to have new covers made for our quilts; yesterday I bought camping bottles which had been unavailable. Today I have taken linen to be dyed. Can you imagine medium blue bed-linen, sheets, work clothes (former maid's and working clothes)? Yes, one can't wear light things for peeling potatoes or working in the fields and particularly if one has to be *soooo* careful with soap.

Tomorrow afternoon we are going to Hede's; on Wednesday they are always at our house. On Monday at 4 o'clock I have a meeting; at 5.30 the Taussigs always come. They visit us regularly, they are most loyal and self-sacrificing friends, not only to us but to other people too. Wonderful people. I am already looking forward to when you will get to know them. But you met them already in Karlsbad.

I am very sorry that I can't tell you all sorts of things which I experienced this winter, but it would be going too far. I myself think that you too should keep various things to tell me later if you think they are important. Even if you think it is worth knowing, I am not curious, although there will remain no change in my interest in you and what you are doing. After all, the time when we will see each other again is not so far away and then there will be endless talking, won't there?

Do you know what we had for lunch today? Chopped tripe and potato dumplings. That way one can get 1 kg of meat out of 250 gram meat ration coupon. That is a generous meal.

It is obvious that in our future life together we won't get worked up about acquiring things. It will be such a different way of life. The time of the old ways of thinking is over. He who best understands the art of living is and always has been the person who knows how to adapt to change at the right moment. Have no fear, Ernstili, we won't burden ourselves with big demands and will choose rather to live simply and modestly, so as to squeeze a few more hours of joy and happiness out of life.

Saturday 11/4

The post brought nothing again so now I am hoping for Monday. The weather is still mostly cool while no doubt for you there is sunshine and springtime. My sweet, do go regularly to the vineyard again, at least every other day. Why should you deny yourself such a harmless and yet special delight? Seize the opportunity, go out into beautiful, calming nature without any doubts or guilty conscience. I am sure, if you want it, you will find company for the walk.

Last night I dreamt of you, with you. We were in Karlsbad and were planning a Saturday outing into the Erzgebirge.[42] I was looking forward to it with childlike delight. We were going to go alone. Yes, if the reality isn't possible one has to make do with dreams. Today's letter is again about nothing. The contents could be extremely heavy but I prefer to chat with you.

I have paid another quarter's rent for my accommodation. Will I pay again? Who can know? Here in my house I feel very close to you; strange, here there is peace and calm and I feel very good. I always feel as if you're close by me, I hear you coming, see you looking round with a questioning or ironic gaze, and if I don't like it I have my own ways of cajoling you gently and softly. I'll do it discreetly. That is how I fantasize and just don't want to leave you, but I have to, so farewell, beloved, keep healthy, happy and content. With dearest love and kisses.

Your Mitzimarie.

Prague, 14/4/1942

My dearly beloved

Again one of your letters appears to have gone missing because today I only got your card of 2/4 and last week only one letter. And the content of this card

---

[42]Krušné hory.

is so strange, as if you had had a great upset which indeed, in the present times, would not be at all surprising. Ernstili, whatever happens, so long as it doesn't harm body or soul, don't worry about it. Only thus armed can one cope with these times.

On Monday the 'call-up' was delivered. I must report on 21/4 and leave for Theresienstadt on the 24th.[43] My transport reference is Am. 976. Don't be upset, I'm not. It has to be. This time it is Haus Lanner[44] which is the reason. My biggest headache, is Mutti. She is not included this time. Should I take her with me as a volunteer or not? Everyone advises against this on the grounds of common sense. But imagine leaving her alone. So it is dreadful. Of course I will let Mutti decide and it seems that she wants to stay here after all.

And now to us, beloved. I beg you, don't worry unnecessarily because I don't believe you need to. It is not a nice time that lies ahead of me but what others can bear I hope I too can bear. In any case, whatever happens, I will look for employment as far as possible. It is a great comfort to me that I shall see my sister and brother-in-law again. Besides, the whole business must, after all, end some time, nothing lasts for ever in this world. I'm not much worried about food scarcity, or living very basically. I know the latter from my young days. My life here for the past year has not been pleasant at all, disagreeable, sad and full of worry, controlled by others and driven by circumstances, so the parting will not be hard for me, it can't get any worse. I lived partly alone and cut off, I who by nature so love intimacy. But I knew how to banish my loneliness because I was together with you in letters and in my mind too. The happiness I found in our love helped me to overcome all hardships easily and I know already now that that is how I will survive Theresienstadt as well, because I want to, because I want to experience bliss in your arms and because I want to see a happy you in the flesh. Willpower can do a lot in life, my sweet, so don't be grieved. There are much worse things today and so long as a person is alive

---

[43]It is unlikely that Marie received Ernst's response to the information before her departure from Prague.

[44]Marie thinks she has been selected for this particular transport because she annoyed someone when she refused to sell the house in Karlsbad.

and healthy one must hope and have trust. I do that with confidence. I just have to imagine that I was a man, a soldier, and going onto the battlefield. If I imagine the women and mothers who have to send their sons to the front, then I prefer to go to Theresienstadt because the memory of these worries is still fresh in me.

My birthday will be here soon. Who knows whether I might not celebrate it with you? Or otherwise yours? It isn't so far away either. A lot of people I know are going with me, I won't be alone. Here good friends have taken me under their wing and are helping me. It pains me to have to give you this worry, but it is not my fault, my sweet. It is only your letters that I will miss. I will write to Hede as often as I can. She will send on to you my 30 words and you can write to her.

15/4

Today I am at home, preparing – that is a terrible job. The Jewish bush telegraph keeps talking about a postponement, so there is still hope but, as I said, I don't care either way.

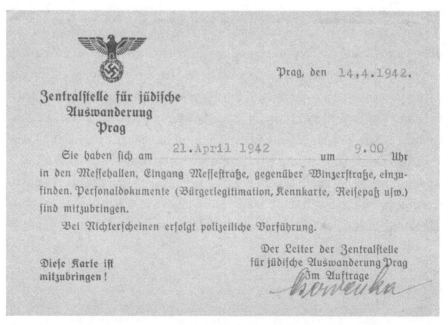

Photo 18 *Card ordering Marie to report at the Trade Fair grounds on 21 April 1942.*

Now Hede and a good, kind friend have come to help so I have to stop and will write again tonight.

Farewell, you will have news from me a few more times. The northern spring is longing for the southern, as always, and if nothing else the autumn must bring the spring.[45]

Where am I sitting? And then? Then I kiss you with all my heart and am entirely

Your Mitzimarie.

Prague, 17/4/1942

My most dearly beloved

Now, four days before I report, I want to try to write to you in as organized a way as possible. I will first of all deal with the most important things.

Correspondence:

(1) via Hede. She will write to you frequently about me. Please will you also write her a card at least once a week? Perhaps she may now and again be able to send you my correspondence. We'll see how it all turns out and what will be allowed or possible. You can trust the whole family, in character and decency like Gusti. Correct to the fingertips. What an irony of fate that today I received a letter from Karel saying that the marriage application will be settled favourably in the very near future. Unfortunately it will be too late for me. I would probably still have had more time if my name had begun with an L instead of a B.[46]

(2) via Emil and Käthe Taussig, Prague X, Rakonitzergasse 1.

Hede and Rudi know all about everything, they know my best acquaintances and friends whom you don't yet know. I am mentioning this particularly because I have a great wish that, whatever happens, you will get to know them

---

[45]The northern spring is Marie, the southern is Ernst, but in the second part of the sentence the spring is their reunion, and if it doesn't happen in spring, as now seems unlikely, then it must happen in the autumn.

[46]Marie means if she and Ernst were married. She seems to have the wrong impression. The list of deportees from 24 April contains surnames starting with all letters of the alphabet, including tens of names starting with 'L'.

some time. If I still have time I will go once more to see Karel and will tell him, too, this wish and everything related. I am leaving my mother behind, as she prefers to carry on staying here. But it may happen that she follows soon.

My future place of residence represents a sort of ghetto, it has the advantage that, if one obeys all the rules, one lives in some ways without the restrictions one has here. Up to 3,000 people live in one barrack and the men can visit the women from time to time. Women up to the age of 55 work, according to their abilities and achievements, the old people go into an old people's home or an infirmary, the children in a children's home. There are already locksmiths, workshops, carpentry shops, laundries, gardens, poultry rearing, etc. If one is lucky one gets a job which suits, if one is unlucky one just has to do something one doesn't enjoy as much. In any case I will look for work, then one spends less time brooding.

So it is communal living. One can take as much food from here as one wants, so I am taking plenty for Gustav and Irene as well, as you can imagine, and if I am allowed to keep the things we won't be in need for a while. The food won't, of course, be what we are accustomed to but there is enough for one to live. And I think everyone keeps getting something from the new arrivals etc. If one is lucky and finds a job which allows one to stay, that is an achievement, but the onward journey to the Lichtmanns on the other hand, is a minus. But even that is no misfortune. From the Lichtmanns one can write here. From Theresienstadt a card with 30 words, only once a month, whereas from the Lichtmanns one can write as often and as much as one wants. Only not from Litzmannstadt, one can't at all, there is no question of it.

I have many acquaintances in Theresienstadt who can show me goodwill if they want to. There are also masses of relatives there. So, my dearest, there is no immediate danger for me and you must not worry. I will do everything I can to hold out and survive this time. What particularly pleases me is that the women can take care of their bodies, wash, etc., even in Theresienstadt, and one hears that there is a nice, friendly social life with informative lectures, both serious and amusing ones, in the evenings, so people – at least some – know how to create some light hearted moments even there.[47]

---

[47]The Nazis invested a lot of effort in the propaganda campaign that presented the life in the ghetto in a good light.

Your letter of the 11th has just arrived, in which you preach such a pretty sermon. At the same time my letter of the 7th to you was returned because it had six sides so I am sending four sides of it again and then I will copy out the rest anew. I am happy with what you write about yourself, thank God it is so and I am reassured. My sweet, you have no idea what an enormous amount of work weighs me down at present, forgive my disorganized letter. I am on edge and in a great hurry before the helpers and visitors arrive, as then it is quite impossible to write.

I embrace you with deepest, most passionate love and whatever my worries I will remain

Your Mitzimarie

Prague, 18/4/1942

My most dearly beloved

Waking from the most beautiful dream (at 4 a.m.) I hop joyfully out of bed. I want to write it all down for you in detail but oh dear, I am starving. Funny, isn't it? Probably a nervous reaction.

Right, I've eaten and now to you. I dreamt that a telegram from the friends summoned us to them. I rang them up and asked them 'What are you thinking of? We are a worry for you.' The answer was 'Everything has been brilliantly prepared. You can throw your worries out of the window and come just as you are.' I said 'Ernstili, what do you think?' You thought for a moment and then you said 'I'll tell you something, Mitzimarie. We will visit them anyhow, since they are making the journey so very easy for us. Let's go and see how it looks where they are, then we'll decide further.' And my preparations for Theresienstadt became preparations for going to the friends. On wings of lightness and joy we put our seven bundles together and then we went off to town.

In reality, too, I now feel a lot lighter in my heart, except for the great worry about Mutti. That is tearing me apart but for the moment one must just think in a matter of fact and practical way. I am making provisions so that, as far as is humanly possible, Mutti will live her life as she is accustomed to. But who can appease her longing for the children? That is such a misery. I worry about her, because sometimes she is as helpless as a two-year-old child. There are good friends around but one can't expect too much. And who knows how soon they will also have to go? And then, when the summons comes for Mutti, that is the worst thought for me. The social welfare service of the *Kultusgemeinde* deals with all that but it is cold and hard, much too hard for my mother. I don't know if you understand completely; it is impossible for you to grasp the present situation. My mother's poor sight makes her helpless, even if people don't realize it. One has to put everything in her hands, she is constantly looking for things. And yet it is better for her to stay here as long as she can, so that is how it must be.

If I keep coming back to whether one or the other of us will be the boss, why shouldn't I? I need to have this point out in the open with you, my beloved, so that you then don't experience any of the disappointments that you often mention. So if you are not rigid, neither will I be; our hearts will teach us to make compromises. But when will that be? I say soon, by your birthday, I am absolutely certain, but it could even be by my birthday that it happens. That is why I am not at all unhappy when I think about my journey, first of all because I hope to see Irene and Gustav. When I say 'hope' it is because I am anxious about Irene's health. It seems odd to me that she has only written once. There are plenty of reasons or excuses for it, but in fact Gustav has written three cards, she one. But I will see them again in good health and then will come the moment when I will be able to bring them all these things! How happy I will be and forgiven for many things. I am not going to worry about the restrictions ahead, I will bear them easily and willingly as a fact of life, thinking all the time of you. I will always have in my mind's eye the moment of reunion with you and the friends and I will think 'What does it matter, something else must come, some time this too will end.'

I have already mentioned Frau Isa Strauss a few times, the well-known philanthropist, the top woman in the I.K.,[48] who has worked so very hard for social welfare. She is the mother of the beautiful Käthe who once stayed with

---

[48]Isa Strauss set up a clinic in Prague to treat the Jewish community early in the occupation. Although she was deported on the same transport to Theresienstadt as Marie, she survived longer, until she was sent to Auschwitz in October 1944. The I.K. is most likely the *Israelitische Kultusgemeinde* (Jewish Community office).

us as a teenager. Kätherl was and is Gretel's best friend. You once met her. Well Frau Isa is coming too this time, I have heard. I hope she will give me the right job in the welfare service. In any case, we will see each other and talk during the three day wait here. Of course, I have many acquaintances there and you must not worry.

I am very much pitied for having to go on my own but I don't feel at all alone because you are with me all the time. I am also enormously admired for my apparent bravery (not conceited, please). I have no intention of wailing or lamenting because there is no reason to and because I am going to live, not in the present, but for and in the future.

I embrace you in deepest love and am

Your Mitzimarie

Karlín, 18/4/1942

My most dearly beloved

As long as I can – so tomorrow and Monday – I will write to you a lot. You must just take these letters as an 'advance payment' and spread them out over the period of the break in our correspondence. Your moralizing sermon in the letter of the 11th made me laugh – don't be cross, my love, I was just amused. I wasn't at all angry but you see, unfortunately I wasn't grousing. It's just that there are always restrictions on how one writes, that is why you misunderstand and get the wrong ideas from my letters. But there is nothing one can do about that. I am very happy about what you write about yourself and if I don't answer certain things it is only for lack of space. As far as the star is concerned I will just say that its consequences are unexpectedly unpleasant. Not that there was any shame, but the practical effect was different from what was expected.[49] And you write to me 'You, as a believer, must think differently.' I would like to discuss with you exactly what my attitude is to belief, and to ask you, if I am not able to see my children again – one is only human after all – to pass on to them something of my thinking.

---

[49] The compulsory Star of David was introduced in Thessaloniki in February 1943.

To you I say I have my own religion, I believe in God, a God who is God to all people. If I enjoyed keeping up the old traditions and made a connection between them and God, it was out of reverence for everything from my childhood and youth and because my belief was enhanced by it. I have never denied my Jewishness, that would have been pointless. But I do not believe in an afterlife and my opinion that every creature has only one life entirely supports the principle that one should shape this one life for oneself as pleasantly as possible. And here I agree unconditionally with you: whoever wants to live in Europe should, in the interests of their descendants, accept the prevailing religion so that these sad experiences do not keep occurring at shorter or longer intervals, for which parents and grandparents cannot escape reproach. So away with it because every person should live their life and anyone who cares so much about Judaism should go to Palestine.[50]

You should only pass on to my children this view of mine if I don't live to see them again, which is not what I hope. So, my treasure, I am and remain a believer, but I too think it is folly that one should have to sacrifice oneself again and again for an idea. Do you understand me? If I now ask you to do everything you possibly can from now on for your own good, that is like a prayer, even if I am praying to you only as my most dear one and not as God. Or is the most dearly beloved more than God? With regard to this request, he is.

So, my sweet, look after yourself, keep yourself healthy and young and smart for me. I will also try to do my best, although that will no longer depend entirely on my will, as I will be living in a community and not on my own. However it may turn out, I hope I won't become ugly because my soul will remain pure and bright. And the soul is reflected in the face. That is what I think and hope. A loss of weight can only make me look younger, so have no fear or worry. But if I become a misery, then rest assured that I would not want to belong to you, whether married or not. I wouldn't be happy about that. I never want to be ugly, at least not at the side of my beloved. But away with these thoughts, it won't happen, I hope.

---

[50]Marie articulates her views on the ideas of Jewish assimilation. Marie's belief that religious assimilation would end the persecution suffered by Jews throughout history fails to recognize that the Nazi persecution was based not on the Jews' religion, but on their racial origin.

It is possible that they will sometimes be able to send your letters on to me, there may come about a relaxation of the rules about sending mail, be prepared for that, please. I asked Hede to keep any letters coming from you unopened, etc. On the other hand, I am going to burn all your letters except for a few which I am taking with me.

I beg you, my best of all, my sweet, good one, my child, my husband, my father and my beloved, on my knees I beg you to keep yourself healthy and not to worry. Trust me and accept my words with the sincerity with which they are expressed.

Believe me, hope with me for a beautiful, happy, joyous future. I press myself into your arms, kiss you most lovingly and am

Your Mitzimarie

Karlín, 20/4/1942

My dearest, my beloved!

The time has come; this is the evening before my departure. I will leave the house tomorrow morning at 8.30. I hope that one more letter will come from you. How am I to take my leave of you now? Tired, utterly exhausted, I'm sitting here and could still be busy the whole night long. In the daytime there are always visits from relatives and acquaintances which take up most of the time and then one has to use the night. Beloved, I remain full of courage and hope. I am confident and determined to hold out and you too must stay calm.

Just imagine, I have 12 pieces of luggage, including a vast amount of food, both cooked and preserved, a lot of provisions, everything possible. Up to now one has been allowed to take unlimited quantities of food. If everything is as it has been up to now and if I keep my luggage in order, then I will give Gustav and Irene much joy and that would give me real satisfaction. There was at last a nice card from Irene. She is well and says her friends there are very good people. That is very important. I too will be travelling with friends and will have friends there. Frau Isa Strauss is going at the same time as me and I will try to work in a team with her when I look for a job. I can only tell you so much, that you must not worry. I can't say more at the moment. Ernstili, trust me, I beg you. Time will pass and then we will see each other again. I keep picturing our reunion and then a lot of things just vanish. Emil was here today, he was very depressed. All my acquaintances were kind and good. The kindest and best of all were Emil Taussig and his wife. Please write to him, he wants to write to you too. It would be good if you could get into correspondence with him because you will hear everything about me from him.

Hede and Rudi Sternschuss were also kind and very, very good, and also my friend Olga. She knows more about me than Mutti or other relatives and acquaintances and she was a great help to me. Please write soon to Hede and Rudi too. You will surely hear something, above all from Emil. Olga too will answer you immediately. She can tell you all sorts of things. The parting from Mutti was heartrending.

Darling, I beg you now just to look after yourself as you promised me. Then everything will come right. We will hold out, follow our goal tenaciously and unflaggingly. It will be worth it, my sweet, despite everything. I don't know how but, try as I will, I cannot see it all as tragic because I am convinced that for us too there will one day be peace, sunshine and joy again. We will just have to be brave for a while. In fact, in recent months I have been very worn out, I wasn't at all well any more. You know how unhappy I was. It was because I could see that I wasn't able to give my mother what I had intended. I was disappointed and unhappy. Emil also did some jobs for me today.

Greet Hella for me, the children and Salvator, see your friends regularly, keep yourself entertained, play poker and bridge and carry on writing letters to me and keep them until it is possible to send them. Send Hede a card once a week because it may be that she can send them on, Olga will do the same. I can only write after 5 or 6 weeks and then only 30 words, so be patient. But perhaps it will be sooner. Who knows?

Thank goodness I feel healthy and strong and everybody is amazed at my calm. Or don't I know what is waiting for me? Am I wrong in what I imagine? I doubt it. Only the fact that I have the determination to be strong so as to be able to be with you makes it all easier for me than for others. It is true that I will miss your letters unspeakably: they were everything for me. Who can change things? Peace. And it will come one day. Darling, I can't write any more, forgive me. You know what you mean to me, be strong and firm and carry on being my support and my hero. Farewell my treasure, keep healthy,

I sit down on your lap, hug you with deepest love and kiss you from the bottom of my heart with all the love and passion I have for you. May God protect you.

Till we meet again soon in joy and happiness.

Your Mitzimarie.

On the same evening that she penned her last letter to Ernst, Marie also wrote the following letter to her daughters in England. This letter did not reach them until after the war. She had left it for safekeeping with Hede Sternschuss until such time as it was possible to send it.

Prague, 20/4/1942

My dear children and dear Franz

Before my departure to Theresienstadt I want to send you a few lines in case it should turn out that I am not able to be with you again. I leave here calm and confident, in the expectation of seeing you in the autumn. If fate should decree otherwise, then you will have to accept it and comfort each other, because it just could not be any other way. You have the Sternschuss parents here; they are wonderful people, they will be much, they will be everything for you. You, my dear Greterl, try to marry and to be happy. Stay close together, may your bond be as strong as iron. Never forget uncle and aunt, they will be parents for you, they may need your support. Grunzi has, sadly, aged terribly from all the dreadful blows; I cannot write about that today. My motherly love surrounds you for always, may my blessing bring you happiness, health, fresh courage and enthusiasm and help you find contentment.

Be brave and courageous in life's struggle. Do everything that is good and just – that will help you. Don't be weighed down by tradition and too much religion. Remember that we were sacrificed because we were Jewish and what we experienced others will tell you. Those who want to live here should accept the religion of the land, so that future generations do not have to undergo these sufferings again. That is what my experiences have taught me. Those who wish to stay within Judaism should live in Palestine. Always, and in whatever place, I will think fervently of you and all my loved ones, so that I can find the strength to face this time of trial.

And now, my beloved ones, I hug you tightly, press you to my heart and pray that God may protect you. I kiss you with all my heart and am, with deepest love,

Your Mutti.

Epilogue

The following morning, on 21 April 1942, Marie reported at the assembly centre in Holešovice, a part of Prague. She spent three days and nights going through all the procedures and harassment together with a thousand other deportees. On 24 April, they were sent by train (transport Am) to the Bohušovice station, about 65 km north of Prague, and then made to walk about thirty minutes to Theresienstadt. Marie had spent months preparing for the trip and life in the ghetto, and planned to bring extra food items for Irene and Gustav.

Marie hoped that once in the ghetto she would be reunited with, or at least see, her sister and brother-in-law, but she arrived in Theresienstadt at a very difficult time. The people of the ghetto, which was created only five months before, were already suffering from deportations to the east. Shortly before Marie's arrival, the ghetto commandant, SS Obersturmführer Siegfried Seidl, had ordered four additional transports to occupied Poland in less than a week, each with a thousand deportees. Facing the difficult task of compiling the deportation lists, the ghetto administration decided to include a large number of people who had only recently entered the gates of this fortress town. Only protected prisoners, important workers, people over the age of 65 (later over 67), and other minor groups, such as World War I veterans or those with foreign citizenship, were exempted.[i] H. G. Adler, estimated that 6,000 prisoners for the transports had to be selected from the pool of 10,700 people not protected by the current ghetto rules.[ii]

Marie, in her fifties, widowed and without any contacts in the ghetto administration, was immediately selected for the next transport departing in three days. She spent the time in the ghetto in the so-called *Schleuse* (sluice), in the Aussig barracks, the place where the arriving as well as departing prisoners gathered. Here she may have met Gustav and Irene, who were selected for the transport scheduled to depart only one day after Marie, though in the chaos that accompanied the massive wave of deportations, most of the prisoners in the ghetto did not even go through the Sluice on the way to the deportation train. Some of them were informed about the deportation only several hours before the train departed.[iii] In any case, Marie could not share with them the food she had amassed, because the Germans had already confiscated almost all the luggage of the deportees while still in Prague. Did her sister and brother-in-law volunteer for the transport when they found out that Marie would not be staying in the ghetto with the hope they would be reunited in the east? The fact the Gustav would soon turn 67 and was not among the prime candidates for the transports offers this possibility, but we will never know.

On 27 April, Marie departed from Bohušovice. Her train first travelled further north to Dresden, before taking a sharp turn eastwards in the direction of Breslau, Łódź and Lublin, until finally, after more than three days, it pulled up at the small train station in Izbica in the Lublin 'Reservation' (transport Aq).[1] The train with Irene and Gustav took the prisoners to Zamość, some 20 km south of Izbica. Marie and Irene never saw each other again. The deportees had experienced years of persecution, but even those who had spent months in Theresienstadt could not have been prepared for the conditions that in the spring of 1942 ruled in eastern Poland, a territory that had already become the epicentre of the 'Final Solution'.

Before the war, Izbica was a small town, with an almost exclusively Jewish population (92 per cent). The Germans turned Izbica into a Jewish town (*Judenstadt*). In a valley, encircled by hills from three sides and by the river Wieprz from the fourth, Izbica was completely isolated from the surrounding territories and the Germans did not have to build walls or fences around the settlement. There were only six water pumps and few latrines in the town.[iv] In

---

[1]Lublin Reservation was a territory created by the Nazis in occupied eastern Poland in late 1939, which was supposed to become the settlement for all European Jews. The plan was shelved relatively quickly, but the term was still in use even later.

Photo 19 *Izbica (Courtesy of the Holocaust Historical Society).*

March 1942, the Germans turned Izbica into a transit ghetto and temporary holding centre for the Jews deported from Germany, Austria, the Protectorate and Slovakia, before they murdered them in the nearby extermination camps. Between 16,000 and 18,000 Jews deported from central Europe were temporarily held in the town. Robert Kuwalek has concluded that 'Izbica was a kind of collection point [Umschlagplatz] on the Lublin–Bełżec line, at which, in short, they were supposed to wait for the death train'.[v]

Soon after the arrival of the first transports from central Europe the Germans sent the majority of the local Polish Jews to the Bełżec extermination camp and Czech and German Jews were moved into their houses. The deportees, accustomed to middle-class life in major central European cities, were truly shocked by the living conditions in Izbica, a poor place that had already suffered for more than two years under brutal German occupation. We have only a very limited number of sources that would allow us partly to enter the minds of the deportees, among them Marie, because not more than 13 deportees of the more than 3,000 people sent from Theresienstadt to Izbica survived the war. One survivor recalled her and her fellow victims' first impressions after arriving in the town:

then they stuffed us into one house, about thirty of us in one room, whose windows were papered over. We could barely breathe, nor could we even sit down there, because we were packed in so tightly that we were actually standing all day and all night. I wanted to open a window at least, because we could not breathe, but as I was peeling off the paper, there were so many bedbugs there that I quickly stuck it back on. And then, about two days later, they divided us up into those little houses, because most of the Polish Jews had already been cleared out somewhere.[vi]

People slept on the earthen floor, often more than twenty people in one small room. The people whom Marie arrived with had no suitcases or even food. Their last personal items, in a special carriage of the train, were confiscated en route. Those who had successfully smuggled in money or valuables could, at the risk of the death penalty, buy things at the exorbitant prices of the thriving black market, but others starved or were forced to sell extra items of clothes they wore. Ida Hermannová and her family, who had travelled in the same train as Marie, first from Prague and then from Theresienstadt, described the living conditions in a letter they managed to send clandestinely back to the Protectorate:

We are, literally, barely scraping by. We live here, like the others, several families in one room. We lie on the ground. Our parents, thank God, were lent a straw mattress by a very nice woman who lives with us. We cover ourselves with our coats. Meanwhile we live in the constant fear that they will send us on, as has already happened several times, just like that. One can get everything here, but you have to pay a lot of money. [...] We are selling everything, the last clothes we are wearing, to be able to buy the absolute essentials. All of us have to work hard all day long, but without pay. We breathe mountain air here, about 800m high, and we would all devour, not eat, food, and are forced to prevent little Eva from eating as much as she would like. [...] We beg you to send us packages as often as possible, mainly sugar, roux, artificial honey, groats, millet. [...] hunger is painful. Please send us as well head scarves, stockings, an apron, everything in bright colours. [...] Please do not let us die of hunger. Send us whatever you can. [...] People here are covered in rashes from being undernourished. The women do not have their periods. In a word, it is horrible here. The houses here do not resemble even our cottages. They are much, much worse, full of bedbugs and fleas. There is also a louse here that carries typhus. Thank God we have, by keeping clean, so far protected ourselves against that. [...] Don't be cross with us; you know well that I have never wanted anything from anybody, but hunger is very painful, and you wouldn't even recognize any of us because we are so thin.[vii]

From Marie's transport, men were already selected in Lublin to do forced labour and sent to the Majdanek concentration camp. Mostly only women, children and the elderly arrived in Izbica. The deportees lived in the small town for several months before many succumbed to hunger, typhus or exhaustion. Others were sent to the Bełżec or Sobibór extermination camps during one or other of the 'Aktions' organized by the Germans and their Ukrainian and Polish helpers. Marie's fate is unknown. The fate of the deportees to Zamość, among them Irene and Gustav, was similar. Almost nobody survived. The Sternschuss family received the last message from either Marie or Irene in July 1942.

Marie's ultimate destination is not known (nor is that of Irene and Gustav). After the war, Hella Cougno wrote to Grete Reichl that, when she was working in the camp administration in Auschwitz, she saw Marie's name on a *Sonderbehandlung* ('special treatment') list, which indicated she had already been killed there. This is, however, unlikely, because the prisoners of the Izbica ghetto either died in the town, or were sent to one of the death camps in the region, to Bełżec or Sobibór.

Ernst had no information about Marie's fate after she left Prague. One wonders what he thought. In her memoir, his granddaughter Erika writes that Ernst 'intelligent, kindly but so very innocent' still believed in the German people as cultured and civilized, incapable – apart from a few rotten apples – of committing the cruelties and atrocities they were accused of. Did he think Marie was alive but not allowed to write or send messages? We can surmise that intellectually he may well have guessed her fate. We shall never know. Ernst continued to live with the Cougno family in Thessaloniki until March 1943, when, after a short ghettoization, the Germans quickly organized deportations of the whole Jewish community to the concentration and extermination camps in occupied Poland. Salvator, Hella, Erika and Heinz were sent to Auschwitz in the first train that left Thessaloniki. They all miraculously survived thanks to their being fluent in German, which allowed them to take administrative positions in the prisoner hierarchy. Ernst was living in hiding with a Bulgarian family at that time and had a good chance of surviving the war. Erika learnt about his fate after the war:

> Grandfather still believed in the German people. He felt so lonely away from his family that one Sunday morning he took all the decorations he had earned as a Captain during the First World War, along with his diploma and went to the Gestapo. Extremely politely […] the SS received him and asked who he was and what he wanted. […] 'To be sent to where my daughter and her family went.' The SS-officer put a junior officer in charge, instructing him, 'Please lead Dr Ernst Loevy to the station. From there in a few days he will have the opportunity to join his daughter.'[viii]

Ernst was deported to Auschwitz-Birkenau and was immediately sent to the gas chambers.

Appendix 1: Letter from Else Auerbach

Hilversum, 7 December 1941

My dear Frau Marie,

When a letter arrived a few days ago and I recognized you from the handwriting I was delighted. Then, when I had read it, I was surprised about a good deal, happy about other things and deeply shaken by some of the news. The content of your letter is a mirror of these times. The loneliness, the separation from your children, the disappointment in people and all the dreadful things we have to live through have made you decide to marry again. I understand your decision entirely and wish, from the bottom of my heart, that all the hopes you pin on this may be fulfilled. I had no opportunity to meet your future husband but often heard his name mentioned in your house. Even if we only write to each other occasionally we both know that we are bound by a real feeling of friendship and for the sake of that friendship I beg you to tell me more about what has moved you so deeply. What do your mother and Irene say about it? Do they understand how you feel?

The news about Else R. shook me deeply. One of the many who cannot cope with the times. One needs to have great strength, resistance and the will to live to be able to bear all the hardship. I liked her very much. How does her poor husband cope with his lot? Where is F. and where is Hans? And now poor Frau Altscherl. Another one to be pitied. God grant that the war will soon end and she can go back home. I presume her husband is with her. We are also very worried about my husband's family (two brothers with their wives) and about my sister with her sick husband and two children of nineteen and twenty. The intention was for my sister to leave today. So you can imagine what sort of a mood we are in. One would so like to help and one is so powerless.

We too have lived through a lot. My eldest brother died almost a year ago in Gurs[1] in the south of France where he had to live in a dreadful camp. But we only heard much later about his death. The poor man went through a lot. We so wanted to help him but couldn't. Even writing from here was not possible. Post sent to him was returned with the inscription 'Postal Service Suspended'. Parcels came back to me half a year later. It is horrific that one cannot help one's nearest in their greatest need.

Then our nephew, the only son of my husband's elder brother, who because of particular problems was unable to accompany his parents to the USA straightaway, met a terrible fate. He died on 18 September, just after his 22nd birthday. Until shortly before his death (about three months ago) he had lived in Amsterdam where he was waiting for his exit permit. Despite all our efforts we couldn't help him. Can you understand our grief?[2]

We have lived through terrible things and as long as the war continues we will not be free of dreadful worries.

What you tell me about Edith and her husband makes us happy. Less so what you say about Grete. I would much rather that she had formed a new relationship with another man because, after all, she went through so much with Otto.

Do the sisters live in the same town? Do they ever go near [my daughter] Hannah? Do tell me. Then I will send you H.'s address. Heaven grant that H. stays as happy as she is at present. She sees her husband every weekend and will have work so long as the war lasts. She is apparently very good at it. After the war I hope she will be a good support for her husband. He is an architect by profession and there will be all sorts of jobs to do then. Hannah is at least 5 cm. taller than me. She is 1.82 tall and Lernhard 1.76. The latter took his *abitur* with particularly good marks in history. Who would ever have thought that possible? On top of that he then spent ten months overseas and is now back at his old school. He will stay there until Christmas and then take a job.

---

[1] Gurs was an internment and refugee camp in south-western France which became a concentration camp for non-French Jews, as well as political opponents of the Vichy government.

[2] Willy Lazar Auerbach, born 30 August 1919 in Elbing, Germany (now Poland) and living in 1941 in Amsterdam, died in Mauthausen Concentration Camp on 18 September 1941. In 1941 several hundred Dutch Jews were sent to Mauthausen in retaliation for acts of resistance in the Netherlands.

Yes, my dear, who would have thought that we, who love them very much, would have to live for years without our children. I often have such a terrible longing for them, but we must be glad to know that they are doing well.

My youngest brother and my mother have been living in Texas, (USA) since '27. Fortunately they are doing well. My brother has work and earns enough for them to live comfortably. There is nothing special to tell you, thank goodness, about my husband and myself. We have only one wish, to be able to carry on with our quiet retiring life until the end of the war. The area where we live is lovely – woods, fields, meadows, moorland. We have also got to know a few very nice people particularly and the local inhabitants are very kind and we treasure them.

Please write to me soon. I would very much like to know how long this letter took. Once again, all the best and warmest greetings to all your dear ones and our mutual friends.

Your Else

P.S. Greetings from my husband for all of you. Please reply soon!

Appendix 2: Post-war letters from Hede Sternschuss written in English to Francis and Edith Sternschuss

1   Prague, 17 June 1945

Dear Francis and dear Edithl

Thanks for your letter from 3/6. It arrived in five days. It gave us much pleasure to have news of you, Catherine[3] and Greta. When a regular postal service will be working again I shall write letters to tell you all that happened since April '39. It will be a novel.

In the meantime I hope you have got several letters from Ernest and therefore you will know what we have been doing during the war and how we have managed.[4] Thank God we have saved our flat and what we want: our clothes, linen, etc. It was not easy but the main thing is we can make both ends meet and it is not necessary that you trouble to support us. We can at present manage and Ernest helps if it must be. We thank both of you for your kind offer and hope that the time will come very soon when we can do something for you and your dear Catherine.

I can imagine how much Edith is longing for news from her dear relatives but it is a pity that we have heard last in July 1942, later on no messages came and therefore we have written to the Red Cross to make enquiries. Gusti and Irene left us in January 1942 and Mary in April. Granny in June 1942 and we were very grieved by their parting because we were very fond of each other and they liked me especially therefore we were very often together.

---

[3]Catherine Anne (referred to as CA in the next letter) later became known as Kate (Ottevanger).
[4]These letters have been lost.

Irene and Gusti have been staying for three months at Theresienstadt. Mary and Granny only for a few days and they all had to leave for Poland. That was a rather bad place and we got seldom messages and could not help them, it was not allowed to write letters or postcards. In the beginning we sent small parcels but later on this was not allowed either.

Uncle Otto and Kamilla are three years away[5] and we had no news at all and therefore we are much afraid that they have not survived all the sufferings. Aunt's sister Mary died at Theresienstadt one year ago and what happened to her family we do not know.[6] I am very sorry that I can not write better news to you but you surely have heard how many people were killed and in what danger we always have been. It is a great wonder that we have survived. At present only a few people we know have returned from the concentration camps and I am sorry to say that of our family only Trude and Eva Schick returned, but we still hope that many more will come when the railway connection will be better.

Father's health is not in the best state, he has aged like myself because of the troubles. If we find a good physician, I hope it will be better again. I am glad father is now every day going out for a walk in the park and is enjoying the radio. It is a great pity that we can not look after our grandchild and it would give us great pleasure to see her and to play with her. When she takes after her father you will know to treat her all right. Please send us as soon as possible a new snap of little Catherine and both of you, it will be delightful.

Was it not a great surprise to you when you heard I have learned E[nglish], is it? I am now happy to have used my spare time so well, but it was difficult enough in my age with so much troubles to have a good memory and if I am making mistakes you must excuse it. Surely I shall get more practice now.

Best regards to Harry and Flo [Bramwell], both Gretes, Mr Lester and all my love to you my dears.

Your mother.

Many kisses to the little darling.

Postscript in Czech: Objímá a libá vás všechny. Váš Táta.[7]

---

[5]Otakar and Kamila Sternschuss were Rudolf Sternschuss's brother and sister-in-law. They were both deported on 27 July 1942 to Theresienstadt, and then, several days later, to Maly Trostenets.
[6]Presumably the aunt is Kamilla (or Kamila).
[7]Hugs and kisses from your father.

Photo 20 *Edith and her baby daughter Catherine Anne (Kate), August 1942.*

2   Part letter, 1945

… … How often I was writing letters to you all in my memory I cannot say, I was only afraid to convey to you all the bad news. Our life was surely not pleasant but, compared with the suffering which our dear ones had to undergo, it was easy. I am now always glad that I could be for all a bit of help and that we liked each other very much, saw each other very much and we were always happy you were spared all the troubles.

Mary[8] has been baking skilfully wafers [and] had many pupils and I was among them and she was pleased to have success. Then she was in good humor because she has found her old friend, Ing. L[öwy] in Greece. They were always corresponding and looking forward to get married. It has been making her happy and when she left us she was determined to be strong and to get

---

[8]Marie.

through. I understand very well that Edith wants to know very many details about her people and I am therefore not troubled if she asks for it. It is only difficult for me to give the right words for it. I can only say that neither her mother nor uncle, aunt or Grannie felt deserted through Edith and they had full understanding that it was not possible to write to them. They were glad to know that you are in freedom.

They took the preparation and the parting very bravely and hoped to return after the war. It made the whole affair easier for them that they were among a great part of acquainted people who had the same fate and they helped each other very much. In the beginning they have not known that they will go later to Poland. I have kept some p.c. from Irene and two letters from Mother written before her leave and I hope I shall find the possibility to send them to you without getting lost. I promised to all to look after their things and now I am glad that I could save the earrings, clothes, linen, etc. The machines and the recipes are existing too and we have one Doomsday book register copy for the house.[9] When the power of attorney will arrive I shall use it.

It is interesting to us that Edith's sister is contented and fond of little C.A. and that the little one is a happy pretty girl. I am only very sorry that we cannot have her here because such a child is a great comfort.

I thank you very much for the news about Greta [Sternschuss]. I am pleased that she is healthy and popular and that you are on very good terms together. ...

---

[9]Hede probably means the deeds to the house in Karlsbad.

Appendix 3: Post-war letters from Salvator and Hella Cougno (Kounio) written in English to Grete Reichl

1   Thessaloniki, 20/11/1945

Dear Gretl

Your letter addressed to my father-in-law Ernst Löwy reached me a few days ago and, as he died, I am replying to your letter. I was very pleased to hear that you are safe.

Unfortunately all the Jews of Salonika have been deported to concentration camps in Germany. All the members of our family have been taken with the first transport and my father-in-law has been taken after a while. If he had the patience to be hidden a little more I think he could still remain here. We have been deported in Auschwitz where it was terrible. We have suffered so much that still today I cannot believe how I escaped death. My father-in-law was burnt (gassed) immediately at his arrival in Auschwitz. My wife Hella, my daughter Erika and my son Henry and I, we were lucky that we have received a better work so that we could resist the first months.

The last six months of the concentration camps, since December 1944, was terrible. I was always together with my son, and Hella and Erika separately in another camp. We have been liberated in Mauthausen with my son together which is now 18 years old, and Hella and Erika together in Belsen Malhow.[10] I returned here in August and only three weeks ago Erika came back alone. Hella has taken other dispositions because she thought we were all dead and

---

[10]Malhow (Malchow) was in fact a sub-camp of Ravensbrück, not Belsen. It was a camp for women.

now she is not willing any more to come here. You see how bitter it is now for all of us. In order to have an idea you must think that from 52,000 Jews who have been deported only 1,000 came back. All the 51,000 died there. I found all my business and home destroyed but I started again and I am very confident that shortly I shall have a good position in my business.

Please write me a few words giving me news of your family. What news about your mother and sister? Have you heard anything from Ilse Spitz? If you have her address, please write it me. I think you will remember when I was in Karlsbad 20 years ago. It was a very happy time. After the hell of these last years, it seems to me like a dream.

I will be very pleased to receive any news from you and if you think I can do something for you, I shall do it with great pleasure.

Yours heartfully, Cougno S.

2　　　　　　　　　　　　　　　　　　Thessaloniki, 18/2/1946

My dear Gretl

At last I came home and I found a charming letter from you. You cannot imagine how I am happy to hear news from you. We are only so few ones from our family. It is alike a wonder that we are all four still alive and only my dear father payed it very hard. He never believed, when we heard by the radio about it and he told that it is only propaganda. He payed it with his life. I know the loss of my father is a big loss for you too, but you see we became all fatalist and we say that is chance, or, as the Turkish say, 'kismet'.

I returned now about 10 days home and I wanted to write to you earlier, but you do understand quite well when I came home I found a lot of things to do and now I am very nervous and restless and I want to work. I do not like to sit and to think. I understand you quite well, that you are thinking always about your dear mother and your family, but you see we have seen so much misery that we are now so happy that we are still alive. You do know quite well the French proverb 'Laissez les morts aux morts'. You see, our best comrade during 3 years has been death. Often we said it would be better to die than to see all this. Tell me, please, who is still alive from our family and send me, please, the addresses. Yes, you are right, we must go on. We must fight and we shall do it. We went to a hard school but we did learn a lot. But we must begin everything from the beginning and sometimes we are very tired. Our children are grown up now and the hard school of Auschwitz taught them a lot. You can be sure that everybody who came out of Auschwitz did learn how to fight in life. Please send me the address of Fritz Ullmann in Palestine. He wrote to me that he would go to Palestine and I would write to him that I returned home.

I am happy to hear that Edith got married. Please send us a photo of her little daughter. I want awfully to see the pride of your family. You are living near her home and I believe that you are often together with her. Tell Edith to write to me. Perhaps she has more time than you. Please do not be late to answer me and I would be very glad to read Edith too.

With much love to you all.

Your Hella

3   Thessaloniki, 8 May 1946

My dear Gretl

Thank you for your dear letter of 1st May. It is just some days I got your writing but I did not feel so well and tonight I will answer all your questions. You cannot imagine how I have been touched by the photo of your dear mother. So many souvenirs are awakened. I believe you understand me very well. I believe we are living in a dream and happily we are not quite awake. It is better to dream and not to be in the present. There are too many people who you miss and you will not believe that everybody you once loved is not any more beside you, but it is better not to remember this time. We must look forwards, not behind. I am very glad that you got the parcel with the dried fruits and I hope I shall send you in near time another parcel, but I will send you only nuts and almonds. Send me the address of Edith so I can send [some to] her too.

I did not get a reply from Hans Bartl and will try to write to him again. He helped me very much during the German occupation and I would like to help him as much as I can now. If you write to him, please tell him to write to me and I will try again but the post with Austria is not in good order. Your dear mother did not know him but my father begged him to meet your mother but he could not manage to go to Prague because he has been a communist and the German Wehrmacht did not trust him and did not send him to Vienna but they sent him to the front. But you see you will not lose nothing to write to him and ask him everything he knows about your dear mother and about my father and tell him to write to me too. Unhappily I did not see your mother because she came before me to Auschwitz. If I had seen her I would have tried to help her, but when I came I found only her name on the list of SB, that meant gassed. SB is Sonderbehandlung, the special treatment for the Jews.[11] That is all that I know about Tante Marie. Only about one thing you must thank God: she has not been suffering. It was better to be gassed the very moment you came into the camp and not many days afterwards. And so to know where they were going. We fight day and night against death. So I am very sorry I cannot write news of your dear mother to you.

I believe you will soon have the occasion to meet Salvator and he will tell you everything that happened and then you can imagine the truth. We cannot write it. It is too dreadful and nobody will believe us.

We have again the house at the sea. The children are all right and we too. I do not feel so well. The camp – you must pay for everything in life. Salvator happily feels well. Please, dear Gretl, write me quick. I am always longing for news from you and give greetings to Edith and kisses for you and little Ann.

Yours, Hella.

---

[11]This comment is unclear. It is highly unlikely that Marie, deported to Izbica from where the prisoners were sent to Sobibór or Bełżec, would eventually be transferred to Auschwitz.

Afterword: Reading messages of love, fear and hope

Discovering my grandmother's letters to Ernst drew me not only suddenly and deeply into the world she was living in during the last year and a half of her life but also into her character. When I had read and translated them, and then re-read them, I felt I had a whole new understanding of a person of whom I had only had a partial and insubstantial picture. Having lived with and digested them for a while, I made more and more connections with my memories of my mother, and revisited both notes I had written after her death and also letters from Marie to my mother and aunt, together with other letters written by relatives and friends to them during 1939–40 which I had read several years ago. Slowly a bigger, clearer picture emerged, loose ends began to be tied up, impressions confirmed.

I looked back at some pages I wrote in the spring of 2008 which started with the sentence 'I went to sleep last night haunted by the voices of the dead'. It had been just over a year since my mother, Edith, had died at the ripe age of 96, safe in the knowledge of the love of her children and grandchildren and even her great-grandchildren, who had been such a welcome late joy to one who had always loved children dearly. But for a time her slow dying was filled with terrible hallucinations, that the residents in the rest home to which she had moved were being stealthily 'marched off', with the connivance of the carers to whom she was now entrusted. When I tried to reason with her, she said lovingly and protectively that I was too trusting and must not be naïve. All this was spoken in German, a language we had never used together but which was the logical one to use as she returned in her mind to almost seventy years earlier when her world, and that of her family and friends, fell apart in Czechoslovakia, a 'far away country', according to Chamberlain, whose inhabitants were 'a people of whom we know nothing'. As she drew nearer to death she began to call urgently for 'Mutti', a heartrending call for those of us who knew how, ever since the end of the war, she had struggled to deal with the guilt of leaving her 'Mutti', as well as her grandmother, aunt and uncle behind in Prague, when she and her newly married husband and her sister Grete were able, quite late, to escape and get to England. Here they had taken refuge – the word 'refugee' was an early word in my vocabulary – and eventually, when the facts of the Holocaust became clear, decided to settle (my mother and father with greater adaptability than my aunt, for whom 'home' always remained the stolen ideal).

But the wounds of forced uprooting go deeper than reason can penetrate. Before his death in 1999, my father, despite his determination to resist nostalgia, once remarked that his life up to his departure from Prague had been the most vital and meaningful part of his existence, a statement that could have been hurtful to us, his family, if we had not understood just what he had had to leave behind, not in a spirit of adventure but with reluctance impelled by an ever-growing fear.

Exile brings with it different feelings: gratitude and resentment, curiosity about the new and yearning for things abandoned, fear, loss of identity, confusion as to how to order one's sense of values, those of the new world and those of the one left behind. Each exiled person must work through these often conflicting emotions and experiences anew and I was always conscious that in the three adults closest to me – my mother, my father and my aunt – there were differences. My father, determined to deal rationally with the new situation, decreed that only English would be spoken (a language that they still had to master, but which they soon spoke and wrote very well). He also decreed that his children would not be told they were Jewish, so that it was not until I was twelve, in 1954, that I found this out quite by accident and my world was turned completely upside down. It had the same effect on my younger sister, Helen when she was told. To my mother the revelation of the truth was an enormous relief: she had always disliked the deception and I now realize how disloyal she must have felt to her mother at not letting her own children know how her mother's life had ended. She at once told me all she could, as gently as possible, and gave me a copy of *The Diary of Anne Frank*, which had recently been published. Of course, I identified utterly with Anne Frank and perhaps it was then that I got my first insight into the idea of chance. It was clear to me that 'if' I had been born a little earlier, 'if' my parents had not escaped or 'if' England had been occupied, our fates would have been what Anne Frank's became. Those 'ifs' could so easily have been fulfilled that the distance between possibility and reality seemed to me almost non-existent and I began to live in my mother's skin and, through her, in my grandmother's, as the people closest to me, and then to try to comprehend the vastness of the suffering. It was an extraordinary awakening and one which brought me yet closer to my mother.

Yet with the knowledge came the frustration at all that which could not be known. Perhaps that was why, a year after my mother's death, I found myself looking through old letters and discovering how, in later life, time plays extraordinary tricks. For the first time I understood how close my arrival in this world was to my parents' flight from Czechoslovakia – only three years – and how the anxiety they were living in at that time was at its height. Never in my childish self-absorption would I have guessed what was going on in my parents' minds. I do have a very early memory of my mother talking to a fellow refugee, from Vienna, and of the word '*schrecklich*' ('terrible') occurring so often that I asked what it meant, but that is my only remembered glimpse into the blackness. My parents' friendship with various people with that familiar accent I had not consciously recognized as Austrian German, the arrival, shortly after the end of the war, of a wonderful magical parcel from Czechoslovakia, my paternal grandparents' arrival in Britain in 1947, even the shortening of our family name and that process of 'naturalization' (which I confused with 'nationalization'), none of these gave me a hint of the horrors my parents had so very recently escaped. By the time I found out about our Jewish identity the war years seemed – and were for me – a lifetime away. Yet there I was, in 2008, revisiting through their letters people now long dead, some of whom I had known as a child: wonderful 'uncle' Harry Bramwell and his wife Flo, who, in their small council house in Sheffield, generously offered hospitality to my parents, aunts and uncle; and my beloved godmother, 'auntie' Maud, whom I loved so much that I would practise dealing with death by trying to face losing her. She and her husband Arthur befriended my parents early on, corresponded briefly with my grandmother Marie, and did all they could to be substitute parents to my parents. Then there were also those letters from my grandmother to my mother and aunt, which my aunt had kept in various bundles around her house and which, after her move into a care home, my mother and I had cleared out and stored away after a cursory reading of some of them. My mother had not wanted to keep them and told me to have them. I wonder now whether she was handing down to me a memory, at one remove, that was too painful for her to revive.

There were letters, also, from Eman, the distant relative in America that my mother had mentioned and whose widow, Louise, sent me my treasured doll at the end of the war. The early letters from Eman and his wife discussed ways in which my family might emigrate to the USA. Eman, despite his lack of money, was eager to do all he could to help the daughters of his cousin Marie, whom he remembered with great affection from the days before his own emigration early in the century. He tried to explain the hardship they might at first face, in view of the unemployment then current in the United States, but encouraged them to feel all would be possible for young people not too proud to try their hand at anything. In later letters, until America's entry into the war, he was the transmitter of news between my grandmother and her daughters, doing his best to reassure both sides.

Intriguingly, there is one letter from Eman addressed directly to my grandmother, giving news of Edith and Grete in a circuitous way designed to escape the censor's notice, and an envelope to Ernst Löwy in the spring of 1941 (after Greece was occupied and when, as the letters from Marie to Ernst would in due course show, direct communication between Prague and Greece was interrupted). All of these were fascinating, conveying the sense of a simple, good-hearted man, full of compassion, so that I felt a touch of real grief when I came across a letter from his wife saying that Eman had died in June 1942, unable to bear the sadness around him any longer. In my grandmother's letters to Ernst, which I had yet to discover, Eman is frequently referred to, often with a touch of exasperation because he sends summarized versions of Edith's and Grete's letters rather than forwarding them. Poor Eman was only doing the best he could and at least my grandmother could know her daughters were safe and were coping. But my grandmother's exasperation is understandable, however unreasonable.

A further two letters addressed to my grandmother were, mysteriously, amongst the papers I was exploring, and at the time, though they were curious, they did not have the significance they were to acquire later. Still, I read them with interest: the first, from a friend Ella, who was the sister of Marie's good friend Olga (the Olga Löwenstein who is mentioned frequently and lovingly in Marie's letters to Ernst) is written in June 1939 from the Philippines and describes her long sea journey and her first impressions of the very un-European country she finds herself in. She comments interestingly not only on the difficult climate but also on the customs and attitudes – for example how, from her perspective, children are brought up to be little dictators. There were also letters from Ella to Grete, completing the picture. She herself was desperately worried about her two sisters, Olga in Prague and Anne Riemer in Vienna, and felt guilty at her own safety.

The other letter to Marie whose presence is unexplained (I guess this correspondence must have been entrusted to my Sternschuss grandparents, though I am unsure why) is dated December 1941 and is from an old friend, Else Auerbach, whose children are in England. She herself is in Hilversum, Holland – by this time also an occupied country, from which she appears to be able to write relatively freely to occupied Czechoslovakia – and she tells of a nephew of hers who recently died in a camp in France, Gurs. She also congratulates Marie on her intention to marry Ernst Löwy – again the mention – and says she fully understands and is glad. Both these letters were to gain additional weight and interest when I finally, in October 2008, came to read Marie's letters to Ernst, Ella's because she was the sister of Olga and Else's because Marie mentions receiving a letter from her and I immediately recognized her as an old family friend from Berlin and the letter as the one in my possession. I even remembered as a small child visiting her children in London. I am unsure whether she herself escaped or not, although I imagine it is unlikely.

Here, though, were two more very sincere writers expressing themselves freely and most interestingly, giving a sense of the network of friendships and relationships which was under such ominous threat, and the way people were dealing with it. I had no idea how the letters of Marie would bring a final touch of life to them (like Giuseppe to Pinocchio!) but already I felt myself surrounded by people who, as I said at the start, were 'voices of the dead', whose presence was vivid.

There were also three letters, from a Tante Rosa Kessler, of whose existence I knew nothing. She was the widowed sister of my maternal grandfather, Emil Bader, and lived in Brno. She comes alive through these letters, the first written to congratulate Marie on my aunt's birth in 1909, the second to my aunt to help her recover her Czech nationality through assembling the necessary documents, and the third was a letter of commiseration to Marie following my grandfather's death. In due course Rosa was also deported and perished, along with her two sons, Fredy and Walter. In my grandmother's letters, Fredy visits her unexpectedly at her flat and causes Marie great delight.

There were cards from Onkel Friedrich, the first cellist in the Vienna Philharmonic and member of the then famous Rosé Quartet. He was a cousin of my grandmother's and they were very fond of each other. Once again, my own memories just touched that world: I have a clear recollection of going with my mother to visit Onkel Friedrich and Tante Käthe in their upstairs flat in London. I was touched to read, in letters my mother wrote to my aunt during a period when my mother was in London in 1940, how they took care of my mother and took her to concerts, a rare treat in a grim world. One of Friedrich's cards describes how he had just met Arnold Rosé, who had recently learnt of his daughter Alma's death in Auschwitz and who was inconsolable.

There was a further group of letters which, to my shame, I must admit to not having understood in all their reality. These were letters which my aunt Grete had photocopied for me in the 1980s in order to give me some understanding of what had happened. Why I did not truly enter into their spirit at the time is a complex issue, to do with a certain sentimentality and nostalgia which my mother always disliked in my aunt and which no doubt affected me. Now, however, immersing myself in an increasingly real and complex world, I had a new understanding. There was a touching letter from Johanna, a loyal maid in my grandmother's house In Karlsbad, discussing how to save some of the contents of the house after my grandmother's forced departure. There was another from Salvator Cougno (Kounio) explaining briefly that he, his wife Hella (my mother's third cousin) and their two children Erika and Heinz had all miraculously survived Auschwitz. And there were several from my father's stepmother, Hede Sternschuss, whose German nationality and non-Jewish background saved her and my Jewish grandfather from death. These latter were written immediately after the war, in hesitant but correct English, and brought the first news of what might have happened to Marie and her family, and of how they had managed up until their deportation. Kindly, Hede assured my mother and aunt that their mother had been only too glad that they were safe in England and had understood how they could not write. She spoke, too, of the happiness Marie had had in the prospect of marrying Ernst Löwy after the war.

All these people – those I had known and those I had not – spoke with their own clear voices, sure in their own identity, speaking as if only yesterday about events which happened so very many years ago. And suddenly my maternal grandmother seemed very close, very alive, in the letters she wrote between May 1939 and the spring of 1940, as she comforted, encouraged and upbraided her daughters in their new land. She would have been younger when she wrote those letters than I was when I read them, and her children younger than my own, and again I was filled with that strange wonder at chance which ordains that we live in this period rather than that, our lives directed by one set of external events rather than another.

Now that my curiosity and empathy had been aroused I began, at last, to look in more detail at the many letters and papers my aunt had left, becoming more adept at reading my grandmother's handwriting in particular and a little later I made another note in my unintentional diary. I had just discovered a letter written exclusively to my aunt on 17 January 1940, the same date as one written to all three (including my father), but mainly to my mother, sending greetings for her approaching twenty-ninth birthday. This second letter had moved me very much when I first read it, as it shows just how much my grandmother treasured my mother:

> When I look back over time, from the first day of your life to the hour when you left me, every memory I have of you, thank God and thanks to you, is beautiful, every memory connected to you is of years and days of great happiness and highest hopes.

It had been a little shocking, then, to read something of an implied threat in the next passage where Marie warns her daughters never even to consider going and settling in different countries but to stick together, otherwise she will not come and live with either of them. In a postscript she apologizes for her typing errors due to her high emotional state and one senses clearly how passionately she feels on this issue, that she can risk spoiling her beautiful and, as it turned out, last birthday greeting in this way. The newly discovered letter to my aunt also sheds light on my grandmother's state of mind as well as on her character. My aunt had asked to have a separate letter sent to her alone and had evidently complained of the way her brother-in-law had treated her. In her reply, her mother, while assuring her that she was fundamentally a good person, tries to get her to accept that she also has faults which a near relative may be right to point out and that she herself is relieved that her daughters have some male protection in that strange new land. She then goes on to speak of my mother's birthday, asking Grete to buy Edith a few flowers on her behalf and put them on the birthday table next to her photo, but it is the next sentence which, for me, is almost unbearably moving, confirming what she wrote to my mother in her birthday letter, but also what is to come out in the letters to Ernst: her deep admiration for both her husband Emil and her daughter Edith, whom she sees as similarly good.

> You are right in your judgement, she is indescribably good, like her father. I knew their wonderful qualities and knew that everyone is made happier by their presence and this makes it all the harder to live without them. But I know, too, the disadvantages their goodness brings; they always need, as one might say, a good spirit to surround them and where is that now possible?

There is such poignancy in this grieving for the loss of her dead husband and her distant daughters that the penultimate paragraph of the letter – after various pieces of news – ordering that they must make their plans for their future together ('Just imagine a future with no-one that belongs to you in the big wide world') can be seen only as the continuing great, if helpless, love of an anxious mother.

Reading these two letters consecutively, so differently put together yet conveying the same two fundamental messages, was like catching a glimpse of my grandmother's character: how diplomatic she could be with her fragile older daughter (after her divorce in 1936, my aunt had suffered a nervous breakdown), tempering tough advice with praise, sending amusing details about the dog my aunt had loved, etc., yet how passionately she felt that a family should hold together, whatever the cost. All this would recur and be discussed in many different ways in the as yet undiscovered letters Marie was to write to Ernst, but for now the insights these two complementary letters offered were deeply moving and more than I would ever have imagined possible.

I was left feeling very sad that I had not been able to comfort my mother, at her end, with her mother's words. She seemed still to be begging forgiveness.

The next entry in my notes comes when I had finally finished translating my grandmother's letters to my mother and aunt, written between May 1939 and the spring of 1940. Continuing my browsing amongst my aunt's collection, I had found a series of letters written by my mother to her sister in the spring of 1940, while Edith was in London doing a course in stenotyping. What struck me so forcibly in these letters was the way Edith, the 'little one', as she is always referred to by her mother and aunt, took on the role of adviser and comforter, with gentle admonitions here and there, the role, in fact, of her mother. As the person who loved Grete and understood her need to be encouraged but also to be reminded to be self-disciplined, she assumed her mother's guiding role. Reading these letters in conjunction with Marie's, the continuity is striking, with the difference that Marie's letters, while forceful, are written with a certain helplessness at not being able to be on hand, while Edith's are written as the younger sister whose authority comes only from the fact that she is continuing to speak in place of their mother. The fact that Grete kept these letters shows that she did not resent or reject them. Edith's voice is very mature, although from the letters from her mother one can see that she herself was living in fear: she is constantly being exhorted not to be so '*bang*' (afraid). Edith is on the lookout for opportunities for Grete, who is not happy in her domestic jobs. She frequently reminds Grete how to treat people with respect and tact, not keeping them waiting, not being longwinded, etc. She herself has met a number of fellow refugees in London and, after a year of constantly meeting new people and new situations, is realizing what comfort familiar faces can bring. Life is still full of all sorts of possibilities – different jobs in Britain, a move to the US, where Eman and three brothers of her grandmother, Grunzi, are living, even the remote possibility of helping their family leave Prague by going first to Italy or Yugoslavia (the only way of escape now open) but which she cannot work out how to explain in a censored letter.

When, in April 1940, Germany invaded Denmark and Norway, Edith encouraged Grete to keep her nerve and to accept that one cannot live sheltered from the realities of events. Like a fellow Czech refugee who has volunteered to go and fight in France, everyone must contribute to the fight against this evil in whatever way they can.

These letters were written just as the last of the ones from Marie were reaching Edith and Grete. One new theme crops up in both groups: on 29 January 1940 Marie mentions that Thesa, Ernst's wife, had died in Thessaloniki in December, and in mid-February she says she has sent a letter of condolence, since Ernst had asked that she be informed. She asks Edith and Grete also to write to Ernst and his daughter Hella, and in March, on receiving a nice reply from Ernst, repeats her request, saying that Ernst sounds very unhappy and that he had written a letter which had 'cleared a lot up'. One might almost imagine that in this letter (8 March) her mood begins to change. Edith, for her part, has evidently heeded her mother's request, as she tells Grete in a letter of 2 May that she will forward to her the reply she has received from Ernst.

These mentions of Ernst Löwy were interesting, since I had known for a long time that my grandmother was intending to remarry at the end of the war and that her future husband, Ernst, was a distant relative. Of his daughter Hella I knew a little more, since my aunt remained in contact with her for many years, but Ernst was as yet but a name, about whom one could only guess.

Apart from this tantalizing glimpse, in my grandmother's letters and those of my mother, the most interesting thing for me, reading them one after the other, was to understand the world Edith and Grete had moved into, which Marie could only imagine, and to sense the continuity of care Edith was trying to offer her sister in her mother's place. It was an odd sensation because my mother's voice was at once the one I have always known – brave and encouraging in the face of difficulties – and different, written, after all, in another language: she is already the mother I knew, yet not yet a mother. It felt like a strange, knowing yet not quite knowing, hiatus, emphasized by her use of German, natural to my mother, as it was to her mother, but not to be used by the mother she was to become. It felt as if I was reading an overlapping moment between two worlds, like two overlapping pieces of material stitched together so that they are one, the one before the first row of stitching being the old, lost world, the one where the materials overlap is the strange moment of transition and uncertainty, the future undecided, languages as yet mingled – the one into which I arrived – and beyond the second stitched line is the new piece of cloth, the land of England.

That night, after puzzling over what memory does and does not retain, I suddenly heard in my head, quite clearly, my mother saying '*Mach' die Augen zu*' (close your eyes). Was that an echo of bed times when my disobedient mother broke the ban on German to tell her little girl to sleep, something I cannot consciously remember but which gives sense to the feeling of familiarity which the soft Austrian German has for me and joins those two worlds together?

And then, in October 2008 came the amazing, totally unsuspected, discovery that was Grete's posthumous gift to us – though one, I believe, she had pushed so far to the back of her mind that she had forgotten it totally. The discovery of the bundle of letters in an old suitcase has already been described in the introduction. As I read the inscription on the package, the significant names Marie Bader and Edmund Benisch, jumped out, as did the sinister word '*vernichten*' (destroy). Marie's physical being had been '*vernichtet*', but something from the person she was had not and was inside that packet. Within the faded blue packaging was an enormous bundle of letters – over 150 – some typewritten, the later ones handwritten. It was the last one that I read first and it almost made my heart stand still: it was a letter of farewell to Ernst Löwy written on 20 April 1942, the evening before my grandmother had to report for 'emigration' (the euphemism used by the German authorities for deportation) to Theresienstadt, the same evening when she wrote her beautiful last letter to her daughters. This latter was well known to us, as it had been kept until after the war by the Sternschuss parents and had always been very precious. In it she had written of her belief that she would see Edith and Grete again in the autumn, but then, into her encouragement, comes the admission that things might possibly not turn out well and the unspoken recognition that this could be her last chance to give them guidelines for their lives. One senses the underlying emotion, yet the tone is calm and comforting and full of a love which will always be there, whether or not she survives to give it.

That last letter to Ernst is much longer and concentrates on plans for when they will meet again and on how to maintain some kind of contact in the meanwhile. It is full of confidence and courage; only once does Marie briefly falter, wondering whether she could be wrong in what she thinks awaits her. She immediately dismisses such an idea and ends her letter with an expression of love which is quite heart-breaking and which showed me at once how passionately my grandmother was in love with Ernst.

It isn't hard to imagine the thrill and expectation with which I then began to read the letters from the beginning: a whole unknown world – the Prague of the Nazi occupation – and an only partially known grandmother were suddenly discovered in the immediacy of the letters – letters which I soon realized were extremely frank, despite the censor.

Slowly it became clear that the earliest preserved letters – October 1940 – dated from the first open declaration of love. That may be why Ernst included two of his own. As a result, a brief conversation opens the collection. The mystery of how, and even why, their love blossomed is gradually revealed in small morsels, but at first reading I could not know how much would be understandable to me as an outsider. In fact, by the end, with the help of a few facts already known to us, much has been explained, almost as in a constructed novel. There is even a sort of dramatic tension in the halting of the letters in the spring of 1941 (coinciding with the German invasion of Greece) which deprives Marie of the strength which love has given her, until she finds a way to at least lessen the deprivation by re-reading old letters and answering them in depth. Tension builds again in October–November 1941, after the arrival of Heydrich, and is never absent from then on and this time their love is put to a different, more imminent test, which makes the last three letters – the one with the beautiful reconciling dream of Marie and Ernst together with Grete and Edith, the one discussing religion and the final farewell – an unutterably beautiful and poignant climax to the correspondence. Could an author have plotted it more sensitively? One almost feels not. And yet none of this is planned, it simply responds to the course of events. Marie's 'dreams' do add a delightful touch of mischief and playfulness and the final dream, where all her preparations for Theresienstadt had led to the wonderful reunion both with Ernst and with her daughters, was, for me, immensely moving. I had been conscious throughout of the paucity of references to Edith and Grete, but on re-reading the letters – and on reading once more Marie's letters of 1939–40 to her daughters – I understand just how difficult it was for her to cope with their near silence over almost two years.

That she never stopped loving them and yearning unspeakably for them shows up now and again when she allows herself a moment of recollection. One such moment is in a letter to Ernst written on 3 September 1941 where the pain of memory is so great that she has to break off. In her mind she is clear how these two loves – the maternal and the passionate – will work out in the future: she must let her daughters live their own lives, but she now has a love-filled one of her own to live and this letter allows for a blending of these two loves, the one echoing the other but each in its rightful place. When she speaks of Grete, there is often great anxiety: the last letters she had received in 1939–40 had been disturbing. Grete was constantly changing jobs and was clearly quite unable to adapt to her new humble role as refugee and supplicant. In addition, Marie was worried that Grete's former husband, Otto Reichl, who had also fled to England, might try to persuade her to return to him and precipitate another crisis or breakdown. There are a number of references to Otto in Marie's letters to Ernst, and one, too, to an unexpected and, for Marie, thoroughly unpleasant encounter she has with his mother, whom Marie blames in great part for the breakdown of the marriage. These worries weigh heavily on Marie but she recognizes that there is now nothing she can do and that she has to trust her daughters.

Re-reading Marie's letters to her daughters, I realized just how much protection and advice she was accustomed to offering Grete and how desperate she must have felt at now being at a distance and out of touch. These two reasons – the inability to help and the terrible yearning – are why, it seems to me, she refers so rarely to Grete and Edith. Her strength and her will to live are all poured into the miraculous love which has just revealed itself so that, despite the distance, despite the censor and despite the apparent hopelessness of the world around, a vivid life is built up between her and Ernst, in which feelings, memories and minute details of existence are shared and contact is as near physical as a distance of nearly 800 miles and a mountain of impossible bureaucratic paperwork can allow.

As I read the letters I became aware of a terrible rift that had occurred between Marie and Ernst and Thesa Löwy round about the time of my grandfather Emil's death in 1936. By the end of the letters it is still not quite clear how this rift came about but it seems possible to surmise. My guess is that Ernst offered help when Emil died, supporting Marie in her wish to accompany her husband when his body was taken away by the burial society. The two couples had always been friends (Marie recalls how she loved to listen to Emil and Ernst discussing things) but Thesa was known to be very jealous of Ernst and may perhaps have been suspicious of his support for Marie, perhaps even sensing the unadmitted attraction of which Ernst seems to have been partially aware. Words were had and Marie, in her grief, must have said more, and been more unforgiving, than she should have, so that she was left to grieve not only her husband but the loss of a precious friendship at a time when the clouds of Nazism were gathering. There is a picture from as early as 1934 of Emil reading a copy of the Nazi newspaper *Der Stürmer*. He holds the front page towards the camera. The headline reads 'Jewish Murder Plan against Gentile Humanity Revealed' and is flanked by a vicious cartoon. Emil's last months were anxious ones, and for Marie at his death, a very difficult time began. She had to help her older daughter recover from her breakdown and at the same time keep the business going in an increasingly hostile environment. It was almost a relief, she says in one letter to Ernst, to find herself hounded out by the invasion of the Sudetenland, and to lose her home and her business. Ernst and Thesa had meanwhile fled to Thessaloniki to their daughter Hella, without any reconciliation, but it was Ernst's wish that Marie be made aware of Thesa's death on 24 December 1939.

The glimpses Marie's reminiscences give of her and Ernst's shared past – memories of childhood and of the significant journey they shared to Leipzig – were fascinating for me, my first images of her as something other than my mother's mother. That she could love Ernst so passionately did not in any way negate the love she had for her 'Emmerl': they were simply two quite different loves, two different lives she might have lived. She is so honest about her love of Emil and how, despite the difficult times that they had lived through during and after the First World War, her family life with him was what had made life worth living, that one can only be glad that she had recaptured her zest for life in her love of Ernst. That love had deep roots revealed almost like in a Marivaux play, where the lovers can say at last '*Je vois clair*', and those deep, unsuspected roots meant that they knew each other extremely well and could fill in, in their imaginations, the laughter, the voices, the facial expressions which distance prevented in actuality.

All this was only slowly revealed as I read the letters and began to know, for the first time, my unknown grandmother with an unexpected intimacy. I learnt, too, that the relationship between Marie and her sister, Irene, which in family lore had always been extremely close, suffered some strain at this time of fear and helplessness. Marie and Irene had made a pact long ago, when Irene realized she could not have children, to 'share' Marie's children, making all the major decisions together and discussing all the little daily details of life. When at one point Grete, and later Edith, needed to be accommodated in Prague, it was with Irene and Gustav, the wealthy aunt and uncle, that they stayed. That this arrangement was not quite as idyllic as it may sound I already knew from my mother. Gentle though she was, inwardly she sometimes bridled at the rather stifling extra parenting of aunt and uncle and on one occasion, when they disapproved of university friends she was associating with, she told them to 'get down off their moneybags'. I was amazed when my mother told me this story, but reading Marie's letters I can see exact echoes of this dislike of the material and the emphasis on possessions and class. My grandmother talks of how she likes the simple people of Prague and later, more critically, blames her sister and brother-in-law for their reluctance to leave their wealth behind in order to escape. When Marie refuses to share her new love with Irene – unlike the sharing of her children – Irene is hurt and cannot understand Marie's secrecy. Reading the letters, I could understand it all too well and thought how alike she and her gentle but determined daughter 'Edithl' were.

What an unsuspected wonder this reading of the letters was for a granddaughter who had never been able to know her grandmother. Now I not only knew her but could understand her thinking, her nature and what she transmitted to my mother. The letters had literally turned my life inside out and for months the world they described became almost more real than the world around me. I believe my mother must have refused to read them. Grete, according to a note she wrote on the inner packaging, read only a few. I, the granddaughter, knew no such scruples, but I understand well how they could not bring themselves to relive the guilt they felt at having abandoned Marie. What they did not know, and what Ernst had wanted them to know, was what extraordinary happiness she had found in the midst of all the fear and misery.

As I drew nearer to the end I read more and more slowly, knowing the dreadful end and longing to keep my vivid, courageous grandmother alive just a little longer. But when the last letter was finally read I began to wonder how Ernst had coped with Marie's silence. If there were any postcards they have not survived and there is no indication that Ernst had any further communication from Marie: she was sent to Izbica, the ante-chamber to the death camps, only three days after arriving in Theresienstadt. Sadly, it is unlikely that she would have been reunited with Irene and Gustav and able to hand over to them her parcels of food.

It was then that we discovered that Ernst's two grandchildren, Erika and Heinz, had each written a memoir of their time in Auschwitz, and from Erika's book we learnt of Ernst's dignified but fateful decision to join them.

The trail did not end there but led me, via Erika's daughter (another Theresa) to a most emotional and precious meeting in 2009 with Erika, her husband Rolly and her brother Heinz, in Thessaloniki. Erika and Rolly lived just above the former vineyard which features so often in the letters and in Marie's dreams for the future. At the bottom of the hill, far in the distance, the setting sun shone golden on the Aegean Sea, a sight I will never forget and one I wish Ernst and Marie, who loved nature and beauty so much, could have enjoyed together. We, the grandchildren, drank to their health and felt an uncanny bond. Erika at first felt that she could not intrude in her grandfather's love life. She had loved him dearly (and he her, as the letters show) and at first asked just to be told a few things. But gradually, as we wrote to each other, she began to feel that this miraculous flower of love deserved to be preserved.

Today, the survivors of the Holocaust are a small and dwindling number and sadly, in December 2010, I had news that Erika had died. I am so glad to have met one of the very last persons alive to have known Ernst and to have established an emotional bond with her. I never knew my grandmother but reading these letters has brought her alive for me and meeting Erika has completed the circle.

And so the discoveries were finally complete. Translating the letters brought a different kind of contact. In attempting to capture the immediacy and the varying tones of the letters, I had to try to avoid ponderousness and sentimentality and I am not at all sure I have succeeded. If not, I have not been true to Marie: her language was so very natural, as close to the spoken word as she could make it, and I wanted to make her come alive. Family lore had a lovely little story about the young Marie: that she kept noticing a gentleman who was clearly interested in her but who didn't have the daring to approach her. So she popped into a greengrocer's and bought a bag of plums, tore a small hole in the bag and let a few fruits drop out one by one as she walked along until my future grandfather, Emil, finally found the excuse and the courage to pick them up and offer them back to her. That is the same person who addresses Herr Censor almost cheekily, begging him to be patient just this once, or explaining to Ernst that she must be brief so as not to make demands on Herr Censor. When one realizes the fear that reigned in Prague at that time, the brave optimism implied in addressing the censor as a fellow human being goes some way to explaining how Marie was able to keep her self-respect despite '*der hässliche gelbe Fleck*' (the hateful yellow spot – meaning the Star of David) and other humiliations. Her feelings for Ernst gave her the courage to retain her own humanity and to believe that, through work and co-operation with others, she would survive the hard present. How she dealt with the final hopelessness I dare not imagine.

Whilst the discoveries were now complete, my understanding of Marie's letters to Edith and Grete between their departure in the spring of 1939 and the spring of 1940 would be greatly enhanced by what I had read in the letters to Ernst. It is only gradually that I have come to realize how much the different sets of letters, from Marie to Edith and Grete in 1939–40, from Edith to Grete in the spring of 1940 and from Marie to Ernst between 1940 and 1942, as well as various ones from Eman and other people added to and explained each other.

I now gave attention, too, to letters to Edith and Grete from Irene, Gustav and Grunzi (although the latter are completely illegible to me and I mention them purely to indicate that she too wrote frequently to her granddaughters), which were amongst the letters which my aunt Grete had kept. Reading Marie's and Irene's letters side by side, I could feel the great love and hopes both had for the younger generation and found touching the little updates each gave on the state of the other. But I could also sense how Marie had insights and advice that she, as the mother, was best able to give. That Edith, at any rate, felt this is clear from a letter from Marie early in 1940 where, responding to a comment of Edith's, she tells her 'I can well understand, little one, how you feel a bit irritated by Auntie … '. It shows that Edith and Marie had their own private understanding and that Marie could empathize with a certain annoyance at Irene's constant prompting and questioning in her letters to her nieces. It is an irritation which Marie herself is to experience and analyse with great pain and guilt in the course of her correspondence with Ernst.

Elsewhere (December 1939) Marie describes to her daughters how Irene awaits her nieces' letters and how she carries them around 'like a cat her little kittens': the deep affection for her sister and the moments of irritation are two strings which tug at Marie's heart increasingly as her love for Ernst grows. But whatever the differences between them – and more and more, in the letters to Ernst, the Lípas' collapse in the face of their desperate situation contrasts with Marie's determination to believe in a happy future – when Irene and Gustav are deported, Marie's thoughts and love are all with them and when it is her turn to go she leaves for Theresienstadt armed with treats to cheer them up.

Having read the letters to Ernst, these small indications in Marie's letters to her daughters of differences and potential friction with Irene became easy to understand, a self-evident part of the relationship. Similarly Gustav's and Grunzi's low spirits and Irene's edginess, all mentioned in passing in these earlier letters, become, with the pressures of the occupation, increasingly oppressive and difficult to handle and Marie is clearly relieved to be able to discuss them with Ernst, as he, in his turn, reveals his own uneasy relations with his daughter and son-in-law.

The re-reading of Marie's letters to her daughters confirms for me what I had sensed to be the reason she so rarely mentions them in the letters to Ernst. She yearns for them so much and is so frustrated at not being able to hear from them and write to them, that she does not dare to let her thoughts dwell consciously on them if she is to keep her optimism. Comments such as those she made in letters just after the outbreak of war show just how much she is having to discipline her longing:

> One must just live from one day to the next and accept that we must just put up with our destiny. Let's thank God for what we have been able to enjoy together, your presence will always surround me and be in me

and

> Next week is [Jewish] New Year. These are serious and hard times, so I don't want to get emotional and will suppress all my memories [of past years] because the present is quite enough to think about. Life without my children is no life at all, a mere vegetating.

Her frustration at not being able to help her daughters is equally obvious: she is very worried at how afraid Edith is feeling and at how she is allowing herself to be overworked. With Grete the worries are different and she has advice to offer on how Grete must take care to hold her tongue and not answer back, etc., but in one letter she is in utter despair that Grete is once again without a job and she clearly longs to be able to tell her a few home truths face to face. By the next letter, characteristically, she has picked herself up and tries to be more constructive. This pattern of near despair followed up by a summoning of forces is one I recognized from the letters to Ernst. By the time of the first preserved letters to Ernst, all direct written contact with her daughters has been lost and she has no way to advise and support them and must, as she says, leave them to care for themselves.

The letters to Edith and Grete were of renewed interest in another way also. Knowing from the letters to Ernst the full power of the restrictions which would gradually be imposed and the way Marie would deal with them, it was interesting to see how she coped with the early ones. (In fact, some were imposed even before Edith and Grete's departure, such as the requirement for exit visas, so they may well have been alert to hints of more.) She mentions them in such a way that it is clear that entry to certain places are, or imminently will be, prohibited, for example swimming pools, theatres, cafés and parks (officially banned in mid-August 1939). As in the letters to Ernst, she uses the oblique formula ' … we can't and we don't wish to go out any more.'

However, she describes beautiful walks she has made in Prague which make her love Prague and its citizens, who are kind and helpful, so that she feels she has lived there for ever. On one occasion in June 1939 she made a chance discovery which brought her great happiness when, on the anniversary of her husband Emil's death she came across the grave of Franz's mother, Ada Sternschuss, in the beautiful tree-lined New Jewish Cemetery in Olšany (Praha-Žižkov). Here is one small satisfying detail linking the two sets of letters from Marie. In September 1941, she writes to Ernst that Ada's grave is a place she always visits when walking in the cemetery: 'That is where I always make my prayers'. Jewish cemeteries have become one of the few spaces still open to Jews to walk in.

A number of references to people become clearer as a result of reading the two sets of letters in conjunction with each other. There are, for instance, references to Grete's good friend Käthe Brock-Strauss, and her family's escape, leaving their little son Hansi temporarily with his grandmother, Frau Isa Strauss, who is mentioned in the letters to Ernst. Marie's admiration for Käthe and for her mother Isa, who had already founded an important clinic which bore her name, helps build a continuous picture: it is with Isa Strauss that Marie hopes to work when they are deported together to Theresienstadt (as she tells Ernst in her letter of 18 April 1942). Her admiration then is undiminished and gives her the strength also to contribute in whatever way she can to relieving people's misery.

Mention of a mysterious American woman, Henriette Eisenberg, whose address Marie gives to Ernst before her deportation, became more intriguing when I realized from the letters to Edith and Grete that this same woman was evidently travelling repeatedly from Prague to London, apparently involved with the *Kindertransports*. A letter from Irene, admonishing Grete for not being grateful to Henriette ('If it hadn't been for her you would surely still be where you were') implies that it was through Henriette that Grete got the job of accompanying children to England in May 1939 and in this way was able to make her escape. Thus another apparently meaningless name, overlooked in a first reading, began to take form, and again one is aware of the continuity of the world Marie inhabits, despite closing walls and diminishing information. An enquiry about Frau Eisenberg *via* the journal of the Association of Jewish Refugees in 2013 elicited a response from Laura Selo who, as Hannelore Gumpel, and with her two sisters, was on the transport which Frau Eisenberg led from Prague on 31 May and who remembers her enthusiasm for her task. This particular transport is referred to in Irene's letter to Grete of 22/05/39.

And so, in numerous ways, both in factual details such as a description of her flat and in insights into other people's personalities and my grandmother's reactions, the two sets of letters together build a single, many-faceted world. On the emotional level, one recognizes the varying tones of advice, encouragement, etc., common to both, and the levels of feeling, from joy in a beautiful walk to moments close to despair.

Marie, Mitzimarie, the girl, the young mother and wife, the widowed mother and finally the mature woman in love and as full of emotion as a young girl falling headlong in love for the very first time, against the deadly serious background of occupied Prague and the threatening unknown beyond: that is the grandmother I belatedly came to know, when I was already a grandmother and when her two daughters were already dead. Now I know for myself the joys of being a grandmother and wish she could have experienced them too (I was born only three months after her deportation from Prague but she knew nothing of my impending arrival). Yet my sister Helen and I have, almost a lifetime later, been given a quite extraordinary and utterly unexpected chance to know our grandmother almost at first hand. She can now live on in that continuum of the generations of which Hitler failed to rob her, not *vernichtet*, not vanished and unknown.

This must be what her Ernst wished to give to her children and her children's children, ensuring that that brave spirit was not entirely erased, and ensuring at the same time his own immortality, that beloved grandfather of Erika and Heinz.

Long ago I had my own reconciling dream about my grandmother's death. I was standing in the doorway to a large, low room and opposite, under a large window, stood a great bed with two figures in it: my mother and my grandmother. My mother was stroking her mother and, as I watched, Marie turned and curled up to Edith and very gently and peacefully died in her arms.

It is strange, the power that vivid dreams have to appear to carry a grain of truth. I fear this one carried no actual truth but for years it brought some unjustified comfort.

Today a different comfort has been given with the discovery of Marie's letters to Ernst. I have puzzled long and hard over why and how he left Marie's letters and can come up with only one conclusion: that he feared, after almost a year's silence, that Marie was already dead and, being very uncertain of his own future, believed it right that something of the beauty of their last eighteen months should be offered to Marie's daughters. For that, and for my aunt Grete's inability ever to throw anything away, we, their descendants must be grateful indeed.

Kate Ottevanger

Notes

Introduction

i Livia Rothkirchen, *The Jews of Bohemia and Moravia. Facing the Holocaust* (Lincoln, NE – Jerusalem, 2005), 120.

Chapter 1

i Helena Petrův, *Zákonné bezpráví. Židé v Protektorátu Čechy a Morava* (Prague, 2011), 206.
ii Marion A. Kaplan uses the concept, introduced by Orlando Patterson, to characterize the situation of the Jews in Nazi Germany during the 1930s. Marion Kaplan, *Between Dignity and Despair: Jewish Life in Nazi Germany* (Oxford, 1999).
iii Erika Kounio Amariglio, *From Thessaloniki to Auschwitz and Back. Memories of a Survivor from Thessaloniki* (London, 2000), 25f.

Chapter 2

i Mark Mazower, *Salonica, City of Ghosts: Christians, Muslims and Jews* (New York, 2004), 422–424.

Chapter 3

i Livia Rothkirchen quotes from Himmler's letter to Heydrich, in her *The Jews of Bohemia & Moravia. Facing the Holocaust*, 123.

ii Callum MacDonald, and Jan Kaplan, *Prague in the Shadow of Swastika* (London, 1995), 97.

iii See Wolf Gruner, *Jewish Forced Labour Under the Nazis: Economic Needs and Racial Aims, 1938–1944* (Cambridge, 2006), 168.

Chapter 4

i Melissa Müller and Reinhard Piechocki, *A Garden of Eden in Hell: The Life of Alice Herz-Sommer* (London, 2008), 124–128.

ii Heda Margolius, *I Do Not Want to Remember. Auschwitz 1941 – Prague 1968* (London, 1973), 14.

Epilogue

i Yad Vashem, Transports to Extinction, http://db.yadvashem.org/deportation/search.html?language=en

ii H. G. Adler, *Theresienstadt 1941–1945: The Face of a Coerced Community* (Cambridge, 2017), 248–251.

iii Ibid.

iv Mark Roseman, *The Past in Hiding* (London, 2001), 227f.

v Robert Kuwałek, 'Das Durchgangsghetto in Izbica', *Theresienstädter Studien und Dokumente* (2003): 321.

vi Archive of the Jewish Museum in Prague, oral testimony no. 162, H. D.

vii Archive of Beit Theresienstadt, 303.014.001, letter from Izbica by Ida Hermannová and her daughter.

viii Kounio-Amariglio, *From Theresienstadt to Auschwitz and Back. Memories of a Survivor from Thessaloniki*, 68f.

Select bibliography

Adler, H.G. *Theresienstadt 1941–1945: The Face of a Coerced Community*. Cambridge, 2017.

Bryant, Chad. *Prague in Black. Nazi Rule and Czech Nationalism*. Cambridge, 2007.

Demetz, Peter. *Prague in Danger. The Years of German Occupation, 1939–45: Memories and History, Terror and Resistance, Theater and Jazz, Film and Poetry, Politics and War*. New York, 2008.

Gruner, Wolf. *Jewish Forced Labor Under the Nazis. Economic Needs and Racial Aims, 1938–1944*. Cambridge, 2006.

Kaplan, Marion. *Between Dignity and Despair: Jewish Life in Nazi Germany*. Oxford, 1999.

Klein, Lisl. *Nobody Said It Would Be Easy*. Brighton, 2012.

Kounio, Heinz Salvator. *A Liter of Soup and Sixty Grams of Bread: The Diary of Prisoner Number 109565*. New York, 2003.

Kounio Amariglio, Erika. *From Thessaloniki to Auschwitz and Back. Memories of a Survivor from Thessaloniki*. London, 2000.

Krejčová, Helena, Jana Svobodová and Anna Hyndráková, eds. *Židé v protektorátu: hlášení Židovské náboženské obce v roce 1942: dokumenty*. Praha, 1997.

Kuwałek, Robert. 'Das Durchgangsghetto in Izbica'. *Theresienstädter Studien und Dokumente* (2003): 321–351.

Lewkowicz, Bea. *The Jewish Community of Salonika*. London, 2006.

Margolius, Heda. *I Do Not Want to Remember. Auschwitz 1941 – Prague 1968*. London, 1973.

Mazower, Mark. *Salonica, City of Ghosts: Christians, Muslims and Jews*. New York, 2004.

McDonald, Callum and Jan Kaplan. *Prague in the Shadow of the Swastika*. London, 1995.

Müller, Melissa and Reinhard Piechocki. *A Garden of Eden in Hell: The Life of Alice Herz-Sommer*. London, 2008.

Münzer, Jiří. *Dospívání nad propastí: deník Jiřího Münzera*. Praha, 2002.

Petrův, Helena. *Zákonné bezpráví. Židé v Protektorátu Čechy a Morava*. Prague, 2011.

Polt, Renata, ed. *A Thousand Kisses: A Grandmother's Holocaust Letters*. Tuscaloosa, 1999.

Pressburger, Chaya, ed. *The Diary of Peter Ginz*. London, 2007.

Roseman, Mark. *A Past in Hiding: Memory and Survival in Nazi Germany*. London, 2001.

Rothkirchen, Livia. *The Jews of Bohemia and Moravia. Facing the Holocaust*. Lincoln, NE – Jerusalem, 2005.

Roubíčková, Eva. *We're Alive and Life Goes On: A Theresienstadt Diary*. New York, 1998.

Schapiro, Raya and Helga Weinberg, eds. *Letters from Prague, 1939–1941*. Chicago, 1991.

Index

Printed in the USA
CPSIA information can be obtained
at www.ICGtesting.com
LVHW020741171024
794056LV00001B/108